Tim Pachirat

over ... ... ion
... power
... gov't is not ...
that exists. p. UC

transnational union organizing

locational mobility

the R of capital

private property...remains a
social construct" p. 221

Ross at his best works on two theoretical
level → his formulations about the mobility of
capital and their socially constructed
underpinnings are very interesting.

POWER IN MOTION

POWER IN MOTION

CAPITAL MOBILITY AND THE INDONESIAN STATE

JEFFREY A. WINTERS

CORNELL UNIVERSITY PRESS

ITHACA AND LONDON

First published 1996 by Cornell University Press

Printed in the United States of America

Library of Congress Cataloging-in-Publication Data

Winters, Jeffrey A. (Jeffrey Alan), 1960–
    Power in motion / Jeffrey A. Winters.
        p. cm.
    Includes bibliographical references and index.
    ISBN 0-8014-2925-0 (cloth : alk. paper)
    1. Capital movements—Indonesia.   2. Investments, Foreign—Indonesia.
3. Power (Social sciences) I. Title
    HG5752.W56   1995
    332'.042'09598—dc20   95-31250

Cornell University Press strives to use environmentally responsible
suppliers and materials to the fullest extent possible in the publishing
of its books. Such materials include vegetable-based, low-VOC inks and
acid-free papers that are recycled, totally chlorine-free, or partly
composed of nonwood fibers.

Cloth printing   10 9 8 7 6 5 4 3 2

FOR ANNETTE M. WINTERS

CONTENTS

FIGURES

PREFACE

Capitalism is a system of production and social organization characterized by extreme asymmetries of power. Those who control capital and other investment resources are not just one among several interest groups competing for the attention of state leaders. Indeed, they often are not even citizens. Many investors do participate in open politics, but this is neither their most potent nor their most reliable form of influence. Far more important is the structural power they wield through their decisions about where, how much, and when to invest the resources they control. These silent signals of support or protest, and the tremendous political power they manifest, are unique and deserve at least as much attention from students of politics as they receive from leaders of state.

The central and enduring tension under capitalist forms of production stems from the separation between economic power and political power. Deep-rooted political arrangements reserve to a small group of unaccountable persons the privilege of deploying economic resources that everyone else relies on. Neither dictator nor democrat gets very far in commanding capital controllers to serve the regime, the community, or the society. And yet there would be no capitalists, no private control of investment resources, and no special political leverage for investors if states did not uphold claims to property and defend the wide discretion that accompanies property rights. The power of capital controllers is deep, structural, and daunting, but it is also contingent—incessantly contested and remade in the daily conflicts that arise when the material needs or demands of a community are divorced from direct control over the resources necessary to meet them.

This book probes this tension. The overwhelming focus is on the *structural* power of capital controllers—power that derives from the capacity to deploy scarce investment resources. Capital tends to flow toward social systems that produce profitable investment climates, rewarding laborers and political elites alike for their capital-friendly policies. Similarly, capital flows away from locations that cannot or will not produce inviting climates, punishing the community with declining investment rates. Power is manifested in the motion of capital itself, into and out of a community or region or country.

The structural leverage of investors is not new—since the earliest days of capitalism investors could withhold resources whenever they deemed it prudent or useful to do so. What is new since the middle of the twentieth century is the rapidly expanding geographic reach of capital controllers and the types of capital involved. The structural power of capital controllers has always been great, and dramatic increases in capital mobility, particularly for direct investment, have augmented that power. Now capital controllers have gained leverage from their capacity to deploy capital across competing jurisdictions that are quite dissimilar in economic, political, and social terms.

This is not to say that governing capital is impossible, though it certainly is difficult. States have varying capacities to manage capital movements, and not all systems are equally vulnerable to structural pressures. As the Indonesian case demonstrates, direct state access to substantial investment resources can undermine the structural power of private investors. The problem is, such moments or opportunities are rare (and in Indonesia, few clear benefits accrued to the broader population when the power of investors was damaged). Alternatively, as capital controllers leave a trail of economic and social devastation in advanced industrial states, key countries responsible for maintaining and defending the privileges and mobility of capital (such as the United States, Japan, Germany, France, and the United Kingdom) could stop doing so. In the unlikely event that the conflicts and political alignments in these countries shifted so as to make such policies possible (at present they are hardly even conceivable), the ripple effect on the global power of capital controllers would be profound.

This book has several objectives. First, it is a theoretical introduction to the structural dimensions of capital's power, with a strong emphasis on capital mobility. How have people thought about the leverage of

investors, and to what extent has the political economy of capital movement among competing jurisdictions or communities been researched?
The ability of capital controllers to relocate among multiple and often
very dissimilar jurisdictions points to the increasing importance of the
politics of place and space even, paradoxically, as capital mobility has
tended to render contending groups and actors within competing jurisdictions less able to control their own economic fate. Second, the last
chapter in particular is intended to suggest the range of topics where a
focus on capital mobility would prove fruitful analytically. The material
presented in the last chapter is illustrative, emphasizing lines of inquiry
that would not only enrich the approach developed here but also shed
considerable light on the relations and events under scrutiny.

In an effort to give the abstraction of "globalization" more meaning,
the middle three chapters offer a case study of Suharto's Indonesia, from
the mid-1960s to the early 1990s. The political economy of Indonesia is
particularly fertile ground for an approach that emphasizes the structural power of capital controllers. Rather than simply asserting that
structural power exists, I trace the way the limits investors impose get
expressed in government policies. I also examine some of the factors that
can augment or undermine investors' structural leverage. As rich as the
Indonesian case is, it only scratches the surface of capital's power in
motion. For building good theory in comparative and international political economy, Indonesia represents a useful window, a reference point
for comparisons and contrasts that undergird or undermine the claims
or conclusions offered here. Understanding how the structural power of
capital controllers varies across place and time is an important step in
subverting that power and, as part of a broader democratic struggle,
enhancing the capacity of different communities and groups to set their
own material and economic priorities.

The Indonesian case is well suited for probing the structural dimensions of investors' power. If one were to design a laboratory experiment
to test the validity of the claim that investors exercise tremendous (and
increasing) structural power over the construction and maintenance of
investment climates around the globe, one would try to isolate the essential nexus of the processes involved—the provision of investment resources in exchange for a set of policies business deems acceptable—and
then, holding constant as many other variables as possible, disrupt that
nexus and observe what happened. To be certain the results were

causally linked to the disruption, ideally one would restore the original conditions and see whether the relations between state and capital returned to the status quo ante.

Political "scientists" notwithstanding, most people recognize that social and political relations cannot be stripped down and squeezed into laboratory models or images. The Indonesian case is probably as close an approximation as one can hope for. Thanks to the oil boom of the 1970s and early 1980s (the "disruption"), Indonesia's policies toward investors have passed through three distinct phases during the past twenty-five years. The first period, from late 1965 to late 1973, began with the collapse of President Sukarno's government and finished with the start of an oil boom. The Indonesian state was bankrupt in 1966 and in desperate need of financial and investment resources to stabilize the economy and society. Real living standards had been declining for years, production and exports were almost at a standstill, and inflation was out of control.

The policy stance adopted during this first phase can only be characterized as highly responsive to the demands and interests of the most mobile investors, both foreign and domestic. In effect, investors supplied the capital needed to stabilize the Indonesian system in exchange for a set of extremely favorable economic policies. The critical *structural* issue was how the private control of investment resources, typical under capitalism, constrained the range of options Indonesia's decision makers felt they could safely and reasonably consider. Equally important in accounting for Indonesia's particular response to these circumstances was the capacity of the Indonesian system to adopt and implement a package of economic policies favorable enough to capital controllers to boost overall investment and production rates.

The sharp increases in oil prices beginning in the last quarter of 1973 introduced a disruptive element to the exchange relationship (capital for policies) established during the preboom phase. Awash in more oil-related resources than it could spend, the Indonesian state unilaterally abrogated the bargain. Although still concerned to have investment occur at politically and economically acceptable levels, state leaders were no longer so structurally constrained to meet the interests of private investors. Reflecting this new reality, a new policy trajectory was inaugurated early in 1974—one decidedly less responsive to capital controllers, particularly the mobile actors who are most keenly interested in having markets regulate access to opportunities for investment and profits. As the personal discretion of state officials increasingly supplanted markets in regulating this access, overall investment levels from the private sector declined sharply. This drop had no deleterious economic or political impact, however.[1] Many investors either took their resources elsewhere, never invested in Indonesia in the first place, or simply sat on their capital and waited for a more favorable business climate.

By the early and mid-1980s the oil boom had become the oil bust— restoring the previous structural positions of both state and private capital. Moving in tandem, the responsiveness of the state to those controlling private capital increased sharply, and the country's economic policies underwent a clear shift back to more market-based access and opportunity. One of the central puzzles is how to account for these pendulum swings in policy. It is obvious that the oil boom played an important role. The more subtle issues concern the precise way political and economic power shifted across these periods and what these shifts can teach us about how the pattern of capital control "ordinarily" obtaining in capitalist systems, and the degree of capital mobility, affect the power relations between state and investors. By extension, our understanding of major policy trajectories and shifts is also advanced. For Indonesia, it is clear that the periods before and after the oil boom most closely approximated ordinary structural conditions under capitalism— the boom itself was highly exceptional.

We must keep a keen eye on two related issues. The first is the possibility that other factors might account in a *causal* way for the changes in Indonesian policy. The second is the role played by additional factors, many quite specific to Indonesia, that mediated how changes in structural pressures and circumstances were (or could be) addressed by state leaders. Although certainly not a laboratory case, Indonesia is well suited for a study focused on structural-material factors because so few other elements changed in significant ways that could make them responsible for the swings in economic policy.[2] The stress must be on *pendular*

---

[1] A major exception (from the perspective of the individuals affected) was the decline in the power and status of Indonesia's economic ministers that occurred during this middle period. It was changes at the structural level in the pressures to be responsive to investors that determined the relative power of the economic ministers, rather than the power of the ministers regulating the relative responsiveness of the state to those controlling investment capital during each phase.

[2] As this book will show, in addition to the changes in the climate for private invest-

swings because factors that changed in a secular way cannot logically account for policy oscillations. For the entire twenty-five years in question, for instance, Indonesia has had the same president and team of economic ministers, and neither underwent any major ideological transformations. Thus we can rule out theories focusing on presidential politics, personnel changes in key cabinet positions, or the impact of ideology or culture to explain major changes in the direction of economic policy and the climate for private investment.

The role of the military and of political parties has declined across all three phases, as has the political and economic independence of the islands outside Java. Arguments based on military, party, and regional politics and power, then, are of little use in explaining the major policy transformations in Indonesia since 1965. Moreover, the country has seen a steady absence of politically powerful societal actors, and the institutional structure of the state, particularly those bodies in charge of economic policy, has remained remarkably stable. Demographic pressures on the state and economy have been constant and heavy and will remain so for decades to come. Again, models that posit these variables as causal factors are an analytical dead end. On the international front, the country has had no enemies and has fought no defensive wars. Indonesia has long been important geopolitically, and even if the end of the Cold War has diminished this, it came too late to have any major effect on the policy shifts examined here. The country's integration into international markets of all kinds has increased steadily, accelerating particularly during the 1980s. Moreover, the character of that integration has changed because of the deep shifts in the pattern of control over investment resources.

Although these many factors did not cause major policy changes in Indonesia, they were extremely important as mediating elements and are indispensable in accounting for the specific ways Indonesia has responded to structural forces that have also constrained decision makers in a wide range of national and subnational contexts. These factors are addressed more fully in the theory chapter that follows, in the substantive chapters dealing with each of the three phases, and in a brief comparative sketch in the last chapter, drawing on quite different policy outcomes in Nigeria.

---

ment, the three most important changes that did occur were themselves more a result of the structural variables I focus on rather than being responsible for change across the three phases.

Although this effort to offer a theoretical explanation for a state's responsiveness to mobile investors (evident in the policies that constitute the investment climate) relates to other studies in international political economy—particularly Krasner's attempt to account for the relative openness of different countries' trade regimes[3]—my approach differs in significant ways. While my theoretical claims are admittedly broad, the method of analysis I employ is highly attentive to the details of the interaction between policymakers and those controlling the investment resources the state seeks to attract and retain. And although it is convenient to use phrases like "the state seeks," it is abundantly clear from the material presented here that the state and its political dynamics are treated as anything but a "black box."

On the contrary, because issues of perception and anticipation are so critical to the actions of both investors and state leaders, I have made every effort to discover what these perceptions were for the central actors in Indonesia and to determine how and why they changed. For state elites, I gathered material from published comments and analyses, from internal government documents and studies (most of them classified), and from scores of interviews with the decision makers themselves. For capital controllers, I made extensive use of business advisory publications tracing changes in the investment climate in Indonesia, published accounts of business perceptions and reactions to Indonesia's policies and those of competing jurisdictions, and extensive interviews with foreign and domestic investors. Economic and investment data from Indonesia's Ministry of Finance and from the International Monetary Fund and World Bank, meanwhile, supply a backdrop to the interactions between state and capital.

What results is a theory that marries elements of Indonesia's political economy that are quite macro in nature—for instance, the society's "investment imperative"—with careful attention to the details and texture of policy making and investment processes. The picture that emerges is one of real actors operating within a political and economic "space" that has an identifiable structure and presents concrete constraints but does not compel or determine any single outcome.[4] How the

---

[3] The theory of hegemonic stability is put forth in Krasner 1976.

[4] Fainstein and Fainstein (1982:11) wrote that the project is "to sort out the determinative effects of economic conditions and the indeterminate consequences of specific political and cultural mobilizations." For a nuanced treatment of structural constraints facing policymakers in a context quite different from Indonesia's, see Howell 1992.

approach developed here can be applied to a broad range of cases and contexts is the subject of the concluding chapter.

The ideas and information contained here reflect the efforts, contributions, criticisms, and support of many people both in the United States and in Southeast Asia. My thanks go first to Jim Scott, Ben Anderson, and Sylvia Maxfield for their guidance. I am very grateful also to Chris Howell, Dan Lev, Jon Pincus, Rizal Ramli, and Ian Robinson for reading part or all of my manuscript—their criticisms helped sharpen my arguments. Friends, advisers, and colleagues at Yale University who helped me greatly include Charlie Bryant, Dave Cameron, Bob Dahl, Mark Harmon, Paul Hutchcroft, Juan Linz, David Lumsdaine, Dave Mayhew, Yoon Hwan Shin, and Mark Thompson. I also thank Roger Haydon at Cornell University Press, as well as the careful and helpful readers of my manuscript. Important support for initial research in 1989 was provided by the Yale Center for International and Area Studies and the Council on Southeast Asia Studies. Support for subsequent research in Indonesia from 1990 through 1994 came from the University of Michigan, the Henry Luce Foundation, and Northwestern University. I am very grateful for these generous resources.

I was guided and assisted by hundreds of people in Indonesia. It is not possible to thank them individually, and anyway most would probably prefer to remain unnamed. My thanks to Juwono Sudarsono; Vice Admiral Soedibyo Rahardjo, former head of the Armed Forces General Staff; General R. Soeprapto (ret.), former governor of Jakarta and vice chair of the *Majelis Permusyaratan Rakyat* (MPR); Kharis Suhud, J.B. Sumarlin, Mohammad Sadli, Julius Tahija, General Ibnu Sutowo (ret.), General Soemitro (ret.), Lieutenant General Sayidiman Suryohadiprojo (ret.), and Bakir Hasan. A very special word of thanks to the many people who, in addition to helping me enormously, became friends and made life in Jakarta so pleasurable. The Faculty of Economics of the University of Indonesia in Jakarta very kindly permitted me to use their institute as a base during my research. I thank everyone there for their generosity. My thanks also to the Institute for Southeast Asian Studies in Singapore.

JEFFREY A. WINTERS

Chicago, Illinois

POWER IN MOTION

THE STRUCTURAL POWER
OF CAPITAL CONTROLLERS

A paradox surrounds the political power of investors under capitalism. Although they enjoy a very special position in society as the private controllers of resources everyone else depends on, investors are not ordinarily seen as wielding significant political power except when they engage overtly in the political process—through parties, lobbyists, as candidates, or through more personal links to policymakers in government. Apart from their simply having more time and money to sway the political process, no additional political power seems to accrue from being a member of a country's exclusive "economic government." The key to the paradox of actors that are so powerful yet do not appear so lies in the *way* the unique political leverage of those controlling investment capital is exercised. This book probes the structural dimensions of investors' political power—those that are built into the very fabric of capitalist systems of production and which are not and cannot be shared or matched by others who lack discretionary control over investment resources for societies. It also explores how that structural power is changing.

If capitalists—who are unelected, unappointed, and unaccountable politically—were all to wear bright yellow suits and meet weekly in huge halls to decide how much investment would occur, where, when, and in what sectors, their enormous social power—which is qualitatively different from other political levers—and its implications for of policy making would be shrouded in considerably less confusion and disagreement. Indeed, people in procedural democracies might even begin to demand a say in the investors' deliberations and choices. But this is not

1

the way it happens. Although like every other discernible "interest group" capitalists have associations and political instruments, they make *investment decisions* for themselves and by themselves. As we will see, it has been argued that because investors control a society's lifeblood as individuals, separately, and under conditions of market competition, and because different fractions of capital disagree on so many issues, they effectively cancel each other out in both political and economic terms, leaving the real power in society to the country's political apparatus and those who control it, democratically or otherwise. A full appreciation of the augmented political power conferred on those controlling investment resources is impossible as long as the view prevails that keeping a diverse group of capitalists separated physically and organizationally ensures that they operate on the same political-power terrain as all other actors.[1]

Direct participation (in whatever form) represents only a small part of investors' total power to influence political outcomes and policy. Outside and in some respects *prior to* the overt political process, those controlling investment resources "vote" in a way that nonpropertied citizens in the wider public cannot. The sum of investors' separate calculations and actions as profit-driven actors in a market environment is translated into very real forces of support for and opposition to key government policies. I will argue that investors need not consciously coordinate their actions to act in concert, that investors' decisions are of enormous consequence for societies and leaders of state, and that the atomized way capital controllers dispose of their resources does not seriously dilute the structural political power they alone enjoy under capitalism.

I offer both logic and empirical evidence to support of these claims. The logical aspects derive from the nature of capitalism (particularly the elements of market competition and private ownership of the means of production) and the geographical division of laboring and consuming populations into national and subnational jurisdictions. The empirical

---

[1] There is a parallel belief that market societies are essentially free of conflict. According to Lindblom (1977:46), "In liberal thought a world of exchange is conflict-free. Everyone does what he wishes. When all social coordination is through voluntary exchange, no one imposes his will on anyone else. But how, we ask, can such a happy state be possible? It is possible only because the conflicts over who gets what have already been settled through a distribution of property rights in society. Was that distribution conflict-free? Obviously not. Was it noncoercively achieved? Obviously not." And, we might add, is it noncoercively *maintained*? Obviously not.

aspects are plainest in the stated and unstated policy interests of investors and in observed policy processes and outcomes. They also are evident as policy-making elites explain their perceptions of the constraints they face regarding investors, and the anticipated consequences for economic and political stability of not attempting to operate within those constraints.

It is taken as an existential fact that in societies where there is a division of labor and production for direct subsistence is limited, an "investment imperative" must be satisfied if the society is to function smoothly, reproduce itself, and—with any luck—experience economic growth. The position and legitimacy of state leaders are inextricably linked to the satisfaction of this investment imperative, since prolonged failure to meet the investment and production needs of a population tends to complicate stable rule—sometimes severely. Although statements by investors suggest that most are aware of the crucial role they play as a group, their capital is not consciously deployed to meet any given population's investment and production objectives. Rather, the calculus that informs the actions of those controlling capital tends to be personal and unfolds in an environment ordinarily marked by some degree of market competition. Among capitalists' core objectives are pursuing the largest profits attainable, protecting their right to private property with the fullest personal discretion that right implies, and keeping risks to a reasonable minimum.

When investors choose not to invest, policymakers are powerless to force them. Except in unusual circumstances (of which the Indonesian case is a prime example), the only way to maintain or increase investment rates is to create a political and economic policy environment that investors find responsive. And it is precisely in designing and implementing policies that meet the population's investment and production needs *by first satisfying the core objectives of those controlling capital* that the structural dimension of investors' political power finds its expression. This book seeks to demonstrate how crucial these considerations are to a satisfying explanation of the economic policies characterizing each of the three phases seen in Indonesia during the past twenty-five years. Furthermore, the application of the concepts developed here is not narrowly limited to Indonesia but has explanatory value in a wide variety of national and subnational contexts and across an equally broad range of policy areas and episodes. The analytic reach of the approach advanced here should become evident as we turn to the ways capital mobility has been changing in recent decades to allow relocation, particularly of direct investment, across ever wider jurisdictional lines.

As a final word of introduction, I should mention the lineage of the theory presented here. Although the literature dealing with the relationship between state and capital is fairly large, the subliterature focusing on the structural power of those controlling capital is narrower. And narrower still is the work dealing specifically with structural power rooted in the mobility of capital.[2] One body of research on the political economy of capital mobility for cities and regions dates back to the 1960s.[3] This work has not dealt with nation-states but has focused instead on the structural power of capital as manifested in the ability, vastly expanded since World War II, to relocate across jurisdictional lines at the subnational level.[4] Material presented here extends the insights and reach of the literature on cities and regions both theoretically and geographically to encompass the power associated with the expanding mobility of capital among nation-states. This book also is one of the first attempts to combine these insights with a detailed case study.[5]

Some Definitions

Most of the terms and concepts I use will be defined in the course of the discussion. Some, however, should be mentioned at the outset to avoid confusion. It will be clear from the context when "capital" refers

[2] Studies focusing on the structural power of investors and at least in part on the issue of mobility include Fröbel, Heinrichs, and Kreye 1978; Bryan 1987; Peet 1987; Gordon 1988; Milner 1988; Sassen 1988; Arrighi 1990; Webb 1991; Goodman and Pauly 1993; Yoffie 1993. On finance capital see Conybeare 1988; Maxfield 1990; Frieden 1991; O'Brien 1992; Mathieson and Rojas-Suarez 1993. Some of the more "footloose" manufacturing processes are examined in Scott 1987.

[3] The journal *Regional Studies* has been especially important in advancing the debate on the structural power of mobile capital controllers over the jurisdictions they move among. Three approaches have been prominent. The first is to look in a rather technical way at the mechanics of how firms make locational and relocational decisions. The second is to examine the different kinds of incentives offered by various jurisdictions and see how they really influence location decisions. These studies are directed at (and indeed often written by) city and state planners trying to design policy packages that will attract and retain investment for a jurisdiction's job and tax base. A third and least developed approach is to step back and address the phenomenon of capital mobility and relocation in terms of the social and political power it represents.

[4] Important work in this area includes Crenson 1971; Perrons 1981; Peterson 1981; Walker and Storper 1981; Ward 1982; and Eisinger 1988.

[5] Gill and Law (1989) address these subjects nicely, but their article offers only a brief theoretical sketch and does not present detailed case material.

to actual investment resources and when it refers generally to the actors who control capital and invest it. The term "capital controllers" is used interchangeably with "investors" and "business." "Capital controllers" is a somewhat awkward term, but there are at least two good reasons for using it. First, in many instances those who own capital do not control it in any meaningful way, as happens with pension funds in the United States.[6] Second, certain huge resource pools that can be used for investment are neither owned nor controlled by private individuals but instead are manipulated and "invested" by bureaucrats in large agencies like the World Bank, the Asian Development Bank (ADB), the United States Agency for International Development (USAID), and foreign assistance consortia such as the Inter-Governmental Group on Indonesia (IGGI), later renamed the Consultative Group on Indonesia (CGI). Capital controllers consist, then, of *private* and *institutional* investors.

The most important analytical subdivision in this book within the group called capital controllers is based on the relative mobility of their investment resources or production facilities across jurisdictional lines, especially national boundaries. Although I will say more about mobility later in this chapter, it should be understood from the beginning that the emphasis on *mobility* is deliberately intended to challenge and if possible displace the more traditional focus on the *nationality* of capital ("foreign" or "domestic"). An approach based on mobility not only elicits more satisfying explanations than are possible with theories stressing the nationality of capital (such as dependency) but can better accommodate the analytical challenges ahead as the mobility of capital across national boundaries continues to expand.

The "investment climate" refers to the constellation of policies within a given jurisdiction that are of primary interest to those controlling capital. Investment climates have always been important for determining the rate of investment, but they have taken on increasing salience as the general mobility of capital has expanded and, more specifically, as the capital controllers based in a given jurisdiction become more able to explore extrajurisdictional investment opportunities and conditions. Although different fractions of capital have interests in different and sometimes contradictory policies, several fundamental policies are of common concern to all capital controllers and take on greater importance as the mobility of an investor's capital or production process increases.

[6] Dahrendorf 1959.

There are countless ways societies can attempt to infringe on the private discretion of investors—thereby increasing risks, affecting the ability to compete, and ultimately threatening rates of profit. At one extreme is expropriation. Also very objectionable, particularly to mobile investors, are state policies that replace market mechanisms for access and allocation with the discretion of officials, who then attempt to manage the opportunities for investment and profit according to their own personal and political agendas. Many government policies have at least an indirect impact on rates of profit for investors. Some, however, can be singled out as elements of an investment climate whose effect on profits is direct and that receive special attention from capital controllers. A jurisdiction's tax regime—which can include basic tax rates, depreciation schedules, and special incentives like tax holidays—is a key component of the business climate. Also important are policies concerning capital controls, environmental degradation, ownership by noncitizens, rights of unions, tariff levels (especially for those sourcing inputs from abroad), and the costs of labor. In addition to policies on minimum wages and benefits, the costs of labor are here assumed to be affected by considerations of skill, productivity, and the discretion of investors to hire and fire employees. Labor organization and militancy are separate matters however.

"The state" is a complicated subject that defies quick definition. Some dimensions of the state are relational and others are more ideological and abstract. Two aspects will be emphasized in this book. One concerns its organizational and physical dimensions. States are complex organizations requiring resources to function—they have what can be called a "revenue imperative."[7] They are also territorially specific, and the reach of state policies is bounded in most instances by a clearly defined jurisdiction. Distinct jurisdictions are a critical element in the exercise of structural power because they make relocation among investment climates possible. The second dimension of the state centers on the processes and power dynamics that result in the policies we observe. States do not and cannot act; it is the people in power within them who act. To say "the state" responded in one way or another is simply shorthand for saying "policymakers within the state" did so. It must be understood

---

[7] See Levi 1981, 1988. On fiscal sociology generally, see Schumpeter 1954 and Goldscheid 1958.

that except for the territorial and organizational dimensions mentioned above, a state is a set of relations—an abstraction. As the Indonesian case makes abundantly clear, those responsible for making policy hardly represent a unified group. It is important to keep divisions and conflicts within the state elite very much in mind as we analyze the political processes resulting in state policy. That said, and despite a constant flux, at any one moment states have a single set of policies that are the law (a given tax rate, a policy on who can invest and where, and so on). When I mention the state's responsiveness to mobile capital below, then, the actions of policymakers and the policy results of those actions are the referent.

Private Property and Resource Imperatives

In building a theory of structural power relations between state and capital, it is necessary to delve more deeply into two matters already mentioned. The first concerns the critical issue of resource control under capitalism, the second focuses on the investment needs of complex societies. Beginning with the pattern of resource control, there are several basic points that are obvious enough but rarely serve as the proper starting point for the analysis of political outcomes in capitalist systems. One is that the defense of claims to private property is more *indirect* under capitalism than under any previous system of production. For instance feudal lords, who were also warriors, defended their lands and property quite directly (both against peasants and serfs from below and against attacks from rivals).[8] Thus, for capital controllers to rely on the state to use its coercive capacities to defend their claims to property, the *right to private property itself* must be so fundamental to the social system that it is challenged only in the most extraordinary circumstances.[9] In practice, successive rulers in capitalist societies do not start

---

[8] Anderson 1974a.

[9] Dahl (1985:1–2) reminds us that the deepest concern of John Adams, Thomas Jefferson, and James Madison, together with all the other members of the American Constitutional Convention, was that "political equality might conflict with political liberty." Many of the framers "had been alarmed by the prospect that democracy, political equality, majority rule, and even political liberty itself would endanger the rights of property owners to preserve their property and use it as they chose." Przeworski (1980:48) quotes one political observer who put the issue much more directly: "The universal suffrage is incom-

from scratch and create the right of private property with each change in government. Instead, they enforce a pattern of resource control inherited from the past.[10] So firmly rooted is the guarantee and defense of private property rights within the capitalist world that in political-economic analysis it must be treated as a structural factor.

Another basic point is that there are no provisos attached to the right of private property stipulating, for instance, that investment resources must be used in ways that advance the interests of society or must somehow benefit the state that serves as the guarantor of last resort. Capitalists can invest their resources where they choose, sit on them and do nothing, or destroy them if the urge takes them. In short, the discretion of capital controllers is total, and the ability of state leaders to insist that private capital be invested or used for purposes other than those that suit private investors is extremely limited, if it exists at all. The institution of private property ensures that the state's influence over the use of investment resources is at best indirect.

The second main issue is the "investment imperative" of society, also necessarily indirect in nature, that exists in complex societies when a substantial number of people depend on someone or something else to invest basic resources so that their standard of living can be maintained or improved. The investment imperative arises when the division of

---

patible with a society divided into a small class of owners and a large class of unpropertied. Either the rich and the propertied will take away universal suffrage, or the poor, with the help of their right to vote, will procure for themselves a part of the accumulated riches." The question of how propertied classes would respond if confronted with a *democratic* threat to their right to private property has long preoccupied socialist strategists. Referring to the debates among European socialists, Przeworski (1980:31) writes, "The main question ... was whether the bourgeoisie would respect its own legal order in case of an electoral triumph of socialism." He concludes that the events of 1851 in France suggest it would not. The fate of the Allende government in Chile, among many other cases, supports this view.

[10] Here I disagree with Lindblom, who writes: "Some people believe that wealth or property is the underlying source of power. But property is itself a form of authority created by government. Property is a set of rights to control assets: to refuse use of them to others, to hold them intact, or to use them up. Property rights are consequently grants of authority made to persons and organizations, both public and private and acknowledged by other persons and organizations" (1977:26). Lindblom intends to emphasize that the right to private property does not float in the ether. But his use of phrases like "created by government" and "grants of authority" is problematic and signals, moreover, that he thinks in liberal-pluralist rather than structuralist terms. Only in those rare instances when grants of authority over property are actually being made (and thus governments are literally *creating* the authority manifested in private property) does Lindblom's claim have any meaning or relevance.

labor in a population becomes fairly advanced and the level of production for direct subsistence is limited or declining. As the efforts of laborers are increasingly concentrated into the production of goods and services that do not *directly* sustain them (you cannot eat a widget), their survival comes to depend on an impersonal process of investment, on the wages they earn, and on markets where exchanges can be made for the necessities of life. Urban populations in particular are extremely dependent on this complex investment and exchange process because the possibilities of retreat into production for direct subsistence are minimal. Leaving aside for now who or what controls the investment process, the fundamental issue too often glossed over in political-economic analyses is that a constant pressure exists to satisfy a population's investment imperative, and that when real investment rates decline or, worse, the process breaks down completely, complications arise in both the economic and political realms.

There is abundant empirical evidence that the investment imperative is real. It is undeniable that some kind of investment process must sustain a social system characterized by a division of labor and by complex relations of exchange. However ordinary this process may seem, it is important to realize that it is in no sense automatic, unstructured, or free of conflict and power relations. Even if policymakers are not fully cognizant of the pressures manifested in the investment imperative, they have nevertheless set up planning boards at every jurisdictional level whose task is to predict and track investment rates. The economists and other officials on these boards are also charged with calculating minimum investment levels needed to achieve the employment, growth, and revenue targets that can be expected to keep challenges to the government at manageable levels. Moreover, it is their responsibility to diagnose the reasons behind investment shortfalls and recommend ways to increase anemic investment rates.[11]

Although the notion of a society's investment imperative is extremely important for any understanding of the structural power of capital controllers under capitalism, it presents sticky problems for students of politics. For one, the concept is vague, difficult to measure precisely, and difficult to "operationalize" because the ability and willingness of different populations (and even the same population at different times)

[11] Wood 1968.

to tolerate investment shortfalls and collapses varies widely. A second matter is that the word "imperative" suggests a sort of determinism where real people and the choices they make seem inconsequential. The term conjures up images of mechanical social processes conducted by robots.

That so many examples exist of state leaders' failure to satisfy the investment needs of their jurisdictions is evidence enough that there is nothing automatic or mechanistic about the processes or relationships described here. This is not to say that the structural forces rooted in the investment imperative do not press themselves on policymakers in all capitalist systems; other factors mediating the intensity of these forces and the ability of state elites to respond to them play an important role in determining specific outcomes. These mediating factors are discussed later in this chapter as well as in the concluding chapter. For the moment it is important to begin specifying the *political* processes and power dynamics that, in a general way, link social forces originating in the need to satisfy a population's investment imperative to pressures that decision makers perceive in order to create an investment climate that responds to the interests and needs of those controlling capital.

Procedural Democracies and Electoral Politics

In discussing investment shortfalls and perceptions of deprivation within a population, it is easy to imagine that the political processes associated with the investment imperative are wrenching and cataclysmic. In fact this is true only in the most extreme cases. In most instances the structural power of capital controllers operates in far more silent and subtle ways. The single most important reason for this is that *anticipation* by policymakers plays a central role in the power dynamics surrounding a jurisdiction's investment imperative and how (and at what level) it is satisfied. In analyzing these dynamics, the work of Charles Lindblom, Bob Jessop, and Adam Przeworski provides a good starting point.[12]

Lindblom and Jessop offer a general analysis of what Lindblom terms "the privileged position of business" in market economies, and Przeworski has analyzed the narrower issue of the tremendous structural

[12] See Lindblom 1977, 1982; Przeworski 1980; Jessop 1982, 1983.

The need for a polity to sustain levels of investment for continued survival of its population (non-subsidized?)

obstacles preventing peaceful transitions to socialism.[13] All three recognize the constraints imposed on state policy when investment resources are privately controlled.[14] Furthermore, they link these constraints explicitly to the investment imperative and the indirect way it is satisfied. Lindblom writes: "Because public functions in the market system rest in the hands of businessmen, it follows that jobs, prices, production, growth, the standard of living, and the economic security of everyone all rest in their hands. Consequently, government officials cannot be indifferent to how well business performs its functions."[15]

Guarantees of private property, as argued above, mean that "although governments can forbid certain kinds of activity, they cannot command business to perform. They must induce rather than command."[16] Inducements are none other than government policies responding to the interests and objectives of capital controllers. Focusing still on the perceptions and actions of *investors*, Lindblom adds: "Any change in their

[13] Przeworski (1980:48) asks pointedly: "How did it happen that the movement that aimed to revolutionize society by changing the very base of its productive organization ended the period of integration into the political institutions of capitalism without even touching its fundamentals?" Even though social democrats held power in Austria, Belgium, Denmark, Finland, France, Germany, Great Britain, Norway, and Sweden, "riches remained nearly intact, and certainly private property in the means of production was not disturbed."

[14] Lindblom (1982:324) goes the furthest in his use of a prison metaphor to convey how difficult it is even to consider policies that capital controllers deem threatening to their core interests. One probably could not design a system of political power that is more "simple and fiendishly clever," Lindblom maintains, than one in which any attempt to alter it "automatically triggers punishment." By automatic, Lindblom means that "the punishment follows from the very act intended to change the system. Punishment does not wait for anyone's deliberation on whether the change is acceptable or not."

[15] Lindblom 1977:172. Jessop (1983:92) concurs, noting that "the general exclusion of the State from private economic activities means that it is continually forced to react to economic events rather than control them and must ensure the continuing smooth operation of market forces as a precondition of its own survival. In this way capital retains significant *indirect* control over the State through the latter's dependence on the continued health of the economy." This formulation, with its vague references to the state and the state's own "survival," is not very helpful in that the political processes threatening the survival of "the state" cannot be specified precisely at such a level of abstraction. Jessop (1983:93) is clearer in his analysis of structural constraints linked to how the revenue needs of the state are met: "In so far as the State depends on tax revenues or other forms of surplus extraction for its resources, its capacities are indirectly determined through the rate and volume of private productivity and profitability. In particular this means that the 'governing groups' in charge of the political system (politicians and officials) have a vested interest in securing capital accumulation as a precondition of their own survival as people who live off (and not just for) politics."

[16] Lindblom 1977:173.

but what about eg. [illegible] economy and where so much of the market seems to [illegible] to the [illegible] ?

not just for taxes, but also for regime legitimization.

position that they do not like is like a disincentive, an anti-inducement, leading them not to perform their function or to perform it with less vigor. Any change or reform they do not like brings to all of us the punishment of unemployment or a sluggish economy."[17] This is, of course, still only one side of the power dynamic. The question remains, Why should this breakdown in investment, or even the prospect of it, affect the likelihood that policymakers will be more responsive to capital?

All three authors agree that the critical issue turns on the complications posed for state officials in procedural democracies when investment rates slow and voters feel the impact. "When a decline in prosperity and employment is brought about by decisions of corporate and other business executives," Lindblom points out, "it is not they but government officials who consequently are retired from their offices."[18] Put another way, the notion of the *privateness* of property is so entrenched in capitalist societies that it is inconceivable to hold investors personally accountable for the economic and political ramifications of their purely self-interested investment decisions. The only target that remains is policymakers, whose vulnerability to defeat at the polls compels them to be keenly sensitive to the likely reactions of capital controllers to state policies. In Przeworski's words, "As long as the process of accumulation is private, the entire society is dependent upon maintaining private profits and upon the actions of capitalists allocating these profits." He continues, "This is the structural barrier which cannot be broken: the limit of any policy is that investment must be protected in the long run." There is, in Przeworski's view, simply no other way to explain how socialist leaders in Europe bent on radically transforming their societies ended up as mere managers of capitalism.[19] Anticipation enters the picture when we add the fairly reasonable assumption that decision makers can appreciate the link between dissatisfaction based on declining investment rates and the complications this dissatisfaction can present for remaining in office.

Block concurs that the ideological commitments of decision makers are of surprisingly little consequence when it comes to the ways they

[17] Lindblom 1982:327.
[18] Lindblom 1982:329. Jessop (1983:94) and Przeworski (1980) make similar observations.
[19] Przeworski 1980:55–56.

respond to pressures to create an investment climate capital controllers find favorable. Under capitalism, he maintains, "those who manage the state apparatus—*regardless of their ideology*—are dependent on the maintenance of some reasonable level of economic activity."[20] Based on his analysis of socialist governments in Europe, Przeworski adds that "the efficacy of social democrats—*or any other party*—in regulating the economy and mitigating the social effects [of real economic decline] depends upon the profitability of the private sector and the willingness of capitalists to cooperate."[21]

At least three issues require further elaboration to strengthen and broaden these ideas about the structural power of capital controllers. The first concerns concerted action by investors. Are the pluralists right that the actions of capital controllers countervail each other to such a degree that one cannot talk of "capital's power" or "punishment from business"? Second, how crucial is the electoral nexus emphasized by Lindblom, Block, and Przeworski? Is the structural power of capital controllers diminished or absent when leaders are unelected? And third, in light of the increasing mobility of capital across national boundaries, how might the approach of these authors be improved by moving beyond their focus on power relations within single jurisdictions?

Concerted Action

The argument that policies judged unfavorable by capital controllers can precipitate an investment decline or crisis challenges a strong current in pluralist theories of business-government relations that holds that the power of capitalists is checked by market forces and by the sheer diversity of interests among investors. As Samuel Bowles and Herbert Gintis explain, pluralists have argued that perfect competition "so reduces the range of decisions open to the controllers of resources as to render these decisions socially inconsequential."[22] Meanwhile, that investors inter-

---

[20] Block 1977b:15; my emphasis.

[21] Przeworski 1980:55–56; my emphasis.

[22] Bowles and Gintis 1983:239. Galbraith dissented from the belief that perfect competition held business in check but went on to argue that pluralism was still not in jeopardy. Admitting that large economic units were forming in society (fewer than two hundred companies controlling the majority of production and investment in the United States), Galbraith argued that even if huge companies arise, other large units will arise to countervail them. See Galbraith 1956, 1970.

ests' vary widely and are frequently at odds with each other (exporters vs. importers, finance capital vs. industrial capital, small vs. big business) serves to further dilute capital's overall power. With all this variety among investors, the argument goes, the chances are good that certain groups will benefit from a given policy trajectory even if other groups find it utterly incompatible with their interests. Any suggestion, then, that investors as a whole exercise significant structural influence over societies becomes somewhat implausible. Even if one were to grant that there is a structural dimension to capital's power, it is effectively canceled out, leaving only nonstructural factors to account for the timing, content, and durability of policies under capitalism.

There are two major problems with this view. The first is that it fails to appreciate how many policies areas are of *common* rather than *fractional* interest to capital controllers. The second is that it underestimates the potential for concerted action by investors, even when there is no conscious effort to organize a response to a real or anticipated change in a jurisdiction's investment climate. The arguments of Jeffrey Pfeffer and Gerald Salancik are especially useful on this point. They note that when a variety of actors have similar goals and face similar cost structures, a logic of sorts obtains so that without actual planning among the actors, "implicit coordination is possible."[23] Thousands of atomized investors—all equally concerned to defend their right to control the capital they "own," equally motivated to earn and keep the highest return they can, exposed to a greater or lesser degree to competitive forces, and endowed with an average intelligence to interpret an average level of information—can act as one.[24] And we could go even further and argue that the atomized nature of the investor's response is precisely

[23] Pfeffer and Salancik 1978:50; also Pfeffer 1981.

[24] Lindblom implies that there are indeed policy issues that affect enough investors to have a substantial negative impact on society. Underscoring that no organized effort need be made, he writes: "Punishment is not dependent on conspiracy or intention to punish. If, anticipating new regulations, a businessman decides not to go through with a planned output expansion, he has in effect punished us without the intention of doing so. Simply minding one's own business is the formula for an extraordinary system for repressing change." He adds that "the system works that way not because business people conspire or plan to punish us, but simply because many kinds of institutional changes are of a character they do not like and consequently reduce the inducements we count on to motivate them to provide jobs and perform their other functions." Capital controllers "do not have to debate whether or not to impose the penalty." Without necessarily having "thought of effecting a punishment on us, they restrict investment and jobs simply in the course of being prudent managers of their enterprises." Lindblom 1982:326–328.

what makes it so potentially devastating. If individual calculations resulted, for instance, in the vast majority of mobile investors' relocating their assets abroad, the destructive consequences of such a move (almost certainly more dangerous than the factor precipitating it) could be both anticipated and prevented if investors were organized and exchanged information on their plans.

When Elections Matter

elections not the only mechanism of legitimization

It is regrettable that all the studies dealing with the structural power of capital have focused on the procedural democracies of the advanced industrial world and the central role of elections in translating the societal pressures of an investment dysfunction to policymakers. This narrow base of analysis, and particularly the emphasis placed on the strategic calculations of political elites to avoid electoral defeat, implies that the political dangers associated with investment declines or crises in less democratic societies are either greatly diminished or entirely absent. If the electoral nexus is a crucial element in the expression of investors' structural power, then authoritarian rulers, for whom elections are more window dressing than substance, ought to be completely insulated. We should not observe, for instance, any parallel institutional bodies dedicated to estimating the investment and production needs of the society, to monitoring the rates at which private investors respond to the existing investment climate, or to analyzing and recommending to decision makers ways policies should be revised when investment rates appear to be declining.

unless they have other interests in favor (such as logging int'l power, sovereignty)

In fact, government bodies of this kind exist in almost every country, and they are typically staffed by elite economists whose skills at monitoring and predicting are often augmented by those of armies of foreign consultants from private firms, the World Bank, the International Monetary Fund (IMF), and bilateral agencies such as USAID. This does not *prove* that parallel structural forces operate in authoritarian states, but it is at least prima facie evidence that they do. Detailed case studies of the sort presented in this book are needed to strengthen the claim still further. The central issue is not the role of elections per se, but the ways state leaders attain and retain their positions of power. It is logical to focus on elections as an essential explanatory factor where elections are the primary mode of replacing state leaders. In places where elections are less important, the focus must be on the processes and power dynamics associated with challenging those in office. It would be a mistake to assume that authoritarian leaders are not encumbered by the need to maintain adequate levels of investment and production or that they do not at least devote some of the state's analytical and monitoring capacity to assist them in anticipating and, if possible, avoiding challenges to the stability of their regimes that could arise from declining or crisis levels of investment. And though the precise way authoritarian rulers fall differs significantly from the way leaders of procedural democracies are removed from office, investment dysfunctions can be every bit as politically destabilizing. Finally, it is important to bear in mind that even the most totalitarian dictators do not choose the pattern of capital control for their societies when they assume power. Although they may attack selected investors who cause trouble, they do not attack entire propertied classes—at least not without enduring the often severe political and economic difficulties that accompany such attacks.

Multiple Jurisdictions

It is not surprising that the literature dealing with the structural dimensions of investors' power has tended to focus on single jurisdictions. Because theories have been based on advanced industrial democracies, and because the investing classes for these countries have been overwhelmingly domestic and, until relatively recently, have utilized their mobility across national boundaries mainly to extract raw materials, a consideration of multiple jurisdictions has been unnecessary.[25] At least two fundamental weaknesses result from the narrow focus on single jurisdictions. First, the responses capital controllers can

[25] A similar limitation is evident in the literature on the relative autonomy of the state, which has focused almost exclusively on advanced industrial democracies. The dependency literature, meanwhile, represents the Third World version of an essentially parallel theoretical construct—the obvious difference being that the capitalist classes confronting postcolonial states were predominantly foreign. The declining relevance of these literatures can be traced to two important changes over the past three decades. First, foreign investors are now playing a far greater role in overall investment in advanced industrial countries, and second, domestic capitalist classes in many postcolonial countries have formed and are far more important in their home (and even some foreign) economies. I argue that a theory of investor power should be predicated less on the nationality of capital than on its relative mobility.

consider when objectionable policies arise are limited to those that are strictly intrajurisdictional. Thus, for example, Lindblom and others stress declines in overall investment rates caused by "less vigorous" activity on the part of capital controllers. The notion is that capitalists hold back when they are not satisfied with the existing (or anticipated) policy climate, and this slowdown sets in motion the economic decline that political leaders seek to avoid. But what about declines that occur because investors can consider a wider market of potential investment sites—in short, because they are mobile? Especially in light of changes occurring in the global political economy, this missing element of the model is particularly limiting.

The second weakness is obvious once we adopt an expanded view of investors' possible responses. If capital controllers can indeed choose among a wider range of jurisdictions, a competitive dynamic exists *between* jurisdictions not only to retain "their own" mobile investment capital, but to attract the mobile capital "of others." A prime consideration in these transjurisdictional flows, of course, is the relative policy responsiveness of the competing sites. A model that fails to take into account multiple jurisdictions—and the relative mobility of capital controllers among them—not only seriously underestimates the structural dimension of investors' power but also cannot begin to appreciate the additional constraints on policymakers and their nonpropertied populations that derive from the mounting pressures (because mobility has been increasing) to compete more directly with other jurisdictions. Mobility as an analytical concept is extremely important to the arguments in this book and will receive considerable attention.

Mobility

Mobility has long been identified as a characteristic or capacity that affects an actor's power. In a variety of contexts, greater mobility translates into greater power. Peasant farmers in both Europe and Southeast Asia during feudal times, for instance, made great use of flight as leverage against lords who extracted too much or did not fulfill their obligations.[26] Robert Bates and Da-Hsiang Lien, in their work on the role that mobility played in the rise of representative institutions of government in

[26] A contemporary variation on this theme is Bunker's study of the relations between

England and France, argue that absolutist rulers eager to increase their revenues were compelled to give a far greater say in the direction of policy to those whose taxable assets were mobile. The more fixed one's assets were, they argue, the more likely it was that the terms of taxation would be fixed. For those whose assets were mobile, the terms of taxation were more likely to be negotiated.[27] The significance of arguments about the structural power of investors lies, as I stated above, first in the capacity of certain actors to provide or deny resources and economic activity that a population depends on to survive and flourish. Second in importance are the competitive pressures between jurisdictions and populations that this capacity creates as the options of investors to choose among them multiply. The best and earliest work on these matters centers on cities and regions in the United States and United Kingdom, literatures that comparative and international political economy have largely ignored.

Studies of business-government relations in the United States were for a long time squeezed into the dominant pluralist or interest group model of political influence.[28] Although it was recognized that the financial and organizational resources of investors gave business certain advantages as they competed for policy outcomes, the view was that their influence was if anything merely greater than that of other groups, not different.[29]

degree, not kind

_____

the authoritarian leaders of the Ugandan state and the small peasant producers, the Bagisu, who grow the lucrative crop of arabica coffee. Bunker found that the state's inability to prevent the disgruntled coffee farmers from exiting into subsistence production gave otherwise weak farmers considerable power: "The Bagisu's capacity to organize effective resistance to the demands of the central state derived in large part from their direct control over land and the means of production of a major export crop and their capacity to withdraw into a subsistence mode." Furthermore, the resources the farmers controlled were of substantial importance to the jurisdiction, in this case the foreign exchange needed by the Ugandan state: "The central state's dependence on small-hold export agriculture in Bugisu for a significant share of its revenues made threats of popular mobilization to reduce or withhold coffee production an effective means of reversing or diminishing actual central control and opening up new avenues to power and wealth for local groups." The withdrawal of the Bagisu and a redirection of their productive efforts into subsistence farming posed such a threat to Uganda's policymakers that their real choices were to "accede to peasant demands or face continued economic decline and political instability." Bunker 1987:253, 243, 254.

[27] Bates and Lien 1985:61.

[28] Pluralist approaches include Aron 1950; Truman 1951; Latham 1952; Lipset 1960; Dahl 1961; Presthus 1964; Rose 1967; Marshall 1970; and Neustadt 1976.

[29] Dahl and Lindblom (1953) stressed the advantages capital-controlling actors have in public political contestations by virtue of the greater resources they can bring to bear in electoral fights (e.g., the way business funds the Republican Party in the United States). Significantly, by the 1976 reprinting the authors had included in their preface references to

In addition, the arguments about investors canceling each other out economically and politically were an important part of the liberal-pluralist approach.

Because capitalists were seen to be like any other interest group, and because interest groups achieve their political objectives through overt and active participation in the affairs of government (it was still unimaginable that other forms of political power might exist), attempts to assess the political role and influence of business focused quite naturally on evidence of direct political participation. Analytical attention was limited to issues actually voiced by entrepreneurs, to their direct role as candidates for public office or their support for other candidates, and to other measurable activities demonstrating business efforts to engage in policy making.[30] As Roger Friedland and William Bielby point out, analysis of this sort was narrow in that it counted (often literally) only those policy issues that made it into public debate. Why these and not other policy issues arose, and any exercise of power in setting the public agenda and blocking issues from emerging, was overlooked entirely.[31]

It was not until the mobility and relocation of capital and firms within advanced capitalist countries became an important political issue in the early and mid-1970s (especially in the United States and Britain) that studies of capital's structural power began to appear. Scholars began seriously to entertain the notion that "the interests of a group, such as business, could be powerful, even though businessmen did not take part in actual decision making."[32] As the pace and volume of corporate relocation to the South and West within the United States increased, often to take advantage of cheaper and less militant labor, and as different subnational jurisdictions struggled to adopt policies that could attract and retain employers and corporate taxpayers, the power mobile investors were exerting without necessarily taking part in any visible political maneuvers was suddenly unmistakable.

Bates and Lien point to Matthew Crenson's pathbreaking study of industrial regulation by municipalities as one of the first major attempts

---

aspects of investors' leverage that were more structural in nature—arguing that a major task of states is to provide an "inducement system for businessmen, to be solicitous of business interests."

[30] Dahl (1961) advanced a very influential argument along these lines. Measuring power in terms of who actually took part in policy making, he concluded that civic groups, bureaucrats, and politicians were at least as influential as business people.

[31] Friedland and Bielby 1981.

[32] Bates and Lien 1985:62.

to incorporate these power dynamics into models of business-government relations. They write, "Crenson found very little relationship between the participation of industry in the public domain and the policy choices of municipalities; rather, it was the threat of industrial defection—relocation by industries to other, more favorable jurisdictions—that influenced policy choices."[33] Crenson's fundamental insight was that when the locational boundary or market for companies does not correspond with the political jurisdiction, the threat of defection from the jurisdiction places real, though mostly unseen and unmeasurable, limits on municipal policy making.[34] The more recent work of scholars like Davita Glasberg demonstrates how far studies in this tradition have come. She shows that early views of the structural power of capital controllers assumed too passive a role for investors. In her study of interlocking networks of bankers and financiers, she demonstrates how these actors went out of their way to "create an actual crisis even where none existed before" to support certain political elites and systems and subvert others. Among the cases Glasberg considers are the debt crisis in Mexico in the early 1980s, New York City's brush with financial default, and the deliberate attempt by bankers opposed to Mayor Dennis Kucinich in Cleveland to pull the financial plug on the city, precipitating a massive default and the political defeat of the mayor. The bankers resorted to these structural levers of power, incidentally, only *after* their effort to have the mayor recalled failed—and this despite their outspending Kucinich supporters in the campaign by a wide margin.[35]

Human Ecology and the Resource Dependence Approach

A fundamental component of investors' structural leverage is the ability to deprive a jurisdiction of crucial investment resources and productive activities. Those working in the field of human ecology attempted to

[33] Bates and Lien 1985:62; also see Crenson 1971. Even Dahl (1961:250) mentioned this structural leverage: "Probably the most effective political action an employer can take," he wrote, "is to threaten to depart from the community, thus removing his payroll and leaving behind a pocket of unemployed families. If the threat is interpreted seriously, political leaders are likely to make frantic attempts to make the local situation more attractive." Regrettably, he did not pursue the matter in his research and theoretical formulations.

[34] Peterson (1981) builds nicely on Crenson's work.

[35] Glasberg 1989:2.

build a model of power in society based on patterns of control over resources critical to human survival.[36] For human ecologists, dominance or power in social systems is defined as the ability to control the conditions of existence for other units. "In ecological formulations," Friedland and Bielby explain, "dominant economic units are those that control the exchange process with the external environment." Formulated with specific reference to jurisdictions and populations under capitalism, then, dominant economic units are "those which control the generation of employment and income growth in a local economy."[37]

Pfeffer and Salancik, two major figures in the resource dependence school, have expanded on these basic tools to construct a theory that accounts for the leverage actors exercise over a wide variety of complex organizations by virtue of their discretionary control over resources that are critical to the smooth functioning (and even survival) of these same systems.[38] Organizational activities and outcomes, in their view, "are accounted for by the context in which the organization is embedded."[39] Stating their findings forcefully, they maintain that it is the control over the supply of critical resources to an organization that "makes the external constraint and control of organizational behavior both possible and inevitable." In such circumstances, they continue, "organizations could not survive if they were not responsive to the demands of their environments."[40]

This is the state operating with the controlled investment environment by business

Determinants of Mobility

The ability of capital controllers to deprive a jurisdiction of the investment resources it depends on assumes two major forms. The first, which is available to all investors and has received considerable attention in the work of Lindblom, Przeworski, Jessop, and Block, can be termed "withdrawal." Sometimes called a capital "strike" or "boycott," it is the act of withholding investment resources in the face of a policy climate that

---

[36] Park 1936; Hawley 1950. It should be said that although certain aspects of the human ecology approach are useful (and these are the ones emphasized by those who have subsequently applied it to resource dependency in complex organizations), its social-Darwinist elements are quite wrongheaded and of no use in the theory developed in this book.

[37] Friedland and Bielby 1981:139–140.

[38] Pfeffer and Salancik 1978; Pfeffer 1981.

[39] Pfeffer and Salancik 1978:39.

[40] Pfeffer and Salancik 1978:43.

capital controllers find unfavorable for profit making or, in more extreme cases, potentially threatening to basic rights to private property.[41] At its most dramatic a plant can be closed and its workers locked out. At a much more subtle level an expansion, a new investment, or some kind of reinvestment can be postponed or canceled. Unlike relocation, which entails initial costs but also holds out the prospect of renewed and often higher profits, withdrawal necessarily involves costs and losses for individual investors that persist for the duration of the boycott. Although the capacity of different capital controllers to endure these costs varies substantially, this variation has become less important as a basis for categorizing investors as the second mode of deprivation—relocation— has grown in significance. For this reason the primary focus will be on the relative mobility of capital and the implications of variations in mobility both for intraclass differences and struggles among capital controllers and for relations with policymakers within and across jurisdictions.

What confers mobility? The answer lies partly in environmental and institutional factors, such as who or what guarantees property rights and how far the geographical reach of the guarantor extends in defending those rights. Policies regulating transactions among jurisdictions, moreover, have a tremendous impact on the mobility of capital and of other units of production.[42] The convertibility of currency is fundamental, but policies that enhance the traffic in both the inputs and outputs of one's production process also augment mobility. The answer is also partly technological, especially for direct investment. Advances in physical communication—such as highway systems, shipping, and air transport—have an enormous effect on the locational options for capital controllers. Advances in signal communication, particularly the explosion in the use of satellites and computers, continue to play a revolution-

[41] For Hirschman (1970) a boycott represents an amalgam lying somewhere between his instruments of exit and voice. Selected aspects of Hirschman's familiar model that are useful to the arguments in this book concerning the structural power of capital controllers will be mentioned in the pages that follow. Most of Hirschman's framework, however, does not apply to the structural power of investors. The main reason for this is that in designing his model, Hirschman had in mind neither capitalists nor their relation to populations and leaders of state. Readers interested in an elaboration of this critique should see Winters 1991, appendix 2.

[42] This point is developed very nicely by Helleiner (1994), who argues against those who place too much emphasis on technological determinants of capital mobility while ignoring major intergovernmental arrangements such as Bretton Woods.

ary role in augmenting the mobility of capital. And finally, the rapid dispersion of skills among laborers, so that the gaps in abilities and productivity across jurisdictions have closed substantially, has opened many new areas to investors. It is only when one thinks in terms of concentrated manufacturing zones and not whole nation-states that the dramatic closing of this gap becomes fully evident. Although the overall skills and productivity of Americans may be substantially higher than those of Indonesians, the differences between laborers in Jakarta, Surabaya, and Medan and in Los Angeles, Detroit, and New Orleans are far less pronounced.

In addition to these contextual factors, mobility is also determined by factors that are specific to capital itself and to those who control it. Among the variables affecting an investor's reach—how many concentric jurisdictional lines can be crossed—one of the most important is the *form* of his or her capital. Jeffry Frieden, for example, has analyzed variations in mobility in terms of how "liquid" or "fixed" capital is.[43] Finance and portfolio capital is highly liquid and can be moved across jurisdictional lines at lightning speed. Various kinds of direct investment are more fixed. Descending still further, fixed investments can range across the entire spectrum of mobility, from sunken to footloose. Yet even those controlling what are ordinarily assumed to be rather sunken (and thus immobile) investments can still manipulate their capital so as to turn policy differentials across all jurisdictions to their advantage in their dealings with each. In resource extraction, for instance, the residual bargaining power of transnationals whose operations are spread over sites in several countries can be substantial. Though relocation is difficult, a *redirection* of money for research and development and the expansion of extractive capacity to sites in competing countries yields potent leverage.

Oil and gas extraction in Indonesia illustrates the point nicely. According to Caltex Indonesia's CEO, when dissatisfied with government policies the company can "send signals to the government" through spending on research and development. "If the rate of return here becomes too low for us, or if the risks become too high, we will begin to disengage. This point must be clearly conveyed [to policymakers]. We don't give ultimatums, we just file our regular budget reports and it's

[43] Frieden 1988.

clear from the figures that we're cutting back. They call us up and ask why our figures are going down, and then we explain."[44] A senior vice president at Mobil Oil Indonesia said: "In terms of the exploration and production environment, Indonesia competes with countries like Nigeria, the U.K., and the North Sea area. We look at a number of factors: the price we can get for the energy products brought up, the costs of production, and the fiscal environment. Of course we also pay a lot of attention to the political and social context. But what is important for us is that the fiscal terms here in Indonesia be kept as good as possible. Here I'm referring to the split—85 percent to the government and 15 percent to us—exploration cost reductions, and tax benefits. We have lots of choices in where to invest around the world, and we keep a close watch on all of them."

Mobil's Jakarta headquarters tries to convince the Indonesian government that the local office is on its side and trying hard to get as big a share as possible of Mobil's global research and development budget so new wells can be tapped and more gas brought up. "These days our money is tight and we have to spend it very carefully," the executive says, explaining the opening gambit. "Speaking globally, Indonesia and Malaysia are pretty much near the bottom in terms of attractiveness based on costs. And we tell them this. A couple weeks ago a top Indonesian delegation visited our New York headquarters, and our people there put the charts up on the screen showing how Indonesia compared with other locations around the world. They understood our message, and they're trying."[45]

In addition to the relative sunkenness of an investment, mobility is also shaped by the trade regime. The option to relocate can depend on a firm's capacity to transport products from a new production site (perhaps chosen because labor costs were low) to an established home market. Alternatively, relocation can be blocked if a firm finds that trade policies or transport costs do not allow the import of inputs to a site across national lines. Providing services for which the consuming population is fixed is another factor contributing to immobility. Thus a private bus service cannot easily relocate to another city. And finally, licensing regulations and requirements can also contribute to immobility.

---

[44] Interview in Jakarta with Haroen Al Rasjid, 17 February 1989. The ninety-minute meeting in Haroen's office was interrupted twice by phone calls from Ginanjar Kartasasmita, the minister of mines and energy.

[45] Interview in Jakarta with John Frannea, 31 March 1989.

Lawyers and doctors must be certified, for instance, before they can practice. Getting such certification can be extremely difficult even across multiple subnational jurisdictions much less across national boundaries.

Size is also an important determinant of mobility. Generally speaking, smaller investors and entities are less mobile—especially when it comes to relocating among nation-states—for several reasons. First, whether a capital controller intends simply to transfer funds from New York to Tokyo or to move a furniture manufacturing plant from Atlanta to a *maquiladora* in northern Mexico, there are costs associated with the relocation. Gaining access to information about the target location and how to transfer one's capital or plant there can be expensive. Also, the move itself involves costs that can make the relocation fiscally untenable. In general, larger investors and firms have greater human and financial resources on hand to meet these costs. Referring exclusively for a moment to fixed investments (plants, firms, etc.), another element related to size that enhances relocational and redistributive options is having multiple rather than single entities. A company with many subsidiaries can spread its component parts across several jurisdictions and manipulate how much reinvestment each subsidiary receives based on how favorable (profitable) each jurisdiction is. And when a company consists of multiple entities, capital controllers can relocate parts of their firm without necessarily having to move personally from a location that is unfavorable only from a profit-making point of view. When one owns a small, single-entity operation, relocation entails moving with the company. The number of concentric jurisdictional lines (city, county, state, nation-state) a small investor will likely consider crossing—even assuming the costs can be met—tends to be lower.[46] That said, it is noteworthy that many postcolonial states have lowered their minimum foreign investment thresholds to lure ever-smaller firms into relocating across national borders. Indonesia's minimum dropped from $10 million to $250,000.

How Mobile Is Capital?

It is extremely difficult to track changes in capital mobility with accuracy. There are regular reports from governments, international agencies like the United Nations, private research institutes, and the press. Some

---

[46] Although Sassen (1988) focuses more on social and cultural factors inhibiting the mobility of labor than on capital controllers, her insights on this point are quite useful.

data are expressed in U.S. dollars, others in local currencies, and still others as percentages of gross domestic product (GDP) or aggregate world trade or output (though these are often calculated using U.S. dollars as the base currency). Each of these currencies represents a different unit of measurement. Over time, these units change in value not only relative to each other but also relative to themselves. It is tantamount to measuring the growth of a forest with a hundred instruments of different size, all of which change daily, and then reporting the findings in terms of one of the instruments (which itself is constantly changing). Depending on the kind of capital movement being tracked, it is possible to count the movements of factories, the opening of foreign subsidiaries, or the volume of financial transactions.

Even if reliable and meaningful data were readily available, it is not clear that such figures would be the most important consideration if one were interested in the *political* issues surrounding capital mobility. The beliefs and perceptions of policymakers and the broader public are an extremely important dimension of capital's use of structural power. Perhaps this explains why capital controllers and those speaking on their behalf tend to exaggerate the degree of capital mobility, alarming all the more those who might want to resist adopting the policies, offering the subsidies, or accepting the givebacks investors say will make them stay put, create jobs, and pay taxes. The simple answer is that capital is dramatically more mobile now than it was even three decades ago, that one of the most important changes in capital mobility is in the vastly wider relocation options for direct investment in plants and factories, but that capital is far less mobile (and the arrangements and institutions that allow it far more fragile) than capital controllers would like everyone to believe.

With these caveats in mind, what are some of the quantitative indications of capital mobility?[47] On an average day in 1993, the volume of foreign exchange transactions was $900 billion. Gross transactions in bonds and equities between the United States and everyone else jumped from less than 10 percent of GDP in 1980 to 93 percent of GDP by 1990. And yet American investors still keep 94 percent of their equity holdings

[47] The figures presented in the rest of this section are drawn from United Nations 1993; Prowse 1993; *Economist,* 19 September 1992, 27; *Economist,* 28 August 1993, 65; *Economist,* 8 January 1994, 16; *Financial Times,* 19 April 1993, 15; *Euromoney* Suppl., 5 September 1993, 1.

in domestic securities. Although fast-growing stock markets in postcolonial states have drawn a great deal of attention in recent years, the figures need to be examined closely to get a sense of what the numbers mean. During the past decade, for instance, total market capitalization of developing stock markets has increased more than tenfold, while that of advanced industrial states has increased only 3.5 times. Yet in 1993 these emerging stock markets, predominantly in Asia, Latin America, and Eastern Europe, still accounted for less than 10 percent of global stock market capitalization.

The story for foreign direct investment (FDI) is equally complicated. In 1992 there were 37,000 transnational corporations (TNCs) controlling one-third of the world's private sector productive assets. These companies collectively generated about $5.5 trillion in sales from their foreign affiliates alone. Although 37,000 certainly sounds like a lot of firms competing vigorously with each other, concentration of ownership and control is staggering. In 1990 the world's top twenty TNCs alone owned $1.4 trillion in assets, of which $563 billion (or 40 percent) was in foreign assets (not surprisingly, as firm size increases, the proportion of foreign assets increases in tandem). By 1992 global stocks of FDI—that is, long-term, cross-border capital invested in hard assets like new factories, equipment, and research facilities—reached $2 trillion. Flows of new investments adding annually to this total doubled between 1975 and 1980. At $203 billion in 1990, flows of new FDI were ten times what they had been fifteen years earlier. As for where FDI gets invested, the lion's share still ends up in advanced industrial countries, but the trends indicate important shifts toward postcolonial states. In 1987 just 12 percent of total global FDI was in developing countries; by 1993 the share had increased to 20 percent. Given the size of existing capital stocks of FDI in advanced industrial countries (making for a big denominator), this increase of 8 percent in as many years means that the rate of *new* FDI in postcolonial states is especially high. Indeed, although widespread recession caused overall flows of new FDI to decline fairly sharply between 1990 and 1993, flows to developing countries increased fully 50 percent during the same period.

Even with these signs of dramatic surges in capital mobility across national boundaries, it is also clear that large chunks of capital remain in place despite strong incentives to relocate. It might be that the obstacles to capital mobility are greater than they seem. It is also possible that capital controllers who can relocate their resources choose, for reasons of high risk and low nerve, to keep a substantial share close to home. Indications from financial markets, where the highly liquid form of capital makes it supremely mobile, suggest that there are some clogs in the pipes. In 1992 short-term real interest rates in the United States were nearly zero, whereas in Germany they were 7.5 percent. If financial capital were perfectly mobile no such gap would exist, because investors would all shift their savings to Germany until the glut of capital in the banks drove interest rates down to the level available in the United States (where interest rates would rise as savings became scarcer). Interestingly, the gap in interest rates between the two countries disappeared on long-term money.

The Implications of Mobility

In assessing the relative structural power of different capital controllers, it is essential to recall that investors of all sizes and in all sectors can simply withhold their resources. It is for this reason that differences in structural power and influence are based primarily on the degree or range of mobility an investor enjoys, as measured by how many jurisdictional lines can be crossed. There are two senses in which actors with higher mobility are more powerful. First, they have at their disposal more than one mode of depriving a jurisdiction of investment resources. As Albert Hirschman rightly notes, although highly mobile actors (those able to "exit") will be less likely to lobby or participate in overt politics (give "voice"), policymakers are far more likely to listen to them and be responsive to their interests and demands. This is even more true when large size and high mobility coincide. Policymakers find it especially difficult to ignore investors who can or do employ large numbers of people. "The chances for voice to function effectively," Hirschman maintains, "are appreciably strengthened if voice is backed up by the *threat of exit.*" This is the case "whether it is made openly or whether the possibility of exit is merely well understood to be an element in the situation by all concerned."[48] Frieden's early work strengthens this

---

[48] Hirschman 1970:86, 83; Hirschman's emphasis. He adds that when seeking policy changes, "the willingness to develop and use the voice mechanism is reduced by [the capacity to] exit," but "the effectiveness of the voice mechanism is strengthened by the

claim. In his study of the ways domestic groups responded to belt-tightening policies in five Latin American states in the wake of the debt crisis in the early and middle 1980s, he found that loud protests came from holders of fixed assets, whereas those with liquid assets simply moved their resources abroad (with devastating results) and remained relatively silent during the political battles that ensued.[49] A key point in the calculations of policymakers is that the ramifications of relocation can be as enduring for a jurisdiction as the costs and losses can be temporary for the mobile investor who has moved to a more forthcoming investment site.

The second aspect of mobile investors' greater power has to do with the range of policies their decisions influence. As one moves inward across concentric jurisdictional lines, the number of elements of the investment climate that can be adjusted shrinks. The city of Chicago, for example, can tinker with its property tax rates, but the state of Illinois imposes a given rate for payroll taxes, and the United States federal government mandates a minimum wage. Investors who can relocate across all these policy boundaries have an effect on the investment climate from its broadest outlines inward to its narrowest details.

Relative mobility also has an impact on the policies different capital controllers will support and the vigor with which they support them. Mobility plays a significant role in determining how committed actors will be to an investment climate in which access to opportunity is based on free markets.[50] Although it is not an iron rule, investors who are more mobile tend to press more strongly for *official* policies based on free markets, for two major reasons. The first is obvious. Since they are mobile, it is to their advantage to widen, not narrow, the range of sites available to them. The second is both more subtle and linked to the greater leverage mobile actors have in getting responsive policies from

---

possibility of exit." In their work on mobility, Bates and Lien (1985) reach a similar conclusion.

[49] Frieden 1988. Felix and Sanchez (1989) provide further insights into the ways those with mobile assets were able to respond to debt problems in Latin America.

[50] I am not suggesting that mobility is the only factor affecting commitment to free markets. Rather, it is an additional one that has not received nearly as much attention as others. A very important consideration will always be how competitive one is. Highly efficient and competitive firms are far more committed to a level playing field because such an environment ensures their advantageous position over weaker and less efficient competitors.

decision makers. A key element in an investor's ability to make a handsome profit is the presence and competitiveness of other investors and firms. The main reason capitalists support free markets is to keep their opponents from enjoying the competitive edge that interventionist policies confer. But if investors have good reason to believe they alone could negotiate a side deal with policymakers, yet still have market-oriented policies be a jurisdiction's *official* stance that applies to everyone else, the incentive to support free markets as a formal policy is tremendous. Conversely, if a group of investors are aware that selected competitors are receiving special dispensations and that there is little hope of preventing them from enjoying these benefits, and even less that they themselves will get similar treatment, they will quite naturally be strongly opposed to a general policy climate based on free markets. Such a climate leaves immobile and unconnected actors with all the disadvantages and none of the benefits that market-based policies create.[51] The evidence is clear that what is being described here is more than hypothetical. The work of Peter Eisinger and others on cities and regions in the United States and United Kingdom finds that mobile investors take full advantage of their added leverage over policymakers to cut precisely such special deals for themselves on taxation, subsidized credit, accelerated depreciation schedules, and guaranteed markets for a specified period—while all the time supporting free markets for the jurisdiction as a whole.[52]

The political economy of mobility extends well beyond the bounds of intracapitalist conflicts. Changes in the *overall* mobility of capital, particularly during the past thirty years, when the capacity to relocate production facilities has been dramatically expanded, have had a profound impact on the intrajurisdictional balance of power between labor and capital and on the interjurisdictional friction between labor and labor. Both these dynamics have contributed to a massive net gain in power for capital controllers when considered on a global scale.

Part of the explanation for these developments rests in the relative immobility of laboring populations. Quite apart from considerations of family and culture, which, as Saskia Sassen points out, complicate the

[51] In pressing for a policy regime to replace free markets, immobile or uncompetitive actors direct their efforts along lines that distinguish them most from mobile and competitive players. A nonexhaustive list of examples might include nationality, size, race, and being in "traditional" sectors, so-called infant industries, strategic sectors, etc.

[52] Eisinger 1988.

mobility of people, the barriers erected by nation-states to population shifts across national boundaries have slowed relocation significantly (even as the costs of long-distance transport have declined).[53] Furthermore, some of the elements of an investment climate that make a location desirable from the perspective of investors—for instance, low-cost and weakly organized labor, few restrictions on environmental degradation and worker safety—make it undesirable from the perspective of workers. The result is that forces that pull investors in one direction push laborers (especially poor ones) in the other. The movement of labor is a one-way street—from poorer locations to richer ones. And it is precisely the inflow of poor laborers that countries have worked most vigorously to prevent. Ironically, despite sharing equally in an environment marked by technological advances that have made the world smaller, the mobility of capital and that of labor have moved in opposite directions. It is not technology, of course, that accounts for these differences, but rather the *relative permeability* of states to labor and capital.

Another factor that helps account for changes in the balance of power between labor and capital within jurisdictions centers on the absence of structural levers for labor. Lindblom shows that the structural dimensions of investors' power are unique in capitalist societies. "Children may sulk," he writes, "when they do not like the way they are being treated. Professors may grumble. Workers may slow their work. But their responses differ in a critical way. The dissatisfactions of these other groups do not result in disincentives and reduced performance that impose a broad, severe and obvious penalty throughout the society, which is what unemployment does [when investors do not invest]."[54]

By and large, the gap separating resources flowing in and expenditures flowing out is much narrower for laborers than for investors. Laborers work without any special incentives from the state because, as Lindblom puts it, "their livelihoods depend on it."[55] He continues: "The test of the difference is an obvious one. All over the world men work at ordinary jobs because they have no choice but to do so. But in many parts of the world the conditions that call forth entrepreneurial energy and venturesomeness are still lacking, and the energy and venturesomeness are therefore not forthcoming. *The particular roles that businessmen are*

---

[53] Sassen 1988.
[54] Lindblom 1982:328.
[55] Lindblom 1977:176.

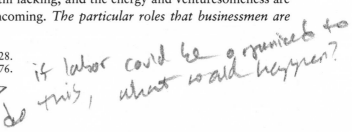

if labor could be organized to do this, what would happen?

required to play in market-oriented systems they play well only when
sufficiently indulged."[56] Capital's ability to exercise structural leverage
without first having to organize as a class, moreover, contributes still
further to the power imbalance.[57] For labor to endanger a system to such
a degree that political elites would feel the same compulsion to act as
when investors merely threaten withdrawal or relocation, they must, as
Lindblom points out, "successfully stop production, not simply in one
firm or industry, but broadly as in a general strike."[58] Not only is this
extremely difficult to accomplish logistically, but when such strikes last
more than a few days, political elites, "even in the polyarchies," deploy
the coercive and hegemonic instruments of the state to break the resolve
of labor.[59] By contrast, no example exists of state leaders' using the
coercive instruments at their disposal to force private capital controllers
to invest or to repatriate all resources and facilities relocated to foreign
jurisdictions. "In short," as Lindblom concludes, "the rules of market-
oriented systems, while granting a privileged position to business, so far
appear to prohibit the organizational moves that would win a comparable position for labor."[60]

A final point about the effect of the changing mobility of capital
relates to the competitive pressures it introduces between jurisdictions.
The free movement of goods, finance capital, and currency across jurisdictional lines has long placed constraints on policymakers, and the
enormous literature in international political economy dealing with this
subject testifies to its importance. But these constraints and pressures
have increased noticeably with the expanded opportunities that exist for
the relocation of factories and other productive facilities. Nowhere is
this more evident than in the postcolonial societies that are beginning to
witness transnational relocation by their own formerly immobile investing classes. The literature on cities and regions was the first to examine
changes in political influence rooted in mobility.

---

[56] Lindblom 1977:176; my emphasis.

[57] Offe and Wiesenthal 1985.

[58] Lindblom 1977:176.

[59] Lindblom 1977:176. Lindblom cites the example of the aborted British general strike
of 1926. Authoritarian governments in postcolonial societies are even less tolerant of
organized labor. Corporatist control of unions is combined with the torture and assassina-
tion of labor leaders to ensure that workers cannot withdraw their side of the production
bargain and threaten an economy and regime with destabilization.

[60] Lindblom 1977:176.

In a piece first published in 1961, Robert C. Wood noted that "zoning" was born as municipalities tried to cope with increasing capital mobility. At first as an element in their revenue-generating strategy, cities divided their jurisdictions into net revenue producing and net revenue using zones. With time this instrument was used with ever greater sophistication and precision to cope with mobile investors. Coincidental with the development of zoning, Wood notes, was the appearance of "policies of municipal mercantilism," or what became known as "beggar-thy-neighbor" strategies. County and city governments all established special commissions whose job it was to "review existing public policies for their effect on private location decisions" of investors. "Influential citizens," meanwhile, were "designated as 'economic ambassadors.' Special tours for outside industrialists [were] arranged to emphasize both the natural and political advantages of a given jurisdiction."[61]

Initial public reaction to this added dimension of competition was decidedly negative. "Not infrequently, these activities engender[ed] hostility among a municipality's neighbors, with accusations of 'pirating' of industry or social irresponsibility."[62] As the practice became more widespread and as arguments were put forth justifying the policies on free-market grounds, the tables were turned. The moral view that one jurisdiction was irresponsible for adopting policies that tempted investors to relocate—thus undermining the tax and employment base of their neighbors—was inverted and replaced by the view that jurisdictions that could not attract and retain investors were "unfit" and "uncompetitive" on market and efficiency grounds. At no time was hostility directed against the investors doing the relocating. The ideological hegemony reflected in this fact is unmistakable and will be discussed further in the last chapter.

Before leaving the discussion of mobility and structural levers of power, I should mention the concrete processes involved in the expression of this power. Anticipation by government officials plays an important role. Lindblom and Hirschman both emphasize the role of strategic calculations by policymakers, who are aware of the varying mobility of investors, the one-shot nature of the costs of relocating, and the negative

---

[61] Wood 1968:79.
[62] Wood 1968:80.

consequences for the jurisdiction left behind. In the context of their taxation study, Bates and Lien write, for instance, that "knowing that the holders of taxable assets can exit, the demanders of taxes would surely take into account the potential for that behavior in calculating their best revenue strategy." They conclude that "the capacity of strategic calculations by maximizing monarchs results in the owners of *mobile* factors . . . being given greater voice over the policy choices of government."[63] By this they mean a greater say in shaping a jurisdiction's policies—even if these mobile actors never actually "speak."

Pfeffer and Salancik's work on the processes and dynamics between complex organizations and those who can deprive them of the resources they depend on to function is also helpful here. Important considerations, adapted slightly for present purposes, include:

1. Those in charge of the organization (policymakers) must be aware of the interests and demands of those who control key resources.
2. The ability of policymakers to control the resources must be minimal; that is, "external" control over the resources must extend to their allocation and use.
3. For the leverage of resource controllers to be effective, the organization's (jurisdiction's) access to alternative or replacement resources must be limited or nonexistent.
4. It is essential that the relevant actions (policies) of the organization's leaders to meet the resource controllers' demands and interests be visible to the resource controllers so that they can assess them and respond.
5. For these processes to operate in a predictable manner, it is important that those in charge of the organization be keenly interested in staying in power.[64]

Items 1 and 4 concern signaling and communication, items 2 and 3 concern the pattern of resource control and the availability of alternative supplies, and item 5 is simply a reasonable assumption about the actors in charge of the organization. This chapter has already touched on most of these points. When investors are not actively "voicing" their interests by participating in some way in policy-making, they transmit signals through their investment activity, ranging, as we have seen, from a slow-down in new investment to outright relocation. I have also mentioned

---

[63] Bates and Lien 1985:61; emphasis in original.
[64] Pfeffer and Salancik 1978:43.

state bodies and state personnel devoted to monitoring the "barometer" of investors' satisfaction and interpreting upward and downward movements for policymakers so that possible changes in the jurisdiction's investment climate—which constitutes a set of signals to investors—can be considered. Item 5, meanwhile, has been an unstated assumption in this book from the outset. Points 2 and 3, although discussed in passing in previous sections, are of a slightly different character in that they represent what I have already referred to as "mediating" factors— variables that shape the ways the structural leverage of capital controllers is felt and dealt with in widely varying contexts. The final element of this theoretical discussion is devoted to fuller consideration of these important contextual factors.

Factors That Mediate Structural Power

Although the structural aspects of investors' power are built into capitalist systems of production and thus present real constraints for decision makers in capitalist societies, they do not have the same effect everywhere. Several important factors mediate how strongly pressures from capital controllers are felt and how willing or capable different jurisdictions and their policymakers are to respond to these pressures. It is for this reason that so much variation in investment climates exists throughout the capitalist world—ranging from jurisdictions that are highly unresponsive to capital controllers to those that respond both rapidly and favorably. It is for this reason too that the power and policy-making dynamics discussed in this chapter are not deterministic in the narrow sense of the word.[65] Rather, they provide us with insights into the sometimes devastating difficulties political elites can encounter when, for whatever reason, they ignore the policy demands of actors whose private and independent investment decisions have wide-ranging ramifications for the rest of the population. For clarity only, I group the mediating factors to be discussed (presented here as propositions) into two broad, and in many respects overlapping, categories. The first focuses on those factors that make a jurisdiction more or less vulnerable to the structural pressures capital controllers can create. The second

---

[65] For a nuanced discussion of determination, see Wright 1978.

highlights those factors that make decision makers more or less likely to respond to the demands of investors.

The first proposition is particularly relevant to the Indonesian case and will require more explanation than the others. *The impact of investors' structural leverage on a jurisdiction decreases as access to and control over investment resources that can replace those controlled privately increases.* Here the issue of end-use discretion is critical. The types of capital that can be used to meet the investment needs of a jurisdiction can be ordered along a continuum that ranges from complete private discretion over end use to complete policymaker discretion. Table 1 presents a selected list of capital types to illustrate this ordering.[66] The direct discretionary control of policymakers over the allocation and use of private and portfolio capital is extremely low. Interstate loans, by contrast, are substantially less restricted in how precisely they are used. Though the demands attached to flows of state-to-state funds vary greatly and depend on the channels they pass through and the reasons they are supplied (e.g., because the recipient is important geopolitically), they are almost always weaker than those placed on capital supplied privately for direct investment. Lending states audit the books of borrowing states to ensure that the resources are used for the intended purposes, but this form of end-use control is nothing like that of direct investors overseeing their own projects. Policymaker discretion over commercial credit, the next step down on the list, is even greater— particularly during those rare periods when finance capital is in oversupply. Commercial banks tend not to have the personnel to monitor in detail how the funds they provide are used by policymakers. The final category, state capital, is by definition controlled and allocated by policymakers. State leaders need not coax or induce anyone or anything to gain access to these resources and have them invested in ways that are economically, politically, or even personally sustaining. The only limits on these resources stem from characteristics of the state itself, such as the degree of power concentrated at the governing center.

The important analytical point in setting forth this continuum of discretionary control is to suggest that as policymakers gain increasing access to resources toward the bottom of the list, the structural influence

---

[66] Stallings (1985) focused on the first four of these categories; Wood (1980) analyzed the interstate loan category. Also see Khoury 1990.

Table 1. A framework for analyzing capital control and end use

Sources/types	Constraints/motives	Intermediate channels	Policymaker discretion over end use
Private direct investment	Supplier has clear purpose for end use. Constraints on resources very high.	None. Supplier deploys resources directly.	*Low.* As intended by original supplier. Source monitors and directs end use fully.
Portfolio investment	Often multiple suppliers. Purpose of end use less clear. Resources moderately constrained	Through a recipient firm. Motives and intentions of firm's owners/managers intervene.	*Low.* End use may diverge from intentions of portfolio investor, but not owing to state actors. Capacity of source to monitor and direct end use is reduced.
Interstate loans	Often multiple suppliers. Suppliers can have contradictory purposes for end use. Weaker constraints on resources.	Through recipient state. Competing intentions of state (or state component) intervene.	*Medium.* End use may conflict with one or all supplier factions. Capacity of source(s) to monitor exists. Ability to direct end use varies but can be high.
Private loans	Suppliers often syndicated. Sovereign guarantee is key. Supplier concerned less with end use and more with risk. Quite weak constraints on resources.	Through recipient state. Often more discretion for executive branch than with bi/multilateral credit.	*Medium to high.* Intended end use, if specified, can be avoided. Weak capacity (and inclination) of suppliers to monitor and enforce end use.
State capital	No additional constraints that policymakers do not ordinarily confront.	None. State deploys resources directly, though internal channels through which this is done matter.	*Highest.* Discretion limited only by state coherence and internal capacity to implement policies.

of private capital controllers to constrain the policies decision makers can safely consider diminishes in tandem. And it is precisely these dynamics that made possible the reduced responsiveness of the state to private investors during the oil boom period in Indonesia. Although periods like this are exceptional in capitalist systems, they are extremely useful for what they reveal about the structural power relationships that exist in nonexceptional circumstances.

A second type of variable affects the mobility of capital for a jurisdiction and thus affects the structural leverage of investors that is rooted in relocation. *As the integration of a jurisdiction into extrajurisdictional markets increases, the exposure to pressures from mobile capital controllers increases as well.* This is not to say that investors have no structural influence at all when poor integration into markets hinders mobility. Simply withholding investments is still available. This mediating factor is less important when the basis of extrajurisdictional integration is a sector controlled and owned by the state, such as Pertamina in Indonesia of the Nigerian National Petroleum Company.

Yet another factor affects the impetus for relocation. *Jurisdictions are less constrained by mobile capital when the differential in investment climates with competing jurisdictions is small or nonexistent or when competitors' climates are clearly less favorable.* Although capital mobility has caused considerable convergence across a wide range of jurisdictions, significant variations in investment climates persist.

A fourth consideration has to do with mobile investors themselves. *A jurisdiction is relatively insulated from the structural power of mobile capital when the fraction of all capital invested they control is small, or when their investments are not heavily concentrated in sectors that employ large numbers of people, are important to access to new technology, supply significant amounts of foreign exchange, or are important to the state's revenue base.*

Quite apart from the climate within jurisdictions, the capacity of investors to relocate presupposes that relations between jurisdictions are relatively free of conflicts and crises so that relocation is reasonably feasible and safe. *As world or even regional economic and political stability decreases, the mobility of capital decreases, and the vulnerability of jurisdictions to the structural power of these investors decreases as well.* Fred Block, for instance, notes that major crises greatly enhance the bargaining power of the state with private investors because their options for relocation in the face of major and unfavorable policy changes are drastically reduced. The possibility that class-based conflict can erupt during these periods and threaten the ordinary sanctity of private property also gives state leaders more leeway in the policies that they can consider and capital will tolerate. He writes that "there are certain periods—during wartime, major depressions, and periods of postwar reconstruction—in which the decline of business confidence as a veto on government policies doesn't work. These are the periods in which dramatic increases in the state's role have occurred." During wars "international business confidence becomes less important, since international capital flows tend to be placed under government control."[67]

A core element of the theory of investors' structural power concerns how the ramifications of disinvestment and relocation for a population—whose reproduction and survival depend on an investment process neither they nor political elites control—result in pressures on policymakers to respond to investors' policy demands. Several factors that are quite specific to different jurisdictions shape how severely both the ramifications and the related pressures will be felt. *As the mobility of labor from a jurisdiction increases, the indirect pressures on political elites from investment difficulties are moderated.* On the other hand, *jurisdictions where demographic pressures are high, unemployment rates are already at socially intolerable levels, the welfare apparatus and resources are weak, and the avenues for retreat for dislocated persons (such as into the "informal sector") are unavailable or already saturated are more vulnerable to investors' pressures.* Furthermore, the willingness of populations to endure the deprivations of an investment decline can be increased when revolutionary, nationalist, anticapitalist, or other feelings are widespread and run high. The last factor to be mentioned in this category also relates to the dangers associated with a population's reaction to investment dysfunctions. *A jurisdiction in which the opposition to the regime in power is unorganized, co-opted, fractured, destroyed, or otherwise rendered ineffectual will be less vulnerable to pressures exerted by capital controllers than those in which the societal forces of opposition are united and well equipped to react to economic stress.*

---

[67] Block 1977b:24. Skocpol (1980) tried—unsuccessfully, I think—to downplay the importance of Block's insight.

Fragmentation along regional, religious, racial, ethnic, or ideological lines can severely dampen a population's ability to apply destabilizing pressures on state leaders.

Assuming an average degree of exposure or vulnerability on the variables noted above, we now turn to contextual factors that focus more specifically on the jurisdiction's institutional apparatus and on the willingness and ability of policymakers to be responsive. *A ruling group that is both willing and able to make extensive and ongoing use of its jurisdiction's coercive instruments to counteract societal pressures can diminish its vulnerability to structural pressures from capital controllers.* An important element in this ability is that policymakers must have the full backing of the jurisdiction's police force and military. Sharp divisions in the military, in particular, can greatly increase the vulnerability of civilian leaders to the pressures investors can set in motion. Note that this point does not contradict the earlier claim that not even dictators are not fully insulated from investors' structural power. Indeed, such a high level of coercion represents the kind of political instability that accompanies economic difficulties related to investment rates.

The unresponsiveness of some policymakers to capital controllers can occur not because the actors in charge are not aware of the difficulties they might face or are unwilling to respond, but rather because the nature of policymaking and policy implementation effectively prevents them from acting. *A high degree of institutional and organizational incoherence—marked by high turnover of officials, little policymaking continuity, frequent coups, or a weak center for decision making—can lead to unresponsive state policies despite the clear presence of structural pressures from those controlling investment resources.*

In concluding this discussion, I must note that pressures that can threaten the position of policymakers do not arise exclusively from the breakdown of the investment process for a population. Indeed, being responsive to capital controllers can itself precipitate strong reactions from workers and other groups in society. In addition, it is entirely possible that existing circumstances make it completely reasonable *in the short run* for those interested in their political survival to ignore the demands of investors. This does not mean that further complications arising from investment shortfalls will be avoided; acting in ways that anticipate or prevent these complications is simply not an option. Again, the point is that we cannot "read" policy processes and outcomes directly from existing structural constraints. Rather, the careful identification of structural forces supplies us with important information about the limits on policymakers that, if crossed, pose identifiable and predictable consequences for their ability to rule, and in extreme cases even to remain in power.

The Indonesian Case

The next three chapters deal with the three major policy phases in Indonesian political economy since General Suharto came to power late in 1965. The dynamics surrounding Indonesia's investment needs, changes in the sources of and control over major resources used to meet these needs, and the potency of structural levers of influence for mobile investors are all critical elements in explaining shifts in policy that have occurred during the past twenty-five years. I will specifically mention several major points at the outset to alert readers to critical issues in the story of how the structural constraints explored in this chapter were felt and dealt with in the Indonesian case.

I cannot stress enough that this book is not about oil booms or even about oil-exporting countries. Rather, it is about the structural dimensions of investors' power under capitalism, the degree to which different actors have access to this power, how and with what intensity it is manifested concretely, and the constraints on policymaking that are imposed as a result. The oil boom of the 1970s and early 1980s is important because it was exceptional. In Indonesia the boom meant that state leaders had direct access to a huge resource pool that could be used to replace a sizable share of the investment resources for the country that had been supplied from private capital controllers—thereby damaging the underpinnings of their structural power. With the pillars of investors' structural leverage severely weakened during this interlude and with the range of policy options decision makers felt they could consider widened enormously, the structurally based limitations present under capitalism in *unexceptional* periods are brought into sharper focus.

The primary tension in policy across the three periods centered on Indonesia's official policies regulating access to opportunities for investment and profit. At one extreme was a system of allocation and distribution based on impersonal market criteria, and at the other extreme was one based on policies that put discretion firmly in the hands of officials. The degree of mobility of capital controllers helps account for which actors favored which mode of distribution, and why. Investors who were more mobile tended to favor the markets, whereas capital controllers who were less mobile tended to favor intervention by officials. This was even more true when international mobility and competitiveness coincided. Added to these interests on the part of capital controllers were the interests of political elites. Except for the special group of economic ministers in the cabinet, Indonesian officials from the president down to the village heads have preferred a system of distribution that supports rather than conflicts with the patron-client structures that pervade the Indonesian state. It is for this reason that the policy trajectory away from market-based terms of access during the relatively more "flexible" oil boom years was in no sense arbitrary.

I will pay considerable attention to the processes of communication between policy makers and capital controllers. Although mobile and immobile actors transmitted direct and indirect signals about their policy interests in a steady way across all three periods, which group policy makers paid attention to varied sharply. A parallel pattern of influence is also apparent for the economic ministers within the state. Mobile investors and the economic ministers were ascendant when the state's ability to replace the resources of private investors was minimal—before and after the boom—and weakest in the middle period when alternative resources were in abundant supply.

Two other points to watch for as the story of Indonesia's political economy unfolds have to do with change that occurred in secular rather than pendular ways. One developed within Indonesia's extremely important indigenous class of investors known as the *pribumi*. During the first two periods they comprised decidedly immobile and relatively noncompetitive actors. For the most part the *pribumi* were small and medium entrepreneurs who pressed hard for official state policies giving them special advantages the market consistently denied them. By the third period, however, an important rift had developed within the *pribumi*. The entire group could no longer be lumped together as immobile and minor players in Indonesian capitalism. A small but politically significant leading edge of the *pribumi*, whose interests as investors now more closely approximated those long pursued by other mobile actors, broke with the more immobile indigenous capital controllers and defended an official policy of access based on market criteria. That this rift coincided with the end of the oil boom and a restoration of the structural leverage of mobile capital controllers is extremely important in accounting for both the extent and the pace of "deregulation" and liberalization after 1982.

The second point centers on the increasing intensity with which policymakers felt competitive pressures from other investment sites. From the beginning of Suharto's New Order, the pressures on Indonesia to compete with other jurisdictions for mobile investors were apparent. In debates about how far Indonesia should go to entice capital controllers to come or return to Indonesia, the benefits of investing in other places were frequently mentioned as an important consideration. Meanwhile, complaints from mobile investors during the oil boom years about how uncompetitive Indonesia's investment climate had become were consistently ignored. Some officials openly invited these investors to go elsewhere if they were not satisfied with what Indonesia was willing to offer. By the early 1980s capital was vastly more mobile than it had been during the preboom days, and the pressures to compete with places like Thailand (which had experienced no oil boom during which officials could easily ignore structural pressures from investors) were markedly greater.

Before commenting briefly on the material chosen to illustrate the character of the three periods, I should mention the policy making process in Indonesia and the role some of the factors mentioned above played as mediating variables. It is important to recognize that decision making in Indonesia is extremely concentrated and centralized. Even if ministers act independently to promote a certain policy line, no official policies of any national significance are adopted without the approval of President Suharto. One noteworthy implication of this is that the success of competing groups within the state in having their policy agenda enacted depends on Suharto's assessment of the implications for his strategy of anticipating or countering challenges to the stability of his rule. Other mediating factors are treated schematically below:

Integration into transjurisdictional markets. For all three periods, and particularly during the postboom phase, Indonesia has had rather high and steadily increasing integration into markets for capital, goods, and services of all kinds. Although it is now the fourth most populous country in the world and is well endowed with natural resources, Indonesia did not try to insulate itself as China and India had. Since the mid-1960s, the Indonesian rupiah has consistently been fully convertible.

Differential of investment climate with competing jurisdictions. Though Indonesia was not notably less favorable to investors than neighboring sites once the economic ministers were in firm control after 1965, by 1974 the gap separating it from its competitors began to widen markedly. Major efforts were made after 1982 to restore the competitiveness of the country's investment climate.

Significance of mobile investors. A large share of capital controllers involved in modern sectors are highly mobile in Indonesia. This includes foreigners, ethnic Chinese, and in recent years a small but significant number of *pribumi* investors. In terms of foreign exchange earnings, state revenues, access to technology, and urban employment, these mobile actors are tremendously important.

Demographic and other societal pressures. Despite remarkable progress in slowing birthrates, demographic pressures have been and continue to be extremely intense in Indonesia. Unemployment and especially underemployment are high, and job creation has at times lagged significantly behind the number of new entrants into the labor force. There is no state welfare apparatus, though possibilities for retreat into family-based relief in especially hard times do exist, especially in rural areas. Stress lines in society are greatest in urban areas (in part because retreat is more difficult) and most volatile among high-school, academy, and university graduates—for whom the job creation rate and quality have barely been adequate.

Regime opposition and coercive capability of state. The Suharto regime has worked as diligently to destroy, fragment, and generally enervate forces of opposition in society as it has to unify and insulate the state's forces of coercion. The population of nearly 200 million is divided along racial, ethnic, religious, class, and regional lines. But as material presented in the last chapter will show, communal and regional divisions in Nigeria run far deeper. Suharto's government has succeeded in making it illegal to have any ideology other than that sponsored by the state. Because of an extensive system of pyramidal government structures reaching down to the village and neighborhood level, and because all outsiders are expected to report to the lowest level of officials, it is nearly impossible to disappear or hide in Indonesia—despite its being a vast archipelago. Suharto has repeatedly demonstrated his willingness to use brutal force against the urban and rural poor as well as to make more subtle strikes on middle- and upper-class figures who dare oppose him. The abortive coup of 1965 and the bloody destruction of the Communist Party that followed was traumatic for Indonesian society. There is no organized opposition or leadership of any significance—overt or underground. Since the late 1980s and early 1990s, calls for more openness, human rights, and democracy have increased. In June 1994, Suharto closed down three major weekly publications for their critical political reporting. Police descended with batons upon a peaceful protest against the bans, arresting several while others were hospitalized.

The period from 1965 to the present is much too large to discuss in full detail in a work of this size. Although not every policy in each of the three periods perfectly reflects the predominance of markets or official discretion as the mode of distribution and access, the overall trajectory in each phase is clear and tends toward one of these two poles. Each chapter presents case studies that convey the character of the responsiveness of state policy to private capital controllers. Chapter 2 offers two that reflect the tension between the pressures to adopt market-based policies to attract and retain mobile investors and Suharto's efforts to secure substantial resources that would assist him in utilizing the country's patron-client structures to consolidate his control over the military in particular and the country in general. I examine the 1967 investment conference in Geneva in considerable detail because it represented the earliest and single greatest effort by Indonesian policymakers to communicate with—and satisfy the policy demands of—some of the world's most powerful and mobile investors. At no time since has a presidential decree been issued to authorize a delegation of Indonesians to represent the president at such a summit with capital controllers. Suharto's efforts to gain access to resources whose end-use was far less constrained are examined through a study of the president's relationship with the head of Pertamina, the state oil company, and I also explore how this "second channel" to resources ended in Pertamina's devastating financial collapse. The strength of the economic ministers as well as the sources of that strength are treated briefly. The point of chapter 2 is to account for the responsiveness of the state to capital controllers during the preboom phase of the New Order.

Chapter 3 is devoted to the oil boom period. The impact of the huge increases in oil prices is examined in conjunction with the decline in the state's responsiveness to the policy demands of mobile investors. A detailed case study of a special state body, "Team 10," is presented to illustrate the command position Indonesian officials assumed at the height of the oil boom, when the discretion of policymakers over access and opportunity for investment and profits was at its zenith. This development is linked explicitly to the weakening of structural levers of influence over policymakers as investment resources replacing private capital came on line in massive quantities. It is linked as well to the decline within the cabinet of the economic ministers, who had set the trajectory of economic policy until the onset of the boom.

Chapter 4 focuses both on the demise of Team 10 and on the controversies surrounding Indonesia's tax reform package in the postboom phase. I describe and explain the restoration of private investors' structural power, the rehabilitation of the economic ministers, and the return to a posture of higher responsiveness to capital controllers. The changing role of Indonesia's own *pribumi* investors is highlighted, together with the heightened competitive pressures facing Indonesia in the 1980s owing to greater capital mobility.

The last chapter is intended to suggest that the theoretical approach developed here can be fruitfully applied to other cases and contexts. I make no effort to present full case studies. Rather, my objective is to illustrate the range and depth of this structuralist-materialist perspective by mentioning the issues, questions, and tentative answers it would generate. The last and longest section compares Indonesia with Nigeria, emphasizing the importance of mediating factors discussed above in accounting for how rather similar structural pressures (linked to a resurgence in the power of capital controllers after the oil boom) resulted in quite divergent policy trajectories for the two countries.

THE PREBOOM YEARS, 1965–1974:
INVESTOR CONFIDENCE AND
POLITICAL CONTRADICTIONS

A major factor in the collapse of the Sukarno government in 1965 was the breakdown of investment and production caused by policies begun in 1957, when the nationalization of foreign firms commenced and the climate for private enterprise turned stormy.[1] Mobile investors who could escape did so. Others, turning to short-term transactions in trade and currency exchange, did their best to shield their property and holdings from the risks and dangers of the time.[2] By the early 1960s capital flight was rampant, spare parts and raw materials were unavailable, exports were declining, and both consumer and capital goods were becoming scarce. Profitable production, either by private firms or by state-owned agricultural estates, was all but impossible.[3] The Sukarno government lacked the real resources to fill the investment gap, and running

[1] Crouch 1988.

[2] Christianto Wibisono, an observer of business and economy in Jakarta and an Indonesian of Chinese descent, claims that the 1963 government takeover of the Oei Tiong Ham sugar conglomerate—the country's first real multinational (which still exists as P. T. Rajawali Indonesia)—sent a strong signal to the Chinese that their capital was in danger. "Capital flight to Hong Kong and Singapore had already begun in the early 1960s," according to Wibisono, "but picked up after this ominous sign." Interview in Jakarta with Christianto Wibisono, 7 February 1989. Although such observations are helpful, reliable data on ethnic Chinese capital flight for this period are unavailable. Even if Chinese capital did not leave the country on a massive scale, it certainly was diverted away from investment for production.

[3] Emil Salim, an important economic minister under Suharto, summed up the situation this way: "Most economic resources were diverted to activities with quick returns. Money went into commodities, creating a sellers [sic] market. Normal long-term investment stopped. Unemployment rose, and the whole economy deteriorated rapidly." Indonesian Embassy 1967.

the government printing presses in Kebayoran only accelerated the inflation of the rupiah. Using 1957 as an index year of 100, the cost of living was 348 in 1960, 36,000 in 1965, and 150,000 by July 1966.[4] Although no one could predict what would happen politically, many observers sensed that continuing down the path of alienating private capital without having anything to put in its place was not a viable option.

In the wake of the "coup" of October 1965, hundreds of thousands of Indonesians were slaughtered, and the country's first president as well as the Communist Party (PKI) were decisively swept aside. General Suharto proved himself adroit in utilizing the country's coercive forces to undermine Sukarno and crush the leadership and popular following of the PKI. But his military training and limited education left him ill equipped and unsure of his ability to design a policy package that would reverse the destabilizing economic decline that marked the final years under Sukarno. As part of his overall strategy to consolidate his hold on power, Suharto turned to a group of otherwise powerless economics professors based at the University of Indonesia in Jakarta. "Everything Suharto does is calculated to help him maintain his power," explained Sarbini, who worked closely with Suharto in the months immediately following the 1965 putsch but was subsequently pushed out because he opposed an indefinite period of military rule. "That's what motivates him, and all his decisions are rooted there. He was very confident of his political skills from the start. On economic matters he listens more. He realizes he must be development oriented. If he learned nothing else from the failure of Sukarno, it was that his downfall was rooted in a neglect of economics. Obviously it's easier to stay in power if there is growth."[5] Many capitalist hands had been burned under Sukarno, and Chinese Indonesians and foreigners (the only private investors who mattered at the time) viewed Indonesia's investment climate as highly unfavorable.

This chapter traces how and why Indonesian officials worked fran

---

[4] World Bank 1966:2.

[5] Interview in Jakarta with Sarbini, 13 November 1989. According to Ali Budiardjo, who headed one of Indonesia's largest foreign mining concerns, Suharto relied on the professors to prepare him for public statements. "I remember talking with Widjoyo, and he was very concerned because the president was going to give his first press conference on economics. Afterward he was astonished. Remarkably, the president just said what Widjoyo had told him to say, and without a mistake." Interview in Jakarta with Ali Budiardjo, 24 March 1989. A former U.S. ambassador to Indonesia said this of Suharto: "He was not what you would call a sophisticated thinker, but he was ready to listen to the right people." See Martens [n.d.], interview with Marshall Green.

tically from the earliest months of the New Order to address the investment and production crisis that gripped the country. Not only was the
economy in shambles, but the state itself had no resources whatever with
which to create the jobs or produce the goods Indonesians required.
Meanwhile, the huge following attracted to the PKI made it evident to all
that class-based agitation could generate mass support. The task, if
General Suharto was to increase his chances of ruling Indonesia with a
modicum of political stability, was to create a policy environment that
would induce those who controlled the investment resources the country
desperately needed to supply them without delay. The challenge was not
only to ascertain which policies investors would find most favorable, but
also to convince these resource controllers—both private individuals
and officials from foreign governments—that Indonesia could and
would adopt and implement responsive policies.

This chapter spans the years 1965 to 1974, during which the state's
policies toward capital controllers became highly responsive, with access
and allocation increasingly determined by market forces. The evidence
will show that this policy trajectory was initiated by General Suharto
and carried out by his enormously influential team of economic ministers because they understood clearly that gaining access to investment
resources was critical to the country's economic and political stability,
that the state did not itself have the needed resources, and that attracting
and retaining the resources controlled by others would in effect entail
exchanging state policy for investment resources. The relative mobility
of capital is central to this story. It accounts for which groups would and
would not find the state responsive, as well as the order in which responsive policies were adopted and actions taken. Equally important is the
signaling that occurred between policymakers and capital controllers.

It is not the intention here to describe every policy and every dynamic
that justifies characterizing these years as highly responsive to capital
controllers.[6] Instead, selected case material conveys the nature of the
power relations between state and capital during this first phase. The
responsiveness to capital controllers was by no means simple, conflict
free, automatic, or even natural. This was most evident in President
Suharto's efforts to circumvent the difficult constraints that being responsive to investors imposed on other modes of power consolidation

[6] Mohtar Mas'oed (1983) presents a fine description of this period.

and maintenance he attempted simultaneously to employ. Suharto used the state oil company to gain access to discretionary resources that could be utilized to operate more effectively within Indonesia's extensive and important power network of patron-client links. The tension between creating a favorable investment climate and playing hardball patrimonial politics is an important subtheme throughout this book.[7]

Desperation

Investment, production, and trade had collapsed under Sukarno. By 1966 factories were operating on average at just over 20 percent of capacity,[8] output in the oil sector was stagnant, receipts from the sale of petroleum abroad had declined 50 percent between 1964 and 1965, exports had dropped steadily since 1961 (in both value and volume), and after balancing export receipts against import needs and debt service, the country was facing a foreign exchange shortfall in 1966 of more than half a billion dollars.[9] The dysfunctionality evident in the private sector was exceeded only by the fiscal breakdown of the state.[10] To meet

[7] Two excellent sources on Indonesian patronage are Anderson 1990 and Robison 1977. Although it is difficult to argue about beginning motives based exclusively on final results, the enormous wealth Suharto has amassed for himself, his wife, and his children makes it tempting to suggest that personal greed was also important in his calculations from the very start. Though exact figures are unavailable, Suharto is widely believed to be much richer than was Southeast Asia's better-known kleptocrat Ferdinand Marcos. It should be said in Marcos's defense that he never had windfall oil receipts to stash away.

[8] The first foreign consultants to survey Indonesian industry after the fall of Sukarno wrote: "Not since 1958 or 1959 have industries in Indonesia experienced conditions that would allow them to push their equipment to its maximum annual output." The only notable exceptions were cement and urea plants, which had been priority sectors and enjoyed special access to raw materials and spare parts. World Bank 1966:15.

[9] Even today much basic information on Indonesia remains highly unreliable. In 1966 virtually no facts and figures on the economy could be trusted. The figures presented here represent the best guesses of the time and are drawn mainly from reports in the *Far Eastern Economic Review* (hereafter *FEER*), which probably got its data from World Bank and IMF consultants in Jakarta. I am deliberately presenting the *Review*'s perspective because it would be one of the main sources consulted by investors watching developments in Indonesia. See Davies 1966; Panglaykim 1966; and *FEER*, various yearbooks. Other good sources on the crisis include Mas'oed 1983 and Palmer 1978.

[10] This collapse could even transform successes into sources of instability and crisis. A case in point is rice output, which reportedly increased by 20 percent in 1965. Much of this product would not make it to market and to the cities because uncertainty about the value

current routine expenditures, government revenues would have to be about 10 percent of gross national product. Actual receipts were just 2 percent. By one early estimate, the budget deficit for the first quarter of 1966 alone was equal to all government expenditures for the previous year.[11]

Reversing the investment and production crisis that helped seal the fate of the Sukarno government would not be easy. Indeed, the early years of Suharto's New Order were marked by tremendous uncertainty, which itself discourages private capital controllers from investing. Pulling the economy out of its debilitating downward spiral was the first job for the economic ministers. Imposing austerity on the public sector, which was estimated to be 30 to 40 percent overstaffed, would be a logical starting place, but there were severe limits on how far leaders could go in this direction because one way investment and production crises manifest themselves is in unemployment—particularly in urban areas.[12] One prominent Indonesian economist explained the obstacles to cutting jobs in the public sector this way: "These surplus officials cannot be dismissed out of hand. . . . because Indonesia is suffering from chronic unemployment. Retrenchment of civil servants cannot take place until other jobs are available for them. New employment opportunities will only be created when the economy starts to function again. Economic recovery is itself dependent on the ending of inflation which in turn largely depends on economies in government spending."[13] Those "other jobs" would be available only after the foreign and domestic

of the rupiah caused farmers to hoard. Restoring confidence in the currency was critical. "If peasants insist on hoarding as a hedge against inflation and new political difficulties," wrote one reporter, "draconian measures may be necessary to extract the rice." Davies 1966:521. There is no indication that Suharto was politically willing or militarily able to consider such measures seriously in 1966.

[11] Panglaykim 1966. Not that 1965 was any better. The deficit that year exceeded all resources collected by a factor of three. See World Bank 1966:2.

[12] The public sector was cut in three important ways by mid-1966. First, Sukarno's expensive prestige projects, none of which added to the country's productive capacity, were put on hold. Second, at the local, provincial, and national levels a large number of Sukarnoists and civil servants linked to the Communist Party (PKI) were cut from the government bureaucracy. Those associated with the PKI were the only targets who could safely be fired, because there was no chance they would receive wide support were they to challenge the regime in the streets. And third, some cutbacks in military spending were pushed through.

[13] Panglaykim 1966:607. It was also clear that the armed forces could not be demobilized for the same reason. See Adam Malik's comments to this effect in Bank Indonesia 1967:5.

actors controlling the investment capital that creates employment decided to inject their resources into Indonesia's economy. From the vantage point of mid-1966, such resources looked far away indeed. Instead of civil servants being fired, their salaries were increased in a losing effort to keep up with inflation. In January 1966, salaries for civil servants were raised by 500 percent. They were doubled again exactly one year later and increased by another 50 percent in April 1967. That same month, the rice allowance for all government employees (including members of the armed forces) was increased by 25 percent.[14]

Too many rupiah were chasing too few goods. An antidote that slowed the growth in the money supply while increasing the availability of goods (especially food and clothes) was desperately needed. Even though domestic immobile investors would be hurt badly by government efforts to take rupiah out of circulation, a tight credit policy was announced in October 1966. Bank lending rates leaped from a range of 6–29 percent per year to 6–9 percent *per month*. The austerity plan designed to shock the economy back into balance had begun in earnest.

Slowing the growth of the money supply was only one part of the battle. Displaying an immediate responsiveness to the more powerful and mobile elements of capital was essential as well if policymakers wanted to gain access to consumer goods such as food and clothing in time to mollify people in the cities. Those controlling "institutional" capital (supplied by creditor states and agencies) were the key to getting foreign debts rescheduled and new credit extended. Another reason for haste was that the employment, production, balance of payments, and state revenue benefits of private sector action (again, mainly from Chinese Indonesians and transnational investors) would not be felt for at least two or three years.

The first steps taken by policymakers were calculated to elicit the quickest material and financial rewards. Given the country's dreadful commercial credit rating, the only conceivable suppliers of resources would be creditor countries eager, for political and economic reasons, to have Indonesia in their camp and behaving properly. The very tense and desperate period from March until November 1966 was dedicated to winning the confidence and material support of those controlling *institutional* resources. Suharto and the economic ministers had three objec-

---

[14] *FEER* Yearbook 1968:200.

tives, all pursued simultaneously: reschedule debt payments due in 1966, get rice and clothing, and negotiate new credit (if possible, in the form of untied cash).

Several symbolic actions were taken immediately after General Suharto took over power from President Sukarno in March. The sultan of Yogyakarta, one of Suharto's close aides and a figure Western leaders trusted enormously, made a speech indicating that the government was abandoning the failed policies of hostility to investors that had characterized the last years under Sukarno. Foreign embassies were cautiously sympathetic, but the predominant view was that words, even spoken so royally, were cheap. "Despite its frank and manly tone," wrote one reporter in Jakarta, "the speech was a statement of policy intention rather than a firm commitment to a series of concrete measures. Cynics commented that sensible slogans had replaced silly ones."[15] Although anticommunist foreign governments, led by the United States, clearly wanted to tilt Indonesia in their direction, they had to move carefully. "If overly generous credits and aids are extended now," this same reporter wrote, "they will act as a powerful disincentive for the new men in Djakarta to put their political house in order. For their own good, they should be told that all out support cannot be expected until this is accomplished."[16]

From the creditors' perspective, the first meaningful moves were allowing an IMF team back into the country in July of 1966 and inviting a World Bank mission in August to identify which imports were most critically needed. Working closely with Indonesia's economists, the IMF officials and other foreign consultants processed what data there were and diagnosed the economy's ills. The economic policy pronouncements of October 1966 built on these efforts and sent a clear signal to creditors that Suharto would permit the economic ministers to orient Indonesia's economic policy. The World Bank team, meanwhile, tried to figure out how to get a "quick return" from the limited foreign exchange Indonesia

[15] Davies 1966:520.

[16] Davies 1966:519. Of course, not all the "men in Djakarta" needed prodding. The economic ministers were firmly behind the country's new economic direction, and the United States consciously tried to give them maximum support without undermining their domestic position by being too public about it. At the same time, efforts were made to subvert the agenda of those disagreeing with the economists—many of whom were counted among Suharto's closest friends and allies in and outside the military. For an excellent description of this strategy, see Sullivan 1969.

had or could expect in the near term. The team gathered what amounted to wish lists from various Indonesian government departments, sent them back because they were utterly unrealistic, and finally received revised requests totaling more than $600 million in imports in the transport, agricultural, and industrial sectors. The team recommended a figure half as large.[17]

Some rice and cotton credit had been offered by the United States under the Public Law 480 program back in April, though the terms were extremely tough because the Americans were being very cautious. More rice, cotton, spare parts, and raw materials were offered on slightly better PL 480 terms after the moves described above were taken, and especially after Indonesia signed an accord ending the aggression against Malaysia. In November 1966, agreement was reached on Sukarno's debts to the Soviet Union and the Eastern Bloc, and the stage was set for a meeting in Paris in December for the nations backing Suharto to reschedule the debts falling due in 1966 and 1967. Satisfied that Indonesia had replaced words with actions, the creditor nations finally proposed $200 million in new loans in February 1967.[18] Summing up the U.S. view of Suharto's efforts, Ambassador Marshall Green reflected, "It was a great moment in history in which Indonesia, the world's fifth most populous country, strategically located at the junction of two continents and two oceans, reversed its course 180 degrees."[19] The general's three objectives of rescheduling old debts, tapping into external supplies of rice and clothing, and receiving new pledges of credit had been met.

Wooing Mobile Investors: 1967

If 1966 was the year for gaining access to the highly liquid resources of institutional capital controllers, 1967 was the year to focus on the

---

[17] World Bank (annex 1) 1966:1. The reason for the discrepancy was not differences in perceived need: the mission was appalled at the dilapidation it witnessed. Rather, the issue was Indonesia's limited ability to absorb more goods. The country's spinning capacity, for instance, was gauged to be just 28 percent of requirements and textile finishing capacity not much better. East Germany was supplying thirty thousand spindles to Palembang to produce textiles, but the plants to house them would not be ready for at least two years.

[18] Posthumus 1972:55.

[19] Quoted in Martens n.d.

longer-range task of jump-starting the country's productive capacities.[20] The two groups of private investors that had the greatest resources for and longest experience in production were transnational investors and Indonesia's own tiny but important ethnic Chinese population. These two groups happened also to be the most mobile, and because of the turbulent and risky circumstances during Sukarno's Old Order, both groups had withdrawn or relocated the investment resources they controlled. It was to these most mobile private actors that the attention of policymakers turned next.

Among mobile private capital controllers, the specific policy concerns of transnational investors would be addressed first, mainly because domestic hostility toward Indonesia's ethnic Chinese community for its alleged associations with the PKI and the 1965 putsch was still high. Meanwhile, the country's more immobile domestic investors, consisting of both ethnic Chinese and *pribumi,* were mostly ignored by policymakers, despite their raising their voices in opposition to the country's austerity program and other policies that were devastating them financially.

Communicating with private investors is very different from communicating with institutional capital controllers from foreign governments or international agencies. Companies do not, for example, have embassies and envoys. Policymakers in Indonesia were painfully aware that, to the extent that transnational investors were aware of their country, with few exceptions the impressions were intensely negative. How could these actors be reached, and what conditions would they want for supplying their capital in abundance?

International press reports chronicling the changes in 1965 and 1966 helped Indonesia's case. But many of these changes, although of tremendous significance, were intangible from an investor's perspective. Word of the World Bank's and IMF's return, cabinet changes, action by creditor nations, and the formation of the IGGI was a plus but could not by

---

[20] Remarking on the efforts of the Indonesian government the restore investor confidence after 1966, Julius Tahija remarked, "The years 1967–72 were our golden period. The most brilliant step the government made was to encourage and give confidence to business in the private sector. Literally billions of dollars of private money poured back into the country." From Ensor 1979b. Tahija, chairman of the Board of Commissioners of Caltex Indonesia and one of Indonesia's more enduring and independent entrepreneurs, sounded this nostalgic note in 1979, just as the country was plunging into its most virulent state-regulated phase of the new order.

itself undo years of horror stories about nationalizations, Communists, labor militancy, hyperinflation, and generalized economic and political chaos. Although Indonesian officials were consumed with more pressing matters in 1966, a few private investors and organizations, eager to consolidate political gains made during that critical year, began to plan meetings and seminars designed to broadcast the news that a tremendous redirection of policy was under way. One such event was the "PIBA Djakarta Meeting" in August 1967.[21] Organized by Julius Tahija, one of Indonesia's leading business figures, the PIBA meeting was a useful first step, but Indonesian government officials did not play a significant role. Private Indonesians did their best to answer questions from mobile investors, but according to a government report, "the ability of part of them to participate actively in the discussions may be doubted."[22] There were other contacts with investors as various missions visited the country in 1967. Table 2 lists the earliest organized visits from abroad. Held as they were in Jakarta, these meetings were preaching mainly to the converted, and their impact was narrow. What was needed was a powerful outreach campaign targeted to the most influential business leaders in the world. If their confidence and interest could be won, other highly mobile players who operate on a more modest scale—fearing in an information-scarce environment that they were missing something—would be more likely to follow in herd-like fashion.

A truly golden opportunity presented itself late in 1966. The sultan of Yogyakarta, in his capacity as head of the Tourism Board, invited several foreigners to the grand opening of a luxury hotel on the island of Bali. Among them was James A. Linen, president of Time, Inc. So taken was Linen with the revolutionary changes occurring around him that he offered to sponsor a summit between the world's top business executives—almost all of whom were his personal friends—and key members of Indonesia's cabinet and economic team.[23] In the words of

[21] PIBA stands for the Pacific Indonesian Business Association, sponsored by Stanford University.

[22] See Bank Indonesia 1967:21. Parts of this document are in Indonesian, parts in English. The section quoted here was written in English. In context, the passage is clearly intended to suggest that few of the private individuals representing Indonesia were qualified to answer questions relating to the rapidly evolving Indonesian laws and regulations constituting the country's investment climate—especially for transnationally mobile investors.

[23] The importance all sides attached to this event is evident from the fact that two

1966 Geneva Conference (handwritten)

Table 2. Earliest private sector missions to Indonesia after 1965

Month	From	Purpose/comments
April	San Francisco	Representatives of several California companies interested in investment opportunities in mining, oil, bauxite, nickel.
May	Oregon	Investigated investment opportunities.
	Belgium	Mission led by the Belgian minister of foreign economic relations.
	Netherlands	Led by Mr. Oyevaar, this was the second Dutch mission to visit Indonesia in 1967. "The Dutch entrepreneurs were considerably interested in expansion and rehabilitation of their former undertakings which have been nationalized since 1958, through new investment in the form of joint enterprise."
July	Australia	"Following a visit of the Australian minister of foreign affairs to Indonesia, and followed by a mission sponsored by the chamber of commerce of Queensland." Investors were interested in industry, housing, forestry, and mining.
August	France	Led by France's minister of industry. Investors were interested in forestry and industry.
	South Korea	Investigated investment opportunities.

Note: All missions listed here visited Indonesia in 1967. Visits from individual corporations are not included. Data from "Foreign Investment in Indonesia" section, in Indonesian Embassy 1967:20.

Indonesia's rapporteur, the summit would allow "both sides, directly and with open hearts, to discuss the possibilities for foreign capital investment in Indonesia."[24] It was agreed that an "Indonesian invest-

---

publications and one internal government report (all three intended for restricted audiences) were generated in its wake. They are Bank Indonesia 1967 (the Indonesian government's own account of the event as submitted by Selo Sumardjan, the secretary for the Indonesian delegation), Indonesian Embassy 1967 (intended for private sector consumption in the United States), and Time, Inc. 1967 (representing James Linen's attempt to reach investors not in attendance in Geneva).

[24] Bank Indonesia 1967:1; my translation. This was the first and certainly the most important meeting between mobile investors and state officials for Indonesia. In subsequent years Business International, a company specializing in managing the flow of signals between mobile private capital controllers and government officials around the globe, has hosted weeklong "roundtables" at which the two sides discuss (always in strict privacy) the status of Indonesia's investment climate and how it can be made more competitive. The first such roundtable for Indonesia was held in September 1968. All have taken place in Jakarta.

ment conference" would be held in Geneva early in November 1967.[25] Underscoring the seriousness with which Suharto viewed this first shot at an international forum on investment, he issued a presidential decree giving the Indonesian delegation full authority to represent the government.[26] Its members included the economic and foreign ministers plus most of the top government economists in charge of investment, trade, and finance. In all, twenty Indonesians went to Geneva, plus two ambassadors with staff in tow.[27] It was a most impressive display.

While the Indonesian officials were certain of their objectives, the means of achieving them through the conference had to be treated delicately. The clearest and most forthright signals had to be sent to these business leaders. But at the same time these were some of the highest officials of the Indonesian government, and they had to maintain at least a public display of dignity and pride. If they appeared too eager or forthcoming, it would provide ammunition to those back in Jakarta who were angered by what they saw as an obsequious posture of the New Order toward creditors and investors. As recently as September 1966 Sukarno had attacked govenment leaders for their "begging." The challenge, then, was to broadcast that Indonesia was actively creating a favorable investment climate while not antagonizing groups back home who interpreted such policies negatively. A balance was struck by mak-

---

[25] Jakarta's facilities were deemed too spartan, and Linen wanted to avoid the feeling that the United States was dominating the whole affair. See Bank Indonesia 1967:1. Pan American Airlines supplied a chartered airplane for the Indonesian delegation, and Inter-Continental Hotels Corporation supplied accommodations. It is not clear whether Linen paid for these services, but it is certain that the Indonesians did not. Mohammad Sadli offers these recollections: "James Linen was the kingpin of the whole conference. I think he paid for it mostly by himself. It must have been very expensive. It was Adam Malik who knew Linen. He had some kind of connection with Bangkok, I think. Our contact with Kuala Lumpur and Bangkok increased dramatically. They wanted to help us open up. Malik introduced Linen to the sultan, and the Geneva conference was pulled together. Linen invited all his friends and cronies." Interview in Jakarta with Mohammad Sadli, 21 June 1989.

[26] KEPPRES 198, 30 October 1967. To my knowledge, this is the only time a delegation of Indonesian officials attending such a conference carried with them a presidential decree giving them full authority to represent their government.

[27] The full attendance list included Sultan Hamengku Buwono, Adam Malik, Mohammad Sadli, Emil Salim, Rachmat Saleh, H. A. Pandelaki, R. A. Kartadjumena, Sri Pamungkas, Sutarjo Sigit, Surjo Sediono, Suhadat Wirjosubroto, Selo Sumardjan, the Indonesian ambassador in Bern (plus staff), U.N. Ambassador Umarjadi in Geneva (plus staff), Director General of Forestry Sudjarwo (and his two assistants, Sunarjo and Moh. Sadikin), Sie Dhian Hoo, S. Soeparto, and Gandasubrata (from the Bank Negara Indonesia office in Amsterdam).

ing the summit a closed-door affair: invited guests only, and no reporters. In addition to private and official views expressed to the press
after the conference, written summaries prepared for selected audiences
would be circulated subsequently. Linen and Time, Inc., would help
reach out to the broader business community through links to world-
wide press channels. The Indonesian embassies in the United States and
Europe, meanwhile, would distribute nicely crafted public relations materials based on the summit.

The conference opened on 2 November with a spirited address from
Linen. "We are trying to create a new climate," he said, "in which
private enterprise and developing countries work together for their mu-
tual interest and profit, and to the even greater profit of the free
world."[28] Linen was impressed with the signs of change in the former
Dutch colony. Now he brought his Indonesian guests to Geneva to impress everyone else or, as *Time*'s report of the proceedings put it, to
"make the case for Indonesia."[29]

The Indonesian ministers carried a message from Acting President
Suharto. Its tone could not have been more accommodating. After extending his "warm personal regards" to the "distinguished gathering of
leaders of international business," he thanked them for taking "precious
time out of [their] crowded schedules" to discuss and consider the role
they might play in his country's recovery and development.[30] Lest anyone suspect that the views presented by the economic ministers at the
conference lacked the full backing of Indonesia's powerful military
leaders, Suharto was uncharacteristically blunt: "We welcome you in
your interest and intention to help in the development of our country.
From our part we are working hard to create the necessary climate of
economic and political stability. It may well be that between now and the
full realization of this goal your presence here and your efforts in Indonesia will have contributed in a very real way. My government and I wish
you every success in your noble endeavors."[31]

With these words, the Indonesian delegates got down to the business
of attracting business. The first segment of the conference was devoted
to speeches from the Indonesians, each one carefully crafted to touch on

[28] Time, Inc. 1967:1.
[29] Time, Inc. 1967:1.
[30] Bank Indonesia (appendix 1) 1967:1.
[31] Bank Indonesia (appendix 2) 1967:2.

the concerns uppermost in investors' minds. The foreign minister, Adam Malik, went first. Stressing how safe and predictable the country had become, he described the dramatic political changes that had occurred during the previous eighteen months. The titanic social and political clashes of the Sukarno days were no more. "This is not to say that there are no issues and controversies," he admitted, "but the conflict situations they produce are of much more controllable magnitudes." "The new government is not vitally challenged by any other power with a radically different political philosophy," he continued, "and the opposition at present is not able to shake the determination of the government or make it alame [*sic*] duck, as the Americans say."[32] Predictability is a critical factor in the investment calculus. Hence "the most important achievement of the post-Sukarno government," according to the minister, "is its firm adherence to the 'rule of law' and its abhorrence of arbitrary, one-man favoritism as a governmental policy."[33] Before making a direct plea for the investors' "own specific resources," Malik assured them that although they were the first *private* capital controllers to consider Indonesia, they were in no sense out front alone. Referring to the money and goods the IGGI was supplying, he said, "Your governments have done what they could to increase the chances of survival of the new government in Indonesia," and they have "pledged their share in the reconstruction."[34]

The next speaker was Sultan Hamengku Buwono, state minister for economic, financial, and industrial affairs. With the opening words, "Today I am experiencing one of the greatest events in my life," the monarch managed to genuflect deeper than any other member of the delegation. The sultan continued: "I am feeling extremely proud of the wonderful privilege of addressing a meeting of top-ranking business executives from the economically most advanced countries in the world. At the same time I feel deeply humble facing the esteemed bearers of

[32] Bank Indonesia (appendix 2) 1967:2–3. Underscoring that the country had achieved a genuine political terra firma, he added, "in the present political make-up, the military dominates."

[33] Bank Indonesia (appendix 2) 1967:4. It is hard to know how many people in the Geneva audience had the experience or intelligence to know how preposterous this claim was. In any event, most of the investors were probably hoping *they alone* would be the exception to this rule. Investors pursue a public policy of fair play and equal treatment mainly to impair competitors. In private they use bribery, intimidation, and any other means available to get a competitive edge.

[34] Bank Indonesia 1967:1, 7.

success in modern big business on four continents, representing a sizeable portion of the world's dynamic industrial and commercial capital."[35] After several more minutes of this preparation, the sultan finally said it was his job to explain the government's economic policies. What followed amounted to an apology for the chaos of the past and a litany of concrete steps that had been taken to stabilize and rehabilitate the economy.

After highlighting initiatives already mentioned above, he turned to matters of direct concern to investors. First was the government's decision to return all non-Dutch companies and assets to their rightful owners (compensating those who declined to take back the damaged firms). Indonesians were no longer gripped by irrational fears that foreign investment necessarily spelled imperial domination, the sultan argued, and anyway, a country lacking substantial domestic capital and in desperate need of productive investment could hardly be choosy. As of the conference date, the sultan announced, some twenty-three foreign companies had been returned.

The second step was the passage of a new Foreign Investment Law in the closing days of 1966.[36] It would be Professor Sadli's job to showcase the new legislation, and so the sultan moved on to his closing comments. He wanted to be certain the investors were convinced that he and his fellow Indonesians understood precisely what business wanted and exactly how the game was played. "I am fully aware of the primary objec-

[35] Indonesian Embassy 1967:13.

[36] The legislation was drafted by an Indonesian team led by Dr. Selo Sumardjan, a member of the delegation to Geneva. Sullivan (1969:333) writes that Sumardjan and his team were at a loss for how to draft the law. They received extensive help from economists at the American embassy and even consulted an American textbook on comparative foreign investment laws. Those familiar with Indonesian nationalism and pride might be surprised to learn that top policymakers are extraordinarily comfortable using foreign consultants to draft the country's legislation. My own observations and direct experience confirm that as late as 1991 American consultants were still drafting major Indonesian legislation (tax reform, capital markets, trade deregulation, etc.). Important private consulting firms for Indonesia (and a host of other countries) have included the Harvard Institute for International Development (HIID), Nathan Associates (based in Washington, D.C.), and Hill and Knowlton (based in New York City). The only other USAID mission in the world that has a larger staff than Jakarta's is in Cairo. The Economic Policy Support Office (EPSO) of USAID-Jakarta is devoted entirely to funneling American consultants into the various economic ministries of the Indonesian government with the explicit purpose of helping the Indonesians monitor the status (competitiveness) of their investment climate and designing and implementing policies that will spur investment, production, growth, and employment.

tives of international investors in general," he said candidly.[37] Reflecting an early awareness of competition between investment sites to attract mobile capital, the sultan added that investors "look for opportunities to make profit in countries that can supply them the best incentives and opportunities for the operation of their capital, and where they can gain a new market or expand existing markets for their products." The perceived dangers of investing in developing countries—particularly ones as patently volatile as Indonesia had shown itself to be—frighten entrepreneurs off. Investors "shy away from the political risks they think they run when investing in newly developing countries." Indonesia had suffered, the sultan explained, because of sensational and biased press reports, and he personally invited everyone in the audience to visit him and his staff in Jakarta and see for themselves how safe the environment actually was.

Emil Salim, deputy chairman for the Planning Council, spoke next. His speech, "The Search for a Place under the Sun," was unique among the presentations offered that November morning. Salim was certainly the most intellectual and philosophical of the economists,[38] and whereas his colleagues kept mostly to the facts, Salim went for the grand overview. Like the others, he recounted the ills of the past, the remedies administered thus far, and the new policy potions yet to be tried. But unlike the others, he attempted to explain some of the whys and hows of the situation Indonesia faced, and in doing so managed to touch on several of the most important theoretical elements of this book. Salim began by locating Indonesia's problems squarely in the arena of investment and production and in the serious repercussions that tend to accompany a breakdown of both. Under Sukarno "normal long-term investment stopped," he argued, while "unemployment rose, and the whole economy deteriorated rapidly."[39] As matters got worse, and as private capital controllers tried to withhold or relocate their investment resources, a battle ensued over their control. "The scarcer the resources

---

[37] This and all subsequent quotations in this paragraph are from Indonesian Embassy 1967:18.

[38] Heinz Arndt, the Australian economist who worked closely with the economic ministers for almost three decades, gives a somewhat less charitable estimation of him: "Emil Salim was the propagandist, the Goebbels of the group, if you will." Discussion in Jakarta with Heinz Arndt, 1 September 1989.

[39] Indonesian Embassy 1967:18.

became, the greater [was] the struggle for control over them," Salim explained.[40]

Efforts to exercise state control over mobile, private investment resources made no sense, he pointed out. Though it was not explicitly stated, he implied that this approach was a strategy for doom because private property controllers usually have plenty of time to relocate their resources abroad or direct them into other short-term, unproductive activities that accelerate the political-economic deterioration of the country. "But the time has changed," he reassured the conference audience. "Indonesia today is back on the path of rationalism."[41] This comment about returning to a pattern of rational action is extremely important. A "rational" course of action for policymakers does not exist independent of the set of objectives the policymakers intend to achieve and their perception of the constraints that separate reasonable from unreasonable policy options and instruments.

General Suharto and those who came to power with him were very interested in consolidating their positions and remaining in power. Suharto and his circle were aware that a basic element in achieving this objective was a restoration of investment and production to alleviate some of the dislocation that existed in society—again, particularly in urban areas. The real options for meeting this intermediate goal were constrained by who or what controlled the investment resources and production units, and what instruments policymakers had at their disposal to gain access to these resources. The "rational" path, then, was one that operated within the constraints presented by the existing pattern of resource control. "Irrational" policies would, by these criteria, be ones that decision makers could anticipate would not spur private investment, would not address dislocations in the wider population, and would not help deflect challenges to their positions of power. In the event that such a policy trajectory was consciously chosen, the option sometimes still exists to use massive state coercion to maintain a regime in power. But as John Lonsdale rightly points out, when other options appear to be reasonably possible, rulers tend not to consciously pursue policies that push the level of violence in society to such heights. "If only for reasons of economy," he writes, "rulers like to be loved."[42]

[40] Indonesian Embassy 1967:18.
[41] Indonesian Embassy 1967:19, 22.
[42] Lonsdale 1981:160.

Salim was explicit in his comments before the world's most mobile capital controllers about the serious pressures policymakers faced because of Indonesia's investment imperative. The highest priority for his government was "to get the economy on the move; to eliminate unemployment and boost [the] economic growth rate beyond the rate of population growth."[43] He continued, "We must meet the challenge quickly. The patience of our people for enduring further hardships has reached its limits. Expectations as compared to achievements show a wide gap of the sort that leads to frustration. As a matter of fact, our problems are so big that we have to run fast in order to stand still."[44]

That officials were painfully aware the state lacked adequate resources to meet the country's investment needs is clear. As Salim emphasized repeatedly, "The need for intestment is too great for the government alone to carry."[45] They were also cognizant that Indonesia did not exist in a vacuum and that, as Sukarno's disaster proved, there existed a marketplace of states to which capital could relocate should the climate in Indonesia became too inhospitable. "More and more countries are competing for foreign funds,"[46] Salim admitted, saying there was nothing Indonesia alone could do about this. "Taking all this into consideration," he added, "it becomes clear that the government should follow the strategy of using its limited resources to produce external economies to stimulate more and higher private investment, either domestic or foreign." "The problem," he added, "is to make the cost of exploitation so low that it becomes attractive enough to lure foreign capital."[47] In short, public funds should be used to enhance the attractive qualities of the jurisdiction so that it can compete globally for mobile capital.

Whereas Malik and the sultan talked of their hopes that Indonesians (read non-Chinese) themselves might someday be the country's prime investors and mentioned a few sectors where transnational investors were not welcome, Salim stated plainly that his country was not in a position to be overly picky. "At this stage all sorts of investments are highly welcome, except in the excluded defense industries. The important thing is not in what sector private investment comes but rather

[43] Indonesian Embassy 1967:20.
[44] Indonesian Embassy 1967:20, 22.
[45] Indonesian Embassy 1967:22.
[46] Indonesian Embassy 1967:20.
[47] Indonesian Embassy 1967:21.

when it comes. *The time dimension is more important than all others.*[48] Waxing poetic, he closed by saying, "A new and reborn Indonesia is entering the family of nations. May God give us our rightful place under His sun."[49]

The last of the formal presentations came from Mohammad Sadli, chairman of the Foreign Investment Team. Perhaps sensing that the audience had endured enough history and philosophy for one day, Sadli devoted all his time to explaining the tenets of the Foreign Investment Law. The leadership in Indonesia wanted growth and development. "To meet these requirements," he said bluntly, "our Foreign Investment Law offers incentives and guarantees."[50] Displaying a clear awareness of every investor's interest in the cost impact of state policy, all the incentives concerned the firm's bottom line. Tax holidays, tariff reductions on imported factors of production, and various transfer facilities were the instruments of choice. Indicating once again a keen sensitivity among the country's decision makers that they were competing directly with other jurisdictions for investment capital, Sadli noted that "tax rates on corporate and individual incomes are still higher [in Indonesia] than in neighboring countries." But the government was "studying proposals to lower average and marginal rates so as to safeguard [its] competitive position."[51]

Although the 1967 law did not explicitly guarantee that Indonesia would never nationalize the property of foreigners, changes of procedure made it so difficult as to provide strong assurances. In any event, Sadli pointed out, Indonesia had subscribed to the World Bank's mechanisms

[48] Indonesian Embassy 1967:22; my emphasis, though from the text it is not difficult to imagine Salim's voice in a crescendo at this point.

[49] Indonesian Embassy 1967:22. It has been said that God works in mysterious ways, but divine intervention through big investors assembled at a hotel in Geneva is novel.

[50] Indonesian Embassy 1967:25. The 1967 law went into considerable detail on which types of investment would qualify for the fiscal incentives being offered. The regulation was not followed rigidly, however. The package of written materials each investor received at the conference constantly pointed out that in fact all investments would be evaluated individually, and those deemed outside the 1967 law guidelines but still of value to Indonesia would be given the full incentive package. (See, for instance, the policy statement of the Department of Basic Light and Power Industries, Bank Indonesia 1967.) Concrete examples of this flexibility in practice abound. Although the 1967 law clearly states that a three-year tax holiday will be given only for investments of $2.5 million and above, British-American Tobacco was granted the holiday for its investment of £56,000, and the Belgian-owned Faroka received the same treatment when it invested just $230,000 in its cigarette factory. See Business International 1968:II-9.

[51] Indonesian Embassy 1967:26.

for settling disputes between governments and foreign enterprises, signaling that the sanctity of private property would no longer be challenged as it had been under the previous regime. A bit defensively, he also
explained that operation permits for foreign companies were valid for
only thirty years. "We know this imposes a long-term risk on foreign
investors," Sadli admitted, but if such a provision allayed residual fears
in Indonesia of unending foreign domination, "it may very well be worth
the risk." Doing his best to downplay the significance of this disincentive, he added that "at the moment we interpret this article as meaning
that the work permit is extendable after thirty years."[52] The last bit of
bad news the chairman felt compelled to deliver was that for "practical
reasons" that could not yet be overcome, investors would not be able to
present their plans to any single government office for approval but
would have to shuttle around to the various ministries and pay "courtesy
calls on officials."[53] Seasoned investors in the audience probably understood that courtesy calls were not all they would be paying. Wanting to
end on a high note, Sadli announced that "early comers" would get
special treatment. "Investors coming in before the end of 1968 will be
treated as pioneers," he said. "Materially they will gain only one extra
year of tax holiday, but there is a lot of good will to be reaped. These
investing parties will catch us in a mood where we still have to establish
credibility, when we will be bending over to accommodate, where the
enthusiasm to attract investors is at the highest, when top officials and
cabinet ministers are relatively easy to approach."[54]

It is clear especially from Sadli's comments that the economists' ability
to meet every demand of investors was limited by countervailing social
and political forces existing in Indonesia. Several officials would have
liked to dispense with the thirty-year limit on permits, but the opposition
to such a move, especially from the military, was much too intense. Also,
the institutional structure of the Indonesian bureaucracy and the dispersion of power and patronage across it made setting up a single body to
vet foreign investments extremely difficult. It was not until 1973 that the
Investment Coordinating Board (BKPM) was established and not until

---

[52] Both quotations are from Indonesian Embassy 1967:27. Perhaps on the belief that
few at the conference understood how powerless Indonesia's parliament was, he blamed
this body for including the thirty-year clause.

[53] Indonesian Embassy 1967:27–28.

[54] Indonesian Embassy 1967:28.

1978 that it was upgraded to a "one-stop" service for foreign investors. Even then it achieved that status only in name.[55] In short, although there were tremendous structural forces pushing Indonesian officials in the direction of creating a highly responsive investment climate, these were not the only relevant forces to be considered by policymakers seeking to stabilize and extend their hold on power.

That said, it is evident that the Indonesian policymakers were doing their best to transmit clear signals to mobile private investors. In a consciously coordinated fashion, they touched on every issue they could think of that impinged on the investment calculus of these powerful actors. Moreover, all the speakers were highly educated, and most were Western-trained economists speaking in English—thus providing even greater assurances to the assembled investors that a shared worldview prevailed in the room. They admitted their desperation and pleaded for a quick response. Although this signaling was an important first step toward reviving investment rates, it was inadequate insofar as the communication was unidirectional. The next and most critical phase of the conference corrected matters.

With the Indonesians' cards in full view, the formal proceedings for the first day were adjourned. Day two, the guts of the conference, consisted of marathon roundtable meetings.[56] The conference participants divided into five groups for intensive discussions, each devoted to a different sector of the Indonesian economy. The officials and the investors would have a "frank and informal exchange of views," according to *Time*'s published record of the event.[57] At least three things should be noted about this phase of the conference. First, the terrain had shifted from an open forum where prepared statements were read to a general audience to tighter, more secluded groups where actors on both sides

[55] BKPM's chair can grant an investment permit only after consulting with interested government ministries, finding out if they have any objections, and then getting the signature of Suharto himself.

[56] Both Time, Inc. 1967 and Bank Indonesia 1967 provide records of these sectoral meetings (with the latter specifically stating that when the Indonesian version was printed, no reference to these exchanges would be made). The Indonesians clearly had less control over what the *Time* publication would include. They do appear to have won agreement on keeping the notes on the exchanges as anonymous as possible. Time, Inc. (1967:18) states, however, that everyone understood that comments would not be "strictly off the record." The next several pages in this chapter are based on these two records. Wherever possible, careful note will be made of how the reports differ.

[57] Time, Inc. 1967.

were specialists in the sector under discussion. Second, the Indonesians were divided up. Even huddled together at the front of the main conference room, they were intimidated by their audience and unsure of themselves as government officials.[58] These insecurities likely were amplified in the individual sessions. And third, the communication was now bidirectional. In fact, as we will see, there are indications that investors used these sessions to give the Indonesians a crash course in the sort of policies mobile capital controllers would find magnetic, while the policymakers took notes and clarified matters where they could.

Table 3 provides an idea of how the sectors were divided, which Indonesian specialists presided, and some of the firms represented.[59] The session on the manufacturing sector opened with Mohammad Sadli lamenting that all the excitement and interest seemed to be in extraction. Only twenty new factories had been proposed by transnational investors since the beginning of the New Order, and none from the big players. The manufacturers wasted no time outlining the kinds of policies that might change their behavior. Investors in manufacturing who enjoyed global mobility in the mid-1960s were looking mainly for new markets, not new places to produce for markets they already had. Indonesia's population was huge and growing fast, but the overwhelming majority was lucky to have enough money to meet basic nutritional needs. In the face of such limited effective demand, the investors wanted assurances that if they invested their operations would be profitable. One of their key demands was for a level playing field for all investors, with no

[58] Mentioning in a general way how unprepared the economic ministers were to seize the reins of economic policymaking (they sought World Bank, IMF, USAID, and private, foreign consultants' help to write almost all the legislation in the early years), Mohammad Sadli made this observation: "The conference in Geneva was very important. It was a first in many senses. Most of us were new at being government officials. We were fresh from the campus, and we didn't know how to act, how to carry ourselves. The sultan took us with him to Geneva. It was our first selling job, and we had no recipe, no guidance. Our ideas were very general." Interview in Jakarta with Mohammad Sadli, 21 June 1989.

[59] Linen had many powerful friends. Among those in attendance were David Rockefeller (Chase), Frederick Jacques Philips (N. V. Philips), Eugene Black (Chase), Rudolph A. Peterson (Bank of America), Howard L. Clark (American Express), R. M. Dorman (Bechtel), John D. Harper (ALCOA), Robert C. Hills (Freeport), Norton Clapp (Weyerhauser), Henry J. Heinz II (H. J. Heinz), Earl C. Daum (GM), Russell R. De Young (Goodyear), Edward B. Hunman (International Paper), Dr. Koji Kobayashi (Nippon Electric), and Shinzo Ohya (Teijen). Almost all these people held the highest positions in their companies. The sources for these names and for the table are Time, Inc. 1967 and Bank Indonesia 1967.

Table 3. Investment conference roundtables, 1967

Sector	Indonesians	Foreign "host"	Selected firms represented	
Manufacturing	Mohammad Sadli Surjo Sediono	James R. Shepley (publisher of *Time*)	Siemens Group British American Tobacco Imperial Chemical Industries Nippon Electric International Paper Compagnie Industrielle Travaux	N. V. Philips Dunlop Goodyear Unilever Teijen Ltd. General Motors
Banking, finance, and services	Rachmat Saleh S. Soeparto	Jerome S. Hardy (publisher of *Life*)	Chase Manhattan Bank First National City Bank Fuji Bank Société Générale de Banque	KLM Airlines Bank of America Ocean Steamship Co. Daimler-Benz A.G. Chartered Bank
Foreign exchange and taxes	R. Kartadjumena H. A. Pandelaki Sri Pamungkas	Ralph Davidson (publisher of *Time* Intl.)	American Express Siemens Group British American Tobacco Eastern Airlines Compagnie Optorg	Swiss Bank Corp. Laird & Co. Deutsche Bank IT&T Dai Nippon Printing
Mining, oil, and other extractives	Dr. Sutarjo Sigit	Arthur W. Keylor (publisher of *Fortune*)	Shell Oil International Nickel of Canada U.S. Steel Standard Oil, California	Bechtel International Union Carbide Freeport Sulphur Alcoa
Agriculture, food processing, and forest products	Emil Salim Selo Sumardjan	E. Stevens DeClerque (publisher of *Life* Intl.)	St. Regis Paper H. J. Heinz Co. Nestle	Massey Ferguson Weyerhauser Co. Dunlop

Source: Data from Bank Indonesia 1967, various pages.

official policies granting special advantages or access to Indonesia's immobile domestic investors.[60] Given the size and power of the firms
attending the conference, such a level field would ensure them a tremendous competitive advantage over most domestic investors.[61]

According to the *Time* report, Sadli and Sediono declared that "on
these matters Indonesian policy has not yet been decided and comment
was invited."[62] This was at best lying by omission in that Indonesia's
entire economic system had long been dominated by the sort of patron-
client relations that make for a very uneven playing field. The matter was
not so much whether policy on these matters had been decided. Indonesian patronage structures were a fact. The issue was how far the economic ministers could reasonably expect to move the Suharto regime
toward establishing a more market-based system of entry and access and
how effective they would be at defending their policy gains against clientelist interests. This struggle between distribution by markets and by
officials has been at the center of Indonesia's political economy ever
since Suharto gave a prominent role to his economic ministers to attract
private capital.

Naturally the manufacturers also raised questions about labor regulations. Although no Indonesian officials from the Manpower Ministry
spoke at the conference, members of the audience did receive a document titled, "Manpower Policy in Foreign Investments,"[63] which reflected the government's pressing desire to have the maximum number of
Indonesians employed. The Indonesian version summarized the discus-

[60] The Indonesian government's version of the proceedings said this issue was *sangat
penting*, or "extremely important." See Bank Indonesia (appendix 6) 1967:2.

[61] It is unusual that some of the investors at the conference openly stated their *individual* interest in monopoly rights so that profits in intermediate and consumer goods would be
guaranteed. The surprising part is not that they pushed simultaneously for an official
policy creating a level playing field for everyone else and monopoly rights for themselves,
but that they mentioned the latter in open session. Such demands are typically made in one-
on-one negotiations with policymakers.

[62] Time, Inc. 1967:19. The Indonesian version indicates that these issues were raised
but does not mention such forthcoming comments from the Indonesian side. This is, in
fact, the most important difference in the way the two reports reflect the contents of the
roundtables. As we will see, the *Time* document makes repeated references to statements
from the Indonesian delegates that great flexibility exists in their government's policies and
that the investors' suggestions will be considered seriously. The Indonesian version, meanwhile, only records the issues as raised, sometimes noting the intensity or frequency of the
comment or objection.

[63] See Indonesian Embassy 1967:109–112.

sion on labor as follows: "An appropriate manpower policy must be promulgated to make good relations between labor and management possible."[64] The *Time* version, however, suggests that the oral exchange on Indonesia's labor laws was more substantial. The relevant notes indicate that the investors called for a new labor law mentioning not only labor's rights, "but its obligations as well."[65]

It appears that the law limiting operation permits to thirty years caused the greatest discomfort for the investors. Quoting a conference participant, one press report said, "The main criticism by international businessmen was the initial 30-year limit on permits for foreign businesses setting up plants in Indonesia. . . . It was impressed on the Indonesians that most companies needed at least 50 years' guaranteed operations to plan ahead."[66] Although the weight of the exchange was once again dampened in the Indonesian version, the *Time* report suggests that Sadli and Sediono were pressed hard on the issue. In apparent exasperation, they said that "the new regime has gone a long way" and "pointed out there may be an opportunity for some further amendment of the laws."[67]

Exchanges like these were repeated in each roundtable, and it would be tiresome to recount the details of them all. Again and again, business would chip away at the laws and regulations and the officials would offer reassurance that nothing was carved in stone and that the investors' role in shaping and refining Indonesian policy was most welcome. The *Time* document overflows with notes reflecting strong and responsive signals to the capital controllers: "The Indonesian officials indicated a willingness to consider this and other problems." "The Indonesians said they would carefully consider these suggestions."[68] Investors at the "Mining, Oil, and Other Extractives" session, where transnational interest was strongest, were extraordinarily blunt about what they wanted and about how their transjurisdictional mobility presented strong structural constraints on policymakers. Pointing out that globally there were more investment possibilities than capital available (an "investors' market," as they put it), they stressed that Indonesia desperately needed to

[64] Bank Indonesia (appendix 6) 1967:2; my translation.
[65] Time, Inc. 1967:19.
[66] *Asian Recorder* 13, 52 (1967): 8087.
[67] Time, Inc. 1967:19.
[68] Time, Inc. 1967:22.

make itself "competitive with conditions in the rest of the world."[69] "The roundtable participants suggested that the Indonesian government take under consideration certain amendments and modifications of its current regulations."[70] Once again putting the accent on their flexibility, the Indonesian delegates responded that their "Parliament had not yet ratified the [controversial] government recommendations and regulations that had earlier been outlined."[71]

We are fortunate to have these fragmentary glimpses into the signaling and negotiations that occurred during that cold November weekend in 1967, but what impact did they really have on investor confidence and perceptions, investor behavior, and Indonesian policy making? Reactions were already evident on the third and final day of the conference. Eugene R. Black, president and chairman of the World Bank until 1963 and a close adviser to President Lyndon B. Johnson since 1965, offered this cautious first assessment to the world's leading capital controllers: "Private capital is a very bashful, shy maiden. It takes an awful lot of wooing. Private capital is not willing to go into a country and receive a grudging welcome. The fact that the Indonesians were prepared to come here is very important. It means they recognize the importance of private capital, and I hope they will be willing not to impose conditions that make it difficult for private capital to invest in Indonesia."[72] He was referring, of course, not just to private capital, but to highly mobile private capital.

Drawing attention to the urgent need for a quick response from investors, J. Burke Knapp, vice president of the World Bank, emphasized that although conditions in Indonesia had improved dramatically, the best way to guarantee smooth sailing ahead would be through a massive inflow of investment. Referring to the economic ministers and the daunting investment imperative they confronted, Knapp exhorted the investors: "These people have got to succeed, and have got to succeed reasonably quickly, in order to sustain in Indonesia the cause which they are upholding there. What I mean is that over their shoulders are 110 million

---

[69] Time, Inc. 1967:21. In an only slightly veiled admonition to those officials bent on skimming untold riches from investors, they added that "just as vital as being fiscally competitive, is that it is important to be competitive in what, for lack of a better word, can be called 'climate.'"

[70] Time, Inc. 1967:21.

[71] Time, Inc. 1967:21.

[72] Time, Inc. 1967:32.

Indonesians . . . [who] are not yet convinced . . . that this cooperation with the western world can be fruitful." In a tone both ominous and urgent, he added, "there could be another swing of the pendulum . . . which would take the whole atmosphere and attitude in Indonesia back, closer to where it was before. What this means is that action is needed soon."[73]

George W. Ball, United States under secretary of state until 1966, gave the most unbridled assessment. Reflecting a clear concern with the geopolitical implications of failing to stabilize the country's economy, he encouraged the investors to heed the sultan's open invitation to visit Indonesia and confirm for themselves what they were hearing in Geneva. "I think we have a real obligation, given the strategic importance of Indonesia," he said, "to investigate with an open mind the possibilities of investment in that country and to undertake that investigation on a comprehensive and systematic basis."[74] Ball then staked his reputation on the claim that worries about Indonesia's political stability were un- founded. "Let me say to you also that anyone who makes a substantial investment in Indonesia should assume that it is going to be there for a while and that there will continue to be a government in power that is basically sympathetic to the ideals that are represented here. . . . And I would tell you as a personal judgement—based on some experience as a diplomat—that I would regard the stability of Indonesia as a first-rate business risk." Boosting Indonesia's standing in the global marketplace for investment sites, he added, "In fact, I have far more faith in the future stability of that great country than I have in many other parts of the world where some of you have put your money." Ball concluded with a flourish: "Let me suggest to you then that we have seen enough and heard enough in the last two days to know, first, that a group of honor- able and able Indonesians is fully determined to meet so far as possible the requirements of the great world enterprises that envisage investment opportunities in their country. And this, gentlemen, is a dramatically encouraging fact."

Press reports indicate that investors were powerfully impressed with the conference. "Sources said it largely convinced many of the world's biggest companies . . . that it was worth their while to explore further

73 Time, Inc. 1967:37.
74 All of Ball's comments are from Time, Inc. 1967:34.

the possibilities of investment in Indonesia."[75] One investor was taken with how candid the Indonesian delegates had been. "They made no attempt to disguise the problems and shortcomings in Indonesia at present," the participant explained, "and if they did not know the answer to a question they simply admitted it." The investors all seemed "immediately convinced of the stability of the present Indonesian Government."

Words of praise and confidence were mixed with assertions of more concrete intentions. According to the same press summary, "Dr. Emil Salim, a senior advisor to President Suharto, said that the majority of the 70 foreign concerns represented had announced their intention of sending representatives to visit Indonesia as a result of this meeting. New York, San Francisco, and Geneva had provisionally been appointed world centres where discussions could be continued between businessmen and the Indonesian Government."

It is difficult to know precisely how influential the conference was for Indonesia's policymakers as they drafted and amended their laws and regulations to suit investors' demands. There are, however, clear signs that the event was significant. The last person to speak at the conference was the head of the Indonesian delegation, the sultan of Yogyakarta. Referring to the roundtable exchanges, the sultan said: "[Your recommendations] have . . . given us a better insight into the shortcomings and inadequacies of our policies in respect to external capital investment. After our return to Djakarta our delegation will report and recommend to our government necessary adjustments in regard to foreign investment policies and regulations."[76] Mohammad Sadli, who went on to hold cabinet posts under Suharto, believes the impact of the investment conference was substantial. Reflecting on the proceedings—more than two decades afterward—he said, "The conference in Geneva was very important. It was a first in many senses. [It] gave us our first opening shot on drawing capital into Indonesia. Immediately after that, we got a big inrush of oil investments. I don't know if there was a direct link between the event and the inrush, but there is no doubt that the conference set the tone for the years to follow. It also gave us experience speaking on behalf of Indonesia in front of the world's top investors. It was very successful.

[75] For the press reports quoted in this paragraph and the one that follows, see *Asian Recorder* 13, 52 (1967): 8086–8087.

[76] Time, Inc. 1967:38.

authorised lang -

The Berkeley group knew how to speak the language of these business people."[77]

He maintains also that the early years of the New Order were marked by an extraordinary sense of urgency, especially to get the country's productive pumps primed. Still referring to the conference, Sadli offered this insight: "Overall, we were extremely forthcoming in our presentation. We were desperate to get new investments, and we were willing to receive anything. With Freeport, which was the first generation of new investments in Indonesia, I all but said, 'Where is the dotted line for me to sign on?' They were ready to invest even before we had an investment law under which to sign the agreement. By the time of the conference, however, we were more ready.'[78] Having major players like Freeport blaze the investment trail is extremely important to others who want to invest but are afraid they will lose everything. Ali Budiardjo explains: "The signing of the contract with Freeport was highly publicized. For the Indonesian government it meant that a big company had confidence in the government. This was important so that others would follow. It did happen, but only after a delay of about a year. Other investors didn't have the same courage as Freeport. They were careful. Especially politically, they wanted to be sure. The big companies wanted to be sure the

[77] The "Berkeley group" refers to the handful of figures at the core of the team of economic ministers who received their doctorates from the University of California at Berkeley in the 1950s and 1960s. It is true that the economic ministers were better qualified than other Indonesian officials to speak to the investors in their own vernacular. But even so, they were by their own admission still extremely new to the posh world of big government and big business. Laughing, Sadli added, "I still recall Emil Salim's reaction to the incredibly luxurious suite provided for us at the hotel. He said to me jokingly, 'I wish they'd offered me the option of taking the cash instead and staying somewhere more simple.'" Interview in Jakarta with Mohammad Sadli, 21 June 1989.

[78] Interview in Jakarta with Mohammad Sadli, 21 June 1989. Ali Budiardjo, who ran Freeport Indonesia for almost two decades, confirms that this aggressive American company (whose top executives lobbied hard on Indonesia's behalf at the Geneva conference) caught the economists by surprise. "Freeport saw that the time had come in 1966. They monitored the news reports and so on, and it was clear to them that the climate had changed dramatically. This was still 1966, when there were demonstrations and everything. Freeport was very courageous because things were far from stable. But they were confident Suharto would win. They talked to people like Tahija [of Caltex Pacific] and me, and we told them. When Freeport approached us in 1966, it immediately became clear that no one had any idea of how to proceed. There was no foreign investment office and there was no foreign investment law. We had our first meeting with the Freeport people in July 1966. Our second meeting was in October 1966. We were in a very awkward position because we had no legal basis on which to conclude the investment agreement." Interview in Jakarta with Ali Budiardjo, 24 March 1989.

PKI was destroyed. They also wanted evidence that the government knew what it was going to do. It was important that Suharto surrounded himself with economists."[79]

From January 1967 (when the Foreign Investment Law was announced) to June 1968—a little more than half a year after the Geneva conference—roughly one hundred applications worth almost half a billion dollars had been received from prospective foreign investors. These were the figures announced excitedly at Business International's round-table meeting in Jakarta in September 1968.[80] "This is far more direct investment inflow," their briefing paper noted, "than many countries that are much more affluent and that have far greater ratings for economic and political stability may expect."[81] Thus investors were responding *unusually strongly* in Indonesia. It appears from both word and deed that the economists, to whom Suharto had entrusted the impossible task of quickly reversing mobile investors' view of Indonesia, had outdone themselves in restoring their confidence.

Chinese Capital: 1968

With a program for reassuring and enticing mobile investors firmly in place, attention turned in 1968 to Indonesia's ethnic Chinese. It is necessary to explore why policies responding to this important group of mobile investors were delayed. Certainly one major factor was Indonesia's deteriorating relations with the People's Republic of China. The PKI had enjoyed Peking's moral and material support and raised suspicions about all Chinese Indonesians. That the ethnic Chinese were Indonesia's most vigorous and dynamic domestic investing class does not appear to have dislodged the widely held view that they supported com-

[79] Interview in Jakarta with Ali Budiardjo, 24 March 1989.

[80] Of the one hundred, sixty-six (valued at $253 million) had received provisional approval from the Foreign Investment Board. Of these sixty-six, final presidential approval had been given to twenty-three. It should be noted that the single investment of Freeport Sulphur ($76.5 million for a copper mine in West Irian) accounted for almost one-third of all projects getting board approval. Even so, the analysts at Business International argued to their audience that these figures were "impressive," especially when viewed comparatively. As of 1966, the historical *total* investment in Pakistan—a country with a population only slightly smaller than Indonesia's—was $400 million. The average annual flow into India in recent years, they continued, had only been in the $50–60 million range. See Business International 1968.

[81] Business International 1968.

munist revolution. Another factor, only superficially related to the communism issue, was that *pribumi* Indonesians were busy bashing the country's ethnic Chinese during 1966 and 1967.[82] Homes, stores, and businesses were smashed and burned. A final factor was the powerful influence of Indonesia's creditors. Unlike other mobile investors, the Chinese Indonesians were more concentrated in domestic trade and consumer goods sectors—neither of which would have an immediate impact on the country's export capacity. It was the large foreign companies in the extractive sectors that were needed to bring in the foreign exchange that would satisfy the World Bank, IMF, and the IGGI countries. Several reasons converged, then, to postpone the state's responsiveness to the ethnic Chinese.

The delay could not go on indefinitely, however, since the investment and production potential controlled by Chinese Indonesians was far too massive to be ignored. By 1968 decisive steps were being taken to bring this capital back. The main legislation signaling the state's new posture toward the mobile elements of Indonesia's own investing class was the Domestic Investment Law of 1968.[83] Sarbini, the main architect of the legislation, explains its origins:

I was the head of the team which drafted the PMDN law of 1968. I worked on it mainly with Soedjatmoko. Our thinking was simple. In order to develop we needed to mobilize capital. In the spirit of a kind of "deregulation," we put forth the 1968 law. Another aspect was the attempt to white-

[82] These eruptions of violence against the ethnic Chinese have been occurring fairly regularly in Indonesia for more than two hundred years. Because Chinese Indonesians are enormously powerful economically (estimates of their control over domestic capital range from 60 to 80 percent), Indonesian leaders of state (who all receive important political money from ethnic Chinese financiers) have adopted the old Dutch tactic of routinely unleashing society's deep resentment of this minority as a way of reminding them of their precarious position.

[83] Domestic investment is termed PMDN for *penanaman modal dalam negri*, while foreign investment is labeled PMA for *penanaman modal asing*. Those writing on Indonesia usually fail to mention that the target of this legislation was specifically ethnic Chinese capital. In no sense was the 1968 law a general, *domestic* counterpart to the Foreign Investment Law of 1967. Most special programs to help domestic investors—even when aiding *pribumi* Indonesians was ostensibly the intention—favored ethnic Chinese. Subsidized credit is an excellent example. Because domestic investors were required to supply a substantial share of a proposed investment in the form of equity, most *pribumi* could not qualify for the special loans that legislators claimed were supposed to give these entrepreneurs their start. Either the economic ministers did not know what they were doing with these laws, or they never seriously intended to give a boost to *pribumi* investors.

wash or launder [*memutihkan*] funds so that those who amassed their riches through illegal currency exchange or smuggling, or whatever, would not fear bringing their money back to Indonesia. We were aware that there was a lot of Chinese capital outside the country. With the 1968 law, we made formal for domestic investors the same incentives and protections enjoyed by foreigners under Wijoyo's 1967 PMA law.[84]

A second piece of legislation targeted mobile finance capital—especially the Chinese "hot money" that had fled to Singapore and Hong Kong when conditions under Sukarno became too dangerous. "In 1968, the big push was to pull the 'hot money' back into the country," a source explained. "This was done with the law on *deposito berjangka,* long-term deposits, with no questions asked as to the money's source. The idea is to draw these resources into investments domestically. This avoids capital flight and gives those who get money here through corruption a safe place to put their money inside Indonesia."[85]

These two major policy initiatives, together with an army crackdown on Chinese bashing, spurred Indonesia's most mobile domestic investors to return their assets and engage once again in production and commerce. Reflecting their decidedly weaker leverage over policymakers, immobile capital controllers were unable to get any major formal policies adopted during this period that addressed their investment interests as generally smaller and less competitive players. That they voiced their dissatisfaction more loudly and steadily than all other investors combined did not matter. The salient difference was not in the intensity of signals sent by this group but in the lack of urgency policymakers felt in listening to their complaints.

Latent Contradictions

Although the resources the economic ministers attracted were extremely helpful to the Suharto regime, the president and his closest noneconomist allies were frustrated by their limited discretion over the enduse of these resources. Institutional capital flowed into Indonesia bilaterally and multilaterally from creditor countries interested in,

[84] Interview in Jakarta with Sarbini, 13 November 1989.
[85] Confidential interview in Jakarta with an ethnic Chinese money changer whose operations were extremely important in the late 1960s, 13 April 1989.

among other things, being responsive to capital controllers in their own export sectors back home.[86] On reaching Indonesia the resources were deliberately channeled into the hands of the economic ministers through Bank Indonesia, the Ministry of Finance, and BAPPENAS (the National Planning Board). Auditors both from creditor countries and agencies like the World Bank watched (as best they could) to ensure that resources were being used for purposes outlined in development plans. PL 480 assistance offered the Indonesians the greatest flexibility because the Indonesian Government would receive commodities that it would in turn sell domestically. These transactions generated "counterpart" funds in rupiah for the government that could be used in a variety of ways— though the United States tried to make sure they were not used for routine expenditures (such as civil servant's salaries). Not long after Indonesia's economy had been stabilized, creditor countries pressed for more "project" and less "program" assistance because the latter allowed too much discretionary control for Indonesian officials.[87]

Although Suharto understood that the economic ministers, their institutions, and their policies were absolutely critical for bringing in fresh resources and getting other relief, he and his political allies were not fully comfortable with an arrangement that, by its very design, constrained their control over the resources.[88] The main reason is that in addition to

[86] The assistance offered by these countries resembles a Sears or Macy's credit card. Customers can make purchases to the limit of their credit line but cannot use the card to shop in other countries. To counter a common suspicion in the U.S. House of Representatives that foreign aid is a wasteful giveaway, John A. Hannah, a top official at USAID, offered the legislators a few relevant facts: "Few people realize that over 98 percent of the commodities financed by AID this fiscal year will be purchased in the United States, thus providing jobs and additional income for American businesses and labor, and market development for our exporters. Many believe the aid program hurts our balance of payments, whereas the very limited spending of aid dollars abroad is more than offset by repayments to the United States on earlier aid loans." See U.S. House of Representatives 1969:121.

[87] Sullivan provides an excellent account of deliberate U.S. efforts to strengthen the economists' hand by channeling resources through them *only*. Sullivan, who worked as an assistant to Rep. Clement Zablocki—an important figure on the House Foreign Affairs Committee—offers an extremely rare perspective on U.S. dealings with Suharto and his associates during the early years of the New Order. He writes, "It was announced Embassy policy that if honest distribution was not carried out, the aid being wasted would be canceled." Sullivan 1969:530. The first U.S. auditor visited Indonesia in 1968.

[88] Important as they were, capital controllers were not the only actors Suharto had to worry about. Although others, especially in the military, did not exercise structural power, meeting their demands was essential—even when, as was often the case, they contradicted or interfered with the policies designed to attract and retain investment capital.

feeling pressures to meet the society's investment needs in a general way, Suharto also understood that his political survival also depended on his ability to manipulate in a far more specific manner the patron-client networks that pervade Indonesia's institutions and society from the presidential palace, through the military and bureaucracy, down to the village level. The financial resources needed to do this had to be abundant and united. Thus, while the ministers at Finance and the National Planning Board were busy spinning economic policy and making convincing presentations at roundtable meetings with mobile investors, Suharto was undertaking the difficult political business of transforming himself from obscure major general, to acting president, to president. In addition, he faced the delicate task of sidelining Sukarno, a man who, despite his role in the conflicts leading up to and following the putsch of October 1965, remained a force to be reckoned with. At first numerous figures close to Suharto tried to redirect some of the institutional resources that began to flow. John Sullivan describes what came to be known in diplomatic circles as the "hunting trips": visits certain powerful Indonesians made to Washington, D.C. to secure large outlays of cash and shipments of goods: "Almost immediately after the new regime became established, and particularly during the summer of 1966, Indonesian generals began to show up in the United States seeking to make 'deals' in surplus commodities. Many times they carried vaguely-worded letters signed by Suharto, which American diplomats came to refer to as 'hunting licenses.' "[89] One of the earliest military men to arrive was General Suryo Wirohadiputro, "whose self-prepared 'aid memory,' dated May 9, 1966, proclaimed the purpose of his trip 'the acquisition of financing of approximately 400,000 tons of rice.' "[90] At 1966 prices this much rice would sell for $72 million and would cost $10 million to ship to Indonesia. A four-man delegation led by Colonel Harsono, chief of the Press and Public Relations Directorate in the Ministry of Information, came in

[89] Sullivan 1969:317. Offering one explanation why Suharto and his men might have believed the United States would go along, Sullivan writes that the officers "conveyed the feeling, either directly or indirectly, that while the United States was spending billions of dollars to kill Communists in Vietnam, the Indonesians had killed hundreds of thousands of their own without a cent from the Americans. In that sense, America 'owed' Indonesia a billion or two in foreign aid." With this reasoning, it is not difficult to take the next logical step that the officers themselves should be the chosen vehicle for delivering the country's blood money.

[90] Sullivan 1969:317n.

search of newsprint, spare parts for printing shops, and fifteen new printing presses.[91] Some hunters showed considerable sophistication by making their requests through American counterparts: "A common gambit was to approach an American rice shipper or a dealer in Texas cotton as a representative of General Suharto empowered to make purchases—providing appropriate credits could be obtained from the American government. Implicit in these approaches was a tacit (or indirect) agreement for a percentage of the sale as a bonus for the Indonesian military man. It was, in the words of [American] Ambassador Green, 'the time honored system of squeeze.'"[92] With the exception of one extremely difficult case, Suharto's men always came hunting unaccompanied by the civilian officials with whom the United States preferred to work. The Americans were startled when a top general, Mohammad Yusuf, arrived in Washington in the autumn of 1966 with Foreign Minister Adam Malik in tow. "Yusuf brought with him a $500 million checklist of military equipment desired by the Indonesian military and presented it to Department of Defense officials during a meeting at the Pentagon. Although the list was received politely and a promise to study it was given, U.S. officials made no commitments."[93] Assistant Secretary of State William P. Bundy was forced to intervene when Yusuf emerged from the meeting to announce to the Indonesian and U.S. press that the Pentagon had pledged $500 million in aid. Yusuf was called back in and given a flat no to his request. He returned to Jakarta embarrassed and empty-handed.[94]

Not all hunters were as difficult to handle as General Yusuf. Sullivan, who watched numerous Indonesian military figures pass through Rep. Clement Zablocki's office, explained that the technique was to feign confusion about why proper (meaning through the economic ministers) channels were not being used to supply aid. He writes, "When lower-echelon officers, some of them armed with 'hunting licenses,' began to

[91] Sullivan 1969:317n.
[92] Sullivan 1969:318.
[93] Sullivan 1969:524.
[94] Yusuf knew that Ambassador Marshall Green in Jakarta was responsible for bringing Bundy into the matter. The generals close to Acting President Suharto retaliated by cutting off the American ambassador diplomatically. Green could not meet Suharto from March until July 1967. In May General Alamsjah, who handled Suharto's appointments, refused to let Green see Suharto unless he first pledged $200 million in U.S. aid. Green did not comply. Sullivan 1969:524–526.

seek out massive American aid in late 1965 and early 1966, [Ambassador] Green asked [Foreign Minister] Malik to contact the Nasution/Suharto leadership to find out if the aid requests had their approval. After some delay, Malik returned to say that the army leadership and he did not believe the time was ripe for a resumption of aid."[95] The Americans were determined to send clear signals to Suharto and his closest associates that assistance would be forthcoming, but that it had to flow through official channels. Said one U.S. diplomat, "We consciously tried to increase their [the economists'] strength by making it clear to the generals that Indonesia would not get aid until they went the way the economists advised. And the top leaders believed it."[96] But there were limits on how far resources could be monitored once they were transferred to Indonesia. Suharto and his allies could still skim money and goods for their own political purposes.

If Suharto had limited control over institutional flows, he had even less access to and control over private capital. Thanks to the hands-off policies needed to attract capital in the first place, even the economic ministers could not control where, when, and how much private capital would be invested. These decisions were squarely in the hands of profit-seeking investors who, to varying degrees, were mobile and could relocate their resources elsewhere should Indonesia try to meddle too much. The issue is one of end-use control, and unyielding efforts were being made by both private and institutional capital controllers to make sure the resources they supplied would remain under their control and, as much as possible, serve their geopolitical or profit motives.

According to Senate testimony of U.S. diplomats stationed in Jakarta during the late 1960s and early 1970s, Suharto made his first serious efforts at tapping a flow of less-controlled resources sometime in 1968. The person best situated to deliver was General Ibnu Sutowo, the top man at the state oil company, Pertamina.[97] Erland Heginbotham,

[95] Sullivan 1969:318–319.

[96] Sullivan 1969:523. Although Sullivan does not say, it is very likely that the person speaking was Ambassador Green.

[97] See U.S. Senate 1978. The senators were considering committing additional money to the IMF to rescue countries experiencing foreign payments imbalances as a result of huge increases in oil prices. Ibnu Sutowo and Pertamina were discussed because those overseeing the Fund were alarmed that private banks lending money to Sutowo had ignored IMF signals that the loans were ill advised. Bailing out countries like Indonesia amounted to bailing out banks that had acted "irresponsibly."

deputy assistant secretary at the bureau of East Asian and Pacific Affairs, explained that "since the Government did not have adequate funds, it was the tendency of the President to turn to General Ibnu, in whom he had great confidence, and say, General, here is an important project, we would like you to get it done, and nobody discussed where the money was to come from."[98] Sutowo's strategy was to use the country's massive parastatal organization as collateral for "sovereign" commercial loans. Of course the economists were immediately alarmed by this development. It was their province to manage Indonesia's foreign credit flows, and they believed the economy was still much too weak to service debts amassed on anything but the most concessional terms.[99] In addition, their inability to control *all* government borrowing reflected badly on them in their dealings with the IMF, World Bank, and IGGI. Especially during the early years, reliable information about this new credit flow was extremely scarce. Even more concerns about the economists' position in Suharto's regime were raised when it was learned that they did not even dare make direct inquiries about Sutowo's activities. "It was quite clear that the IMF was having serious problems in determining the facts," Heginbotham testified. "They could not find Indonesian Government official who were willing to take on inquiring of General Ibnu as to what he was doing."[100] Nevertheless they did, with IMF assistance, attempt to establish "what the limits should be for Government and specifically Pertamina borrowing abroad."[101] Thus began the fight within the Indonesian state over who would control the flow of untied investment resources.

Suharto responded to the constraints of having to be responsive to capital by pursuing a covert policy line that paralleled—and frequently contradicted—the overt policies promoted and defended by the eco-

[98] U.S. Senate 1978:86. Development "projects" are the preferred veil for spreading patronage money throughout the Indonesian system. Projects are deliberately overpriced, substandard materials are procured, and envelopes and briefcases of cash are passed around at every stage—all debited to Indonesia's sovereign account to be paid for with interest twenty or thirty years hence.

[99] Foreign investors in particular pay very close attention to a country's foreign account. If debt payments become too great, the availability of foreign exchange for investors to repatriate profits or collect payment for goods sold to Indonesia is seriously threatened. In short, a country's policy of currency convertibility can be jeopardized and the overall climate for investment ruined.

[100] U.S. Senate 1978:105.

[101] U.S. Senate 1978:86.

nomic ministers. Heginbotham described the entire arrangement as the "two-track" system: "You have the technocrats [economists] running the economy overall and General Ibnu running the oil sector, which was, of course, the most important one in terms of Indonesia's foreign exchange earnings."[102] Each track had its own advantages and "style," as Heginbotham phrased it. The advantages of allowing the economists to do their job have already been discussed at length.[103] Sutowo, meanwhile, acted as the president's political financier, supplying the resources with which he could reward his supporters—via projects and other skim schemes—anywhere in the archipelago. "I helped all the military people with their projects," Sutowo beamed, "and you can't find a single road or school or hospital that wasn't at least partly funded by the money I borrowed through Pertamina."[104] Sutowo was famous for his no-nonsense style and quick results. "He put projects into being rapidly and got a rapid payback," said one analyst, "generally in self-liquidating activities."[105]

Suharto stayed above the fray and allowed the main players in each track, market and clientelist, to fight out their differences. The president was shrewd in realizing that he should not himself become implicated in the emergence or persistence of the Pertamina channel. To do this would have seriously undermined the momentum and confidence that the economic ministers had generated. Instead, Suharto kept Ibnu Sutowo out in front and allowed him to develop a reputation for being a rogue official, the details of whose dealings the president could pretend not to know. Sutowo maintains, however, that the president not only was fully aware of his activities but supported him without reservation. The following interchange with Sutowo is instructive:

[102] U.S. Senate 1978:85.

[103] As to their style, Wellons (1977:209) points out that they tended to develop a "complex array of arrangements with donor governments and international donor institutions, which required many studies, slow, painful processes, with each donor having a different set of procedures." Again, the essential point is that these very procedures were a manifestation of institutional capital's efforts to retain some discretionary control.

[104] Interview in Jakarta with Ibnu Sutowo, 7 March 1989. According to a prominent Muslim politician, who was explaining the way Suharto used Ibnu Sutowo and Pertamina funds for patronage: "Another scheme was the various development projects in the regions. *Puskesmas* [village clinics] and schools would be built all over the place—sometimes with walls that would fall down if you leaned against them too hard. You can collect the anecdotes and horror stories by the thousands. Sometimes they even built schools when there were no students to go to them. The point was to pass around the money." Interview in Jakarta with Ridwan Saidi, 27 March 1989.

[105] Wellons 1977:209.

In those days I was more powerful than the ministers. They objected. But as long as I had the support of the president, they couldn't do anything.

And did you?

Of course. I paid no attention to bureaucratic rules and procedures. If there was a project being considered, I usually said I would have an answer in a month. If I said yes, they could start operations that afternoon. With the ministries, even after you got approval, which took forever, you still had to wait. Without the backing of the president I wouldn't have been able to pull it all together. I just went ahead and made investments without the approval of BAPPENAS. People used to say, "There's the BAPPENAS way and the Pertamina way." It was "three years versus OK start." People in the oil business today tell me nothing has gotten done since I left.[106]

If the details of Suharto's role in creating this dual policy were shrouded in mystery, the animosity between Ibnu Sutowo and the economists was evident to everyone.[107]

To defend their role as the sole vehicle for delivering private and institutional capital resources to the Indonesian system, the economists were determined to shut down the Sutowo channel. Fortunately for them, the IMF, the World Bank, and the countries supplying credit to Indonesia also had their own reasons for wanting to see this flow run dry.[108] The first move to constrain Sutowo came in 1971 with Law 8, stipulating that all state enterprises had to receive Ministry of Finance approval for loans outside specified limits. According to Phillip Wellons, however, this regulation, like most others in Indonesia, could be circum-

[106] Interview in Jakarta with Ibnu Sutowo, 7 March 1989.

[107] Sadli confirmed that the economic ministers were fully aware of the careful game Suharto was playing. Referring to the president's perspective on the resources pouring in from the second channel, Sadli said: "He loved that. He could never get the World Bank interested in projects like Krakatau steel, so he got Ibnu to raise the money for it. And then there were the military links. Ibnu Sutowo provided pocket money for all the top military leaders. And he went around to all the regions of the country building showy things like sports stadiums." Interview in Jakarta with Mohammad Sadli, 6 November 1989.

[108] Heginbotham explained: "The governments, I would underline, had a very direct interest in this because they were making large concessional aid contributions to Indonesia each year, and they had good reason not to want to see these long-term concessional loans undermined by short-term borrowing which would mortgage the future revenues of Indonesia and raise the possibility of a need for further debt rescheduling." U.S. Senate 1978:93.

vented if the president approved—and he did.[109] By the end of 1972
Pertamina's borrowing abroad had exceeded the limits set by the Indonesian government on credits of between three and fifteen years. In the
interim, the economic ministers had succeeded in pushing through an
even tougher law, Presidential Decree 59, in October 1972. This legislation made it plainer than ever that the Indonesian government would not
guarantee loans negotiated by state enterprises without government approval. The law stated, according to Wellons, that "these enterprises
may only accept foreign credits that entail no guarantee by the national
government, BI [Bank Indonesia] or a government bank and that in no
way obligate the national government."[110] In a word, the loans would
no longer be "sovereign." But for reasons that are not entirely clear, the
minister of finance delayed the promulgation of this law—perhaps because he was encountering powerful resistance from General Sutowo
and the president.

In a move that put some bite into the bark of the economic ministers,
the United States government, in December 1972, "suspended program
loan eligibility [for Indonesia] in support of IMF efforts to obtain rem-
edy of Pertamina borrowing excess."[111] The IMF and the U.S. officials
in Jakarta tried to strengthen the economists' hand by threatening to cut
off Indonesia's access at least to institutional capital. This was done
subtly at first through negotiations on Indonesia's standby agreement
with the IMF (which stipulated, among other things, the levels of foreign
borrowing deemed prudent). The Fund agreed to renew the standby in
March 1972 without much fuss. But things changed in 1973 after it
became increasingly clear that the economic ministers were making no
headway in curtailing the activities of General Sutowo. In early 1973 the
IMF reported to the consortium of Indonesia's bilateral creditors, the
IGGI, that Pertamina was engaging in excessive borrowing that neither
the Fund nor Indonesia's economic ministers sanctioned. The U.S.
delegation, for its part, "urged the participating governments to support
the efforts of the *Indonesian Government* and of the IMF to maintain

[109] Wellons 1977:209–210. Robison (1986:236) writes that Law 8 "gave the President
Director of Pertamina full control over oil, LNG, and foreign contractors, subject only to
the authority of the President [Suharto]."

[110] Wellons 1977:202.

[111] U.S. Senate 1978:180; taken from Heginbotham's chronology of events in appendix
C of the Witteveen document. Notice that it was *program* aid, the most flexible kind, that
was withheld.

these [borrowing] ceilings."[112] In late April 1973 the economists were still struggling to get Presidential Decree 59 activated so that punitive actions could be taken against Pertamina. Meanwhile the ceiling violations were becoming more serious, and the IMF response escalated accordingly. Heginbotham explained: "Following the expiration of the 1972 standby agreement, the Fund then reviewed with the Indonesian Government and with the donor countries the situation and further consultations were held between the IMF and the Indonesian Government. [i.e., a strategy was being worked out]. A standby was renewed for the following year with increased ceilings but in this case a very unusual subceiling specific to Pertamina borrowing was incorporated."[113] In effect, the IMF had attempted to lend credence to protests the economic ministers were already making internally by writing a standby agreement that not only mentioned Pertamina by name but explicitly incorporated borrowing levels the Fund and the economic ministers believed were acceptable. By May 1973 the Ministry of Finance, "possibly in response to or assisted by the prodding of the IMF,"[114] was finally able to put some teeth into Presidential Decree 59 of the previous October. Significantly, the law imposed the same loan limitations on Pertamina as contained in the IMF standby agreement negotiated (but not implemented) months before. To wit, Pertamina was prohibited from borrowing beyond a specified limit on terms of one to fifteen years maturity. Loans of

[112] U.S. Senate 1978:92; my emphasis. It is, of course, a fiction of convenience for Heginbotham that those opposing the ceilings were not also the "Indonesian government." He added, "We also made direct representations to United States banks encouraging them to cooperate fully with the Indonesian Government in attempting to maintain ceilings which were acceptable to the donor community and in line with what we felt were responsible policies." It turns out that the United States was doing more than merely "encouraging" its own banks to get in line. Though it was often difficult to discover which banks were lending to Pertamina, regulatory agencies applied whatever pressure they could to institutions when they had concrete evidence of loanmaking. But the pressures they applied could be only with regard to other bank operations (say, a threat to do an audit). In lending to Pertamina, these banks broke no laws. They merely disregarded the signs (such as having the IMF refuse a standby) that would ordinarily mark a client as a bad credit risk.

[113] U.S. Senate 1978:93.

[114] Wellons 1977:212, 202. Wellons's own evidence should lead to a stronger conjecture than "possibly." He writes, "The Minister [of Finance] was to issue implementing regulations [for the beefed-up regulatory law, Presidential Decree 59 of October 1972]. For some reason he sanctioned the regulations only on 3rd May 1973, six months after the Presidential Decision. *On 4th May 1973, one day after the Ministerial Decree, the IMF approved a new stand-by, the previous one having elapsed on 17th April 1973. Stand-by arrangements since 1970 appear to have been approved by the IMF with no hiatus*" (my emphasis).

less than one year were permitted to leave flexibility for working capital financing, and loans of more than fifteen years were perhaps permitted because the IMF and the economists doubted Pertamina could raise many such long-term (i.e., more risky) loans among the renegade banks on the Eurocurrency market.

It is important to interrupt the narrative at this point and look more carefully at the power dynamics that help account for Suharto's decision finally to side with the economic ministers in their attempts to curtail the operations of Ibnu Sutowo. Fully aware that Suharto supported Sutowo and benefited politically and personally from his dealings, the economic ministers targeted Suharto's deep concern for the stability of his rule as the best hope for having the president cut Sutowo loose so the economic ministers and their allies in Indonesia and abroad could shut down his global credit operation. Central to their strategy was Suharto's fear that allowing the development of an investment and production crisis such as occurred in the 1960s could destabilize his regime in the same way it had undermined his predecessor. The technique was to convince the president that it was no longer possible to maintain his two-track system because the Pertamina channel was threatening the hard-won confidence among private investors that the economic ministers had built up since 1966 and 1967. Sutowo undermined investors' confidence in the rule of law, in Indonesia's commitment to market-based access, and in the ability of the economic ministers to direct the country's economic policies. Sutowo's massive commercial borrowing, and the debt-service obligations and draining impact on foreign exchange it entailed, posed a direct threat to the country's capital accounts. Indirectly, the country's ability to maintain the full convertibility of its currency was threatened as well. All these factors converged to send alarming signals to mobile investors, who were already sensitive to Indonesia's inability to maintain a favorable investment climate. As Sadli explained, the president was willing to side with the economists only after "we convinced him that what Sutowo was doing was dangerous for the country."[115]

[115] Interview in Jakarta with Mohammad Sadli, 21 June 1989. If Ibnu Sutowo is telling the truth, the IMF was supporting the economic ministers' position domestically not just through the symbolic pressure of withholding a standby agreement, but also by deliberately manipulating Indonesia's desperate need for food—with all its politically destabilizing ramifications. Without my prompting, Sutowo offered the following description of the IMF's position regarding the country's severe rice crisis of 1972–1973: "It was 1973, I believe, and it looked like it was going to be a good rice crop. But there was a flood and we ended up needing to import a lot of rice. The IMF sent Hoffman to tell the

This is not the only instance in which the credible threat of an investment crisis and the economic and political destabilization that could result has been a key consideration influencing Indonesia's most powerful decision makers to adopt policies advanced by the economic ministers to maintain the state's responsiveness to capital controllers. According to A. R. Soehoed, a former minister of industry and a figure close to Suharto, manipulating the president's fear of failing to meet the country's investment imperative was their most potent instrument for influencing his decisions. He explained: "The technocrats are very good at scaring the old man. They keep him on the razor's edge, and that's how they get their way. They tell him that if he doesn't follow their suggestions the people will go without food and clothes, or the economy won't grow."[116] As we will see, a similar technique was still being used even during the 1980s, when the economists were attempting once again to make Indonesia's investment climate competitive in attracting and retaining mobile capital controllers.[117]

Persuaded that it would be prudent to avoid jeopardizing the country's primary source of capital for investment and production, in May 1973 Suharto threw his weight behind the economic ministers' law designed to limit Ibnu Sutowo to short-term borrowing. As Wellons shows, Sutowo finally changed his pattern of borrowing. The results, however, were startling. Pertamina's short-term (less than one-year maturity) borrowing ballooned during the rest of 1973.[118] The numbers tell much of the story:

	Short-Term Debt
End of 1972	$ 140 million
End of 1973	$ 416 million
End of 1975	$1,000 million

---

government that if I wasn't stopped, there would be no standby of $50 million. Widjoyo and Sadli tried to cut me off, but as long as Suharto agreed with what I was doing I continued." Interview in Jakarta with Ibnu Sutowo, 27 March 1989.

[116] Interview in Jakarta with A. R. Soehoed, 13 December 1989.

[117] As an economist at USAID explained: "An awful lot of this deregulation was done without any analysis of the impact. As far as I have seen, there has been no careful analysis, no modeling. The reforms have come from a few minds, accomplished by horror story analysis presented to noneconomists." Interview in Jakarta with an official at USAID, 7 September 1989.

[118] Wellons 1977:214–215.

Thus, Pertamina's short-term debt tripled by the end of 1973 and more than doubled in the sixteen months that followed. This huge surge in short-term borrowing proved too much for the IMF to tolerate. Applying the most severe sanctions it could, the Fund refused to renew Indonesia's standby agreement in May 1974. By May 1975 Pertamina's short- and medium-term debt was $3 billion, or more than twice the size of Indonesia's international reserves in December 1974.[119] To be sure, it was only in the strictest sense that its sudden surge in short-term loans did not violate Ministry of Finance ceilings on its borrowing. As Heginbotham explained, "Technically, anything less than 365-day credit was not covered by the ceiling, so that this was a violation, if you will, of the spirit but not the letter of the ceiling. There was a loophole in effect."[120] But the 365-day and under window was left open only for working capital needs. Pertamina violated this by signing one-year loans that it and the banks understood would be rolled over and over as the years passed.

Ibnu Sutowo's roll-over strategy proved unmanageable by the last quarter of 1974. Defaults began to occur in September of that year and had accelerated by February 1975. The greatest danger was that all of Pertamina's loans—even the ones contracted *after* Indonesia's laws clearly delineated which loans would not be sovereign—included "cross-default" clauses. Should any of Pertamina's loans go unguaranteed by the Indonesian government, the rest of the country's sovereign loans would simultaneously go into default and immediately become payable in full. Suddenly Suharto's two-track game could no longer be played and, thanks to legislative battles won by the economists two and three years earlier, Ibnu Sutowo's second channel was unceremoniously retired. As one minister intimately involved in the struggle with Ibnu Sutowo remarked, "Once we had the laws limiting his medium-term borrowing in place, it was just a matter of time until he self-destructed."[121]

In the interim, however, Suharto had a flow of relatively untied resources that he could tap for his own political and military consolidation. Yielding only when pressed, he was also able to maintain the parallel policy of responding to institutional and private controllers of capital.

[119] Wellons 1977:215.
[120] U.S. Senate 1978:98.
[121] Confidential interview in Jakarta, 26 May 1989.

By the time Ibnu Sutowo was finally fired,[122] Suharto's need for the commercial resources flowing through the second channel was not nearly as great.[123] Windfall profits from the leap in oil prices in 1973 and 1974 had begun to pour in. The next chapter traces the important changes that accompanied this dramatic increase in Indonesia's access to massive resources under direct state control.

einforcement of need to be responsive

Before turning to the oil boom period, let me emphasize several basic points about the story told in this chapter. First, it was important to begin with a description of how Sukarno's Old Order fell apart, and especially the role that the near-total breakdown in investment and production played in the regime's final unraveling. One reason for its importance lies in the lessons it taught to Sukarno's successor, General Suharto, about the *additional* complications that can be stacked on top of already difficult economic and political circumstances when those supplying investment resources withdraw their capital and the state itself has nothing concrete to put in its place.

A second point concerns the priority given to different resource controllers as Indonesia's officials addressed the policy concerns of each, and the levels of power reflected in the order chosen. The highest priority

[122] Most people assume that Ibnu Sutowo was fired because he bankrupted the state oil company, was corrupt beyond imagination, and nearly caused the fiscal collapse of Indonesia's economy (some go so far as to say he shook world financial markets). Mohammad Sadli and Fikri Jufri (an editor of *Tempo*, an important Indonesian news weekly, and the main reporter to break the Pertamina story) explain that such a view is mistaken. Although Pertamina collapsed early in 1975, Sutowo was not fired until early 1976. They argue that the real reason he was sacked was because he embarrassed Suharto in Bali during a meeting of the leaders of the Association of Southeast Asian Nations (ASEAN). Sutowo, who had not been invited to the weekend affair, went golfing with Ferdinand Marcos on the last day of the summit. Because Sutowo insisted on playing the back nine, the two were late for the closing ceremonies (despite having a Pertamina helicopter rush them back to the Pertamina cottages where the meeting was being held). The dramatic and embarrassing arrival of the Philippine dictator with Sutowo was too much for Suharto. The Pertamina chief was fired first thing the next morning.

[123] Sutowo, having done so much for the president and his supporters, was extremely bitter about the way Suharto had treated him. Reflecting on the events culminating in his fall from power, Sutowo had this to say: "I told Suharto I don't want to be president. I told him to look at my record. I wanted to work and get things done. My ambitions weren't political. He smiled and said OK, but I don't think he really believed me. I became too powerful and he was afraid." Did their friendship cause Suharto to give Sutowo the benefit of the doubt? "He wanted to stay president. When you must suspect everyone of ambitions, how can you have friends?" Sutowo said, leaning back in his chair. Interview in Jakarta with Ibnu Sutowo, 7 March 1989.

was given to what I called institutional capital controllers. Their resources were the most liquid and mobile of all, in that immediate relief comes from having debts rescheduled, and also from having new lines of credit made available to purchase essential imports for urban consumers. It was also of tremendous symbolic importance in gaining the confidence of mobile private investors to first have the imprimatur of guarantor states and international agencies. The next group was mobile investors—foreigners and ethnic Chinese Indonesians. The Chinese Indonesians were addressed after the noncitizens not so much because of differences in importance and mobility as because tensions surrounding the role of the Chinese in supporting the Indonesian Communist Party eased only slowly. Another factor is that part of the implicit bargain struck with institutional capital controllers who were concerned with the country's balance of payments was that Indonesia would make immediate efforts to woo investors whose output would contribute to the country's foreign exchange earnings. It is significant, however, that despite voicing their complaints loudly and clearly to Indonesian policymakers, the most immobile actors received almost no redress from the state. This seems to support similar observations by Bates and Lien, Hirschman, and Frieden.

By contrast, not only did mobile actors receive attention, but policymakers went out of their way to signal how favorable Indonesia's policies were. More than this, potential investors were directly involved at an early stage in shaping the content of the laws that would govern access to investment and profit opportunities in Indonesia. It is because of this unusual state responsiveness and investor involvement that so much attention was given to the Geneva conference of 1967. The events of the conference were important for other reasons as well. It was abundantly evident, for instance, that policymakers have no automatic or preexisting awareness of what kinds of policies mobile capital controllers find irresistible. Furthermore, it is important that policies not be too general, but instead be responsive sector by sector. It is for this reason that attention was given to the various roundtables at the conference.

Two other points about the conference were particularly noteworthy. From Suharto's presidential decree giving special authorization to the Indonesian delegates to the explicit admission by the Indonesians who spoke, it was evident that policymakers understood that they faced structural constraints on the range of policies they might reasonably consider and were also aware that ignoring these constraints could precipitate (or in their case perpetuate) a situation marked by severe economic and political instability. In addition, it is also undeniable from the comments made by the Indonesian delegates that the country's policymakers were keenly aware that in dealing with mobile investors they had to compete head on with the other investment climates these mobile actors could freely consider.

If the first part of this chapter was intended to characterize the high responsiveness of the Indonesian state to capital controllers during the preboom period, and to root that responsiveness firmly in the structural dimensions of investors' power, the second part was designed to show that there was no mechanistic or automatic process of responding to structural forces. On the contrary, this policy trajectory only narrowly survived the challenges presented by the existence of deep and important patron-client networks, the manipulation of which was critical to Suharto's ability to consolidate his position and his regime. That the economic ministers triumphed over Ibnu Sutowo's "second channel" is important in itself, but more important is how and why they triumphed. Their success was linked to their ability to convince Suharto that whatever political and economic benefits he was reaping by using Pertamina to supply resources for his clientelist projects, he was simultaneously jeopardizing the country's political and economic stability by threatening the state's ability to be responsive to mobile investors and competitive with other jurisdictions.

That they succeeded in shutting down the Sutowo channel can be attributed to a number of variables—Suharto's reading of the factors contributing to Sukarno's political collapse; the persuasive power of key economic ministers; that the World Bank, IMF, USAID, and Indonesia's creditor consortium, the IGGI, were all allied with the economic ministers and willing to flex their muscles by withholding the institutional resources they controlled; and finally that by May 1973 Suharto had already gotten quite a lot of patrimonial mileage out of the Ibnu Sutowo scheme, and his position as president and head of the military was much more secure. That the direction of Indonesian policy turned so much on the decisions of a single man was of no small importance in accounting for the country's continuing responsiveness to capital controllers in this period. The key consideration is that powerful structural constraints were pressing themselves on Indonesia's policymakers, that their awareness of these limits was as keen as their determination not to risk violating them, but that the precise ways the state ended up responding have a great deal to do with the twists and turns in the struggles that unfolded.

THE OIL BOOM, 1974–1982: STRUCTURAL LEVERAGE AND STATE INDIFFERENCE

Although the policies during the first phase of Suharto's New Order were somewhat mixed in character, on balance it is accurate to describe the investment climate as highly responsive to capital controllers—and especially to the more mobile among them. Policymakers were aware of the pressures to compete with alternative investment sites, and the design of policies for Indonesia reflects this competitive pressure. Despite the economic ministers' clear victory early in 1973 over Ibnu Sutowo and the clientelist political groups he represented and served, and despite what might be called the "lessons" of Sukarno's indifference and even open hostility to capital controllers, a fundamental shift in the direction of Indonesian policy began to take shape soon after the surge in oil prices late in 1973. And with this shift, the second phase of Suharto's New Order, which would last almost another decade, had clearly begun.

The most important factor accounting for this policy shift was the dramatic change in the pattern of resource control that policymakers in Indonesia confronted and operated within. Because the oil and gas sector is owned by the Indonesian state and surpluses from the sale of fossil fuels accrue to the state treasury, the oil boom placed huge and profoundly flexible resources directly in the hands of Indonesian policymakers, especially the patron-client faction linked to Suharto. The impact of this development on the *effectiveness* of investors' structural leverage was immediate and fundamental. Although the *ability* of mobile capital controllers to withhold or relocate their investment resources was not affected, the state's direct access to substantial replacement resources meant that investors' threats and actions were not nearly as constraining on policymakers. Not only the onset but also the depth and intensity of the country's policy changes can be linked to changes in the Suharto regime's access to windfall oil profits. In addition, the slide in influence *within the state* experienced by Indonesia's economic ministers is linked directly to the diminished power and influence of institutional and private resource controllers, whose policy interests paralleled those of the economic ministers. As the intensity and effectiveness of mobile investors' structural leverage declined and the opportunities to pursue a more vigorous form of patronage politics expanded, opportunities expanded in tandem for immobile capital controllers *who were also well positioned in Indonesia's patron-client structure* to have policymakers be responsive to their demands and interests. It is for this reason that a core group of *pribumi* investors was catapulted to wealth, prominence, and even an elevated status of mobility during the final years of the oil boom.

Assessing the Impact of the Oil Boom: The Macroview

Although the nine-year period beginning in late 1973 represents a clear phase in Indonesian political economy marked by a tremendous increase in direct state access to resources that could be used to meet the society's investment needs, the oil boom itself was in no sense uniform. The period consisted of at least two sub-booms of different size and duration, separated by a devastating financial crisis triggered by Pertamina's inability to roll over its short-term loans. The uneven character of the oil boom phase, especially its weak start and strong finish, helps account for several important developments—but especially the brief "comeback" staged by the economic ministers between 1975 and 1978 and the boldness of the policy shift accompanying the second oil boom. The way the oil windfalls entered the system and were appropriated and used is a second concern of this section. To say that "Indonesia" experienced an oil boom does little to explain the nature and direction of policy. Those officially in charge of making policy, though all members of one government and state, are divided into several groups and factions. This is true of any state, but all the more so of one as patrimonial and authoritarian as Indonesia's.[1] An obvious question, then, is, Into whose institutional, or even personal, hands did the oil revenues flow, and to what purposes were these resources put?

What later became known as the oil boom (for oil-exporting countries, anyway) began as a reaction to the hostilities that broke out between Israel and Egypt (plus Syria) in the last quarter of 1973. In early October the average posted price of a barrel of crude was about $3. By the middle of October, Arab states had pushed the price to over $5, an increase of some 70 percent. By late December the Organization of Petroleum Exporting Countries (OPEC), which for years had been unable to coordinate price increases, succeeded in raising the price to almost $12 a barrel. In under three months the price of oil had quadrupled. What effect did these developments have in Indonesia?

The boom transformed the country's cash flow "with the speed of a wish being granted by a fairy godmother."[2] Beginning with the macroview, it is obvious that the boom had an enormous impact on total government revenues and, more significantly, on the relative shares contributed by different sources. The resource base of the New Order state has always been a mixed bag: part corporate and income taxes, part surplus from state enterprises, part tariffs and duties on trade, and part credit and grants from abroad. Figure 1 supplies an overview of the most important components of the state's revenue base,[3] showing percentages

[1] This was clear in Erland Heginbotham's Senate testimony that the "Indonesian government" had been trying to control the quasi-sovereign borrowing spree of Ibnu Sutowo, who was operating on behalf of President Suharto.

[2] Lewis 1980:54. The impact was all the greater when we consider the country's brush with bankruptcy less than a decade earlier. Although the oil price increases of the 1970s meant a great deal inside Indonesia, it is important to keep things in perspective. In terms of total output within OPEC and any ability to affect the price of oil globally, Indonesia has always been a bit player. The images of oil wealth associated with Saudi Arabia, for instance, do not apply to Indonesia. Its enormous population dampened the overall effect of the boom on Indonesia's economy. Not surprisingly, Indonesia declined the opportunity to participate in the IMF Oil Facilities of 1974 and 1975, when the Fund borrowed SDR 2.8 and 5.0 billion (then $9.4 billion) mainly from the richest oil producers.

[3] The focus here is on the revenues of the central government. Some of these resources are collected by local governments and surrendered to Jakarta, while others are collected directly by the central government. Centralization in Indonesia is extreme, and though local governments do directly collect and use a portion of their budgets, the vast majority of operating resources at the local level comes from the central government (even if initially collected locally). A major tax reform in 1984 changed this only slightly. For a good examination of the way the system works, see Devas 1989.

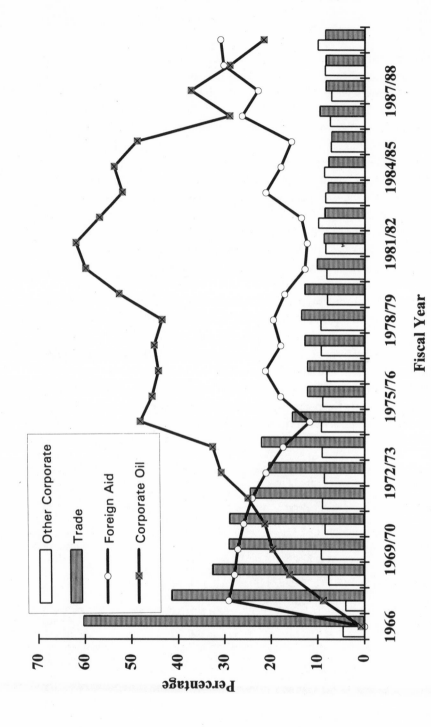

Figure 1. Sources of Indonesian state revenues, 1966–1990. Data from Indonesian Ministry of Finance.

of total revenue for each year.[4] For most years shown, more than 80 percent of all realized resources is captured in the categories of foreign aid, corporate oil, other corporate, and trade-related revenues.[5]

Several key features of the Suharto regime's revenue base are revealed by the graph. There has, for instance, been a secular decline in the state's dependence on resources drawn from trade. Very much reflecting the legacy of Sukarno's pattern of revenue collection, in 1966 the state relied on tariff and duty receipts for 60 percent of its resources.[6] By the mid-1970s the figure was hovering around 10 percent and has remained at that level ever since. Occupying the lower reaches of the graph are government receipts drawn from corporate taxes outside the oil and gas sector.[7] Astonishing both for their relative insignificance and for their consistent flatness, taxes from these corporate sources never pass the 10 percent mark and only in the late 1980s show even a hint of creeping upward. As paltry as this contribution from corporations outside the oil and gas sector may be (especially in light of incessant complaints from private business about high taxes), the figures are even more startling when the sizable share of total corporate receipts from the state's own enterprises is separated from those of the private sector. For the entire period shown in figure 1, the Indonesian government's own enterprises paid an average of 55 percent of all nonoil/gas corporate taxes.[8] During

[4] Total revenue includes foreign credit, which Indonesian officials call "development receipts." This anomaly is discussed in greater detail in the next section.

[5] Since the beginning of the New Order, the Indonesian state has in cumulative terms collected roughly 40 percent of its resources from the oil and gas sector, 20 percent from foreign borrowing, and the rest from domestic nonoil/gas sources. These figures are based on data from the Ministry of Finance.

[6] When smuggling began to displace ordinary trade in the chaotic years leading up to 1965, the state's revenue base was hit especially hard.

[7] Personal income taxes, a major source of state revenue in more industrialized capitalist countries, contribute even less than corporations. Just 2.7 percent of all revenue collected since 1966 has come from personal income taxes. In 1970–1971 they accounted for percent of 3 percent of total revenue, and by 1980–1981 the share dropped to just 1.4 percent. Personal income taxes, already several years into Indonesia's tax reform period, contributed about 3 percent in 1989–1990.

[8] Several additional points should be made about these figures. First, they do not include Pertamina, the largest and most profitable of the state companies. They do, however, include Bank Indonesia and all of the state-owned banks, which dominate the banking sector. Second, of the roughly two hundred state enterprises, only about half are profitable in any given year. Of course the state uses the profitable enterprises to keep the unprofitable ones afloat. Reliable figures on net gains from the state sector are not available, but when oil receipts are included it is fairly safe to say that the state sector has consistently been in the black.

the early years of the New Order government, state firms were a particularly important source of corporate taxes. The line showing levels of foreign grants and credit to the Indonesian state is also noteworthy.[9] This source had dried up in the early 1960s as Sukarno's policies grew ever more hostile to the West. The sharp increase in the supply of capital and resources controlled by foreign governments and international agencies is also evident, rising dramatically in 1967 to almost 30 percent of all state operating resources. Although the share of aid in total revenues moves in almost perfect opposition to the oil sector's contribution, there was an absolute increase in foreign aid for every year until 1980.

The last and most striking element of the Indonesian state's resource base—the rapidly changing share of state revenues from the oil sector—is revealed clearly in the graph. In 1966 oil-related revenues accounted for a tiny fraction of the total. This figure climbed steadily to about one-third of revenues in fiscal year 1973–1974, after which it shot up to half of all government receipts in 1974–1975, and peaked in 1981–1982 at 62 percent. The graph shows that the decline after the oil boom was gentle at first, dropping precipitously in 1985–1986. By 1990 the share of state revenues from the oil sector was projected to be just over 20 percent—roughly equivalent to its contribution in 1970. The picture that emerges from the Indonesian state's revenue data is clear: during the boom years the state was able to collect a huge proportion of its receipts from productive entities directly controlled by the state. The average share of total revenue that was state generated for the periods before, during, and after the boom was 30 percent, 55 percent, and 43 percent, respectively.

As helpful as this macropicture may be in assessing the effect of the oil boom in Indonesia, it is necessary to shift the level of analysis downward and inward to see what happened to control over and access to resources *within* the state, and later to compare these resources with those supplied by private and institutional capital controllers. Only then do the circumstances undermining the structural power of investors and the concomitant decline in the state's policy responsiveness to them emerge clearly.

[9] None of Pertamina's pre-1975 debt is reflected in Ministry of Finance data on the country's sovereign borrowing. This is partly because, as we have seen, the sovereignty of Pertamina's loans through the "second channel" was a matter of considerable dispute. Pertamina single-handedly borrowed more between 1968 and 1975 than the entire Indonesian government had borrowed during the decade and a half after 1960. If Sutowo's loans were included they would alter the picture in figure 1 dramatically.

Control over Discretionary Resources: The Microview

The nature of what I termed in the first chapter "end use" control over resources is at least as important as their relative and absolute size. Some resources are controlled both inside and outside the state, while others are controlled only internally. A good example of the former would be foreign credit, which has always been a critical source for investment in infrastructure in Indonesia. Because foreign governments supply the resources, it is not surprising that they attempt to tie them as much as possible to their own objectives—whether satisfying powerful groups at home or some geopolitical logic in the region.[10] But these same resources are doubly controlled, for once they enter the Indonesian state the struggle begins to determine the ends to which the resources will be used. The Ministry of Finance and BAPPENAS have played the greatest role in exercising internal discretion over foreign credit. That these internal and external loci of control both have strong reasons to support market forms of regulation in Indonesia has been crucial in helping the economic ministers prevent competing political elites within the state—whose own structural and political positions militate strongly against market-based access—from commandeering this key resource pool. A very different situation exists for more autogenous resources—those originating from or generated by the state itself.[11] The primary locus of control for these resources is wholly within the state, and the broader structural environment (capitalism, market penetration, recessions, etc.), together with the position and independent strength of different officials and institutions, becomes much more important in determining who or what will exercise it.

To get a clearer sense of which funds flowing into the state treasury had the fewest external conditions attached, it is necessary to look at

[10] It is for this reason, as we saw, that as soon as Indonesia's economy had been stabilized in the late 1960s, the IGGI pushed for more "project" than "program" credits—the spending of the latter being more difficult for creditor countries to control.

[11] Autogeny should not be confused with autonomy. The term is borrowed from biology. Most female mosquitoes must take a blood meal to produce eggs. "Autogenous" mosquitoes are a rare variety that reproduce without first drinking blood. The autogenous state, then, would produce its own operating resources and would not depend on receipts extracted from other actors such as private business or individual taxpayers. An autogenous state would not necessarily be autonomous, since the society might still depend on private capital controllers to supply resources for investment even if the state itself did not rely on them for revenue.

Indonesia's revenue data in greater detail. Although revenues and expenditures all flow into a single pool, whether as rupiah or as foreign exchange, for accounting and propaganda purposes both are divided into "routine" and "development" subcategories.[12] The routine budget consists, on the revenue side, of receipts from taxes (including taxes on Pertamina) and tariffs and, on the expenditure side, of rice rations and the basic salary for civil servants and the military. "The government's routine outlays are like a retainer paid to a lawyer," said one seasoned observer. "They get the civil servants to the office. But to have anyone actually do anything requires extra money. That's where the development budget comes in. It covers everything from buying office furniture, painting the walls, and paying the ministry's electricity bills to huge development projects costing billions. The entire state machine turns on *proyek*."[13] Money spent on the development budget comes from two main sources: foreign grants or credits and any surplus left over after routine expenditures are subtracted from routine revenues.[14]

From the standpoint of political elites whose power and position rely strongly on patronage relations—and who are thus often opposed to the core priorities and policies of the economic ministers—the part of the "development" budget supplied from abroad is, for reasons already mentioned, somewhat more difficult to control. The greatest source of financial power for those *least* committed politically to being responsive to mobile investors comes, instead, from the surplus that remains after routine expenditures are deducted from domestic receipts. This pool of resources, called "government savings," formed the most critical basis of

[12] The propaganda part concerns the fiction of Indonesia's iron law that expenditures must always equal (or at least never exceed) revenues. Put forth by the economic ministers as part of the stabilization program in the late 1960s, the Balanced Budget Law in reality means that the state cannot print money to cover revenue shortfalls but can borrow abroad instead. Despite much crowing about always operating in the black, the Indonesian state accumulated about $100 billion in red ink betwen 1967 and 1994.

[13] Discussion in Jakarta with Eugene K. Galbraith, 29 August 1989. An expert on the structure and operation of the Indonesian government, Galbraith estimated that for 1989 more than 85 percent of the actual (development) undertakings of the Indonesian government were financed by foreign aid.

[14] In all published data, the Ministry of Finance labels its tax revenues as "domestic receipts" and foreign credit and grants as "development receipts." The World Bank and IMF, in deference to the Indonesians, publish two sets of government budget tables in their annual reports—one with Indonesia's accounting system showing everything balancing, and one in accordance with the way these things are reported everywhere else in the world. When I raised the categorization of loans as revenue to the chief of the World Bank in Jakarta, he shrugged off my objection saying, "Money is money."

power for those who, during the oil boom years, sought to direct state policy away from allocation of opportunity by impersonal markets and toward a system that expanded the discretion of officials to micro-manage access and opportunities. The objective was to use these re-sources in ways that worked with rather than against the grain of Indo-nesian patrimonialism and therefore yielded the greatest benefit to these officials, their friends, and their political allies.

Figure 2 shows how enormous the discretionary funds pouring into the treasury really were (unless otherwise noted, all rupiah figures have been deflated to constant 1980 rupiah). Each bar in the graph represents government savings (domestic receipts minus routine expenses) for each fiscal year as a percentage of the *previous year's* total development ex-penditures (government savings plus foreign credit).[15] When examining this picture, it is important to bear in mind two points: the percentages are on development expenditures that are doubling every three to six years, and the extremely high percentage increases before 1973–1974 were on a very modest base.[16] The figure shows two crucial develop-ments even more clearly than the previous graph tracing overall revenue changes from the oil boom. First, the greatest jumps in discretionary funds available to policymakers occurred in 1974 and again in 1980.[17] The oil boom period, then, actually comprised two distinct booms. Sec-ond, notice that after each boom a slide-off occurred in the size of increases in the years that immediately followed. The downward slope of the first boom was fairly sharp. The more gradual decline after the second boom, however, was followed by a much more precipitous drop by the middle and late 1980s. From the perspective of policymakers

[15] It is impossible to quantify or represent accurately the sense of opportunity or freedom clientelist political elites experienced as the oil windfalls were pouring in. Com-paring levels of new resources coming on line with those allocated the year before more closely approximates what officials perceived than using *current* resources and *current* allocation figures—the latter to some extent already incorporating the opportunities con-tained in the former.

[16] Total development expenditures of just Rp 752 billion in 1969–1970 had exploded to a peak of Rp 7,231 billion by 1983–1984. When adjusted for inflation, this is a tenfold increase in fourteen years. When further adjusted for population increases, it is still a sixfold increase. The sudden jump to 71 percent in 1972–1973 was caused not by oil profits, but by a surge in the price of some of Indonesia's other nonoil exports, especially timber.

[17] Although the figure of 114 percent in 1974–1975 makes it appear to be a bigger boost than in any other year, the actual amount of new and unallocated funds pouring in during 1980–1981 was, in absolute terms, more than twice the windfall of 1974–1975.

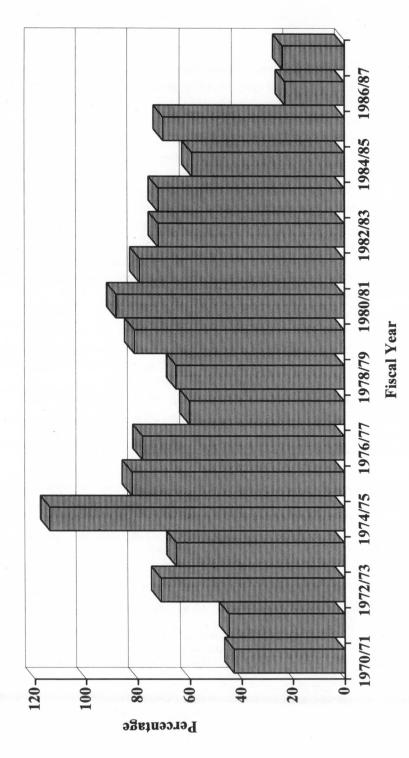

Figure 2. New discretionary development resources as percentage of all development spending in previous year, 1970–1988. Data from Indonesian Ministry of Finance.

(especially Suharto), who had a strong interest in being free to manipulate resources and investment opportunities in ways that resonated with the country's resilient and pervasive patron-client relations, the second boom, with its much larger absolute flows and more sustained character, would have presented a greater and more lasting sense of opportunity. Put another way, the intensity of pressures to pursue market-based policies that induce capital controllers to invest at levels policymakers find economically and politically expedient would be dampened considerably during the second boom.

There were other contextual or environmental factors working both to enhance and to dilute the impact of the oil boom. Focusing for the moment on the surge beginning in late 1973, we see that the opportunities for departing from the policies of the previous eight years were even more short-lived than the downward-sloping pattern in figure 2 suggests. One reason is that the windfall resources that rushed in had to be used almost immediately to contain the damage done by two disasters that sandwiched the oil boom itself. The first was a severe drought that caused a failure of the rice crop in 1972 and 1973. According to Peter McCawley, an economist who studied the macrofinancial context of the first boom, by the end of 1972 "large volumes of rice imports were urgently being ordered despite the fact that international rice prices were climbing sharply."[18] Almost $2 billion was spent during 1973 and 1974—about a third of total imports for these two years—on rice and rice fertilizers. "These imports on government account, most of which were stockpiled," McCawley adds, "absorbed a good deal of the increase in export earnings during these two years."[19]

The second crisis was, of course, Pertamina's insolvency. Slightly more than twelve months after the euphoria of the oil boom started to take hold in Indonesia, the dimensions of Ibnu Sutowo's debt crisis were beginning to make themselves painfully evident.[20] The economic minis-

[18] The sheer size of Indonesia's purchases was very likely responsible for pushing the price of rice through the roof.

[19] McCawley (1977:5) continues, "the crisis came as a shock to the Indonesian government, and the result was that as soon as the immediate problems were past, a policy decision was taken to accumulate domestic stockpiles of rice (one million tons was mentioned as a target) and fertiliser, even though international prices for these commodities were still relatively high."

[20] Early knowledge of the size of Pertamina's short-term debt, to say nothing of billions of dollars in promissory notes and other paper used to lease a fleet of tankers, was limited

ters had to act fast to prevent the total destruction of Indonesia's credit standing, and the cost was high: "Between March of 1975 and the end of the year, perhaps $US 1 billion, maybe more, was paid out by the government to meet Pertamina's short-term debts."[21] In the same year, about $1 billion was also spent on a satellite and other telecommunications equipment. "The result . . . was that foreign reserves plummeted from about five months' supply of imports in September 1974 to about one month's supply a year later."[22] Meanwhile on the global front, the oil "crisis" pulled the economies of most oil-importing countries into recession. Their demand for Indonesia's nonoil exports dropped considerably, especially in 1975, and put still more pressure on the country's balance of payments and government revenues.

The reactions to these developments among many officials followed a parallel roller-coaster pattern. It was clear in late 1973 and early 1974 that a lot of unallocated revenues were flooding into the state. This triggered an immediate scramble to determine who would control the surpluses. The economic ministers, who are always strongest when resources are scarce and the need to induce private investment is greatest, were, for example, adamantly opposed to the satellite purchase. That so huge a purchase went through despite their efforts to direct resources toward other projects is one indication of how much control over discretionary spending had slipped from the hands of BAPPENAS and the Ministry of Finance.[23] But once the Pertamina fiasco began to have its

---

to a very small clique of officials in the government. It would take almost a year for creditors and the wider public to learn about the startling numbers involved.

[21] McCawley 1977:7. These payments were only the first stage in what proved to be a four-year process of negotiation and refinancing needed to undo the damage caused by Pertamina.

[22] McCawley 1977:7.

[23] There are other indications that these two bodies would not be able to contain spending. Having only recently tamed Indonesia's inflation, the economic ministers were concerned that the oil boom would set them back years. Given a free hand, they would have preferred to "sterilize" the inflationary pressure of the windfall revenues by simply not spending all the money that was rapidly becoming available. But, writes McCawley (1977:6–7), this was not to be. "Word soon spread throughout the bureaucracy that the time was ripe for initiating expenditure proposals, and during late 1973 and early 1974 ambitious spending plans were drawn up and several very large projects approved for the coming financial year. The force of upward pressure on government expenditure during this period was such that in 1973/74 and 1974/75 actual expenditure exceeded budgeted expenditure by 35 per cent and 25 per cent, respectively. In comparison, in each of the previous three financial years, government expenditure targets had actually been slightly underspent, so the period during 1973 and 1974 represented a very marked departure from the practice of the early Seventies."

effect, the economic ministers regained some of their preboom control and the "traditional nervousness about balance of payments reappeared" among policymakers and investors.[24] Toward the end of 1975, according to McCawley, "an atmosphere of austerity which was in sharp contrast to the laxity of two years earlier had come to prevail in policymaking circles."[25]

Thus, although from a material perspective the first oil boom presented new opportunities for the numerous power centers throughout the Indonesian government and bureaucracy that, given a choice, preferred to have access and entry based on their signatures and decrees, the situation was mixed. The setbacks accompanying the boom permitted the economic ministers at key junctures to reassert their influence over the trajectory of policies concerning the macroeconomy, government spending for development, and to a lesser extent, policies affecting the interests of mobile investors.[26]

Changes in Policy Following the First Boom

With a better idea of the circumstances surrounding the first boom, it is possible to evaluate some of the key policies that were adopted immediately and during the three or four years that followed. The story begins with the January 1974 riots known in Indonesia as the Malari.[27] By 1970 the positive relationship between students, especially at the University of Indonesia, and the New Order regime was showing clear signs of strain.[28] Protests along a fairly wide spectrum of issues became more frequent and angry as the country entered the middle 1970s. Although not framed in terms of mobility, the state's responsiveness to the most

[24] According to McCawley (1977:8–9), Indonesia's balance of payments situation was not as bad as the indicators available at the time suggested. "During this period the massive size of Pertamina's overseas debts attracted much attention at home and abroad and speculation about the likelihood of a devaluation was rife. As a result, the underlying strength of the balance of payments went largely unnoticed." Whatever the case, the reaction of the economic ministers was strong. So worried were they about having anyone find out how beleaguered the state was that "in May [of 1975] Bank Indonesia actually ceased publication of the main financial statistics including balance of payments data and did not resume publication until September 1976."

[25] McCawley 1977:9.

[26] American Embassy 1979. This report tracks some of the economic ministers' attempts to improve the country's responsiveness to investors.

[27] Malari stands for *Malapetaka Limabelas Januari*, or "the January Fifteenth Disaster."

[28] Crouch (1988) covers this period nicely.

mobile capital controllers was criticized, particularly as a Japanese presence—both physically and through competitive pressures in consumer goods—became more palpable.[29] The students tended to cast the state's policy sensitivity to highly mobile investors and relative insensitivity to immobile investors in foreign and domestic—and even racial—terms. This occurred in part because at the time virtually all *pribumi* capitalists were decidedly immobile. It was possible to view the state's posture in strong foreign/domestic, nationalist, and racial terms because Indonesia's domestic Chinese population—which was well represented in both mobile and immobile categories—was and is viewed as neither domestic nor Indonesian. Attacks were also leveled against the ways funds from Pertamina and payoffs from Japanese and ethnic Chinese capitalists were sloshing around the president's palace, the military commands, and most of the ministries. The students, it seems, believed the Suharto regime would conduct itself with restraint and for the benefit of the wider population, despite the absence of any effective checks or means for oversight to encourage such an outcome. They believed stated objectives of the New Order would materialize as actual policies, and they became enraged when they realized the chances were slim.[30]

Student anger was building to a climax just as the world price of oil was spiraling wildly upward. In mid-January 1974 a large student demonstration broke out in Jakarta just as Prime Minister Tanaka of Japan, who had recently been greeted by angry student demonstrations in Thailand, was visiting the Indonesian capital.[31] Thanks in part to a

[29] As Ali Budiardjo, former president-director of Freeport, explained: "The problem was not foreign investment in general. Many American firms, for example, were investing in minerals and oil and there were no complaints from anyone in Indonesia. Why? Because we didn't have anyone here who could take their place. They didn't compete with *pribumi* investors. But if the foreign investor did the same thing as a domestic investor, then there was anger. Coca-Cola is a good example. It takes the place of other drinks owned and produced domestically. Another example is noodles, like Indomie from Japan. The anger was focused on Japan because it was Japanese investment which was competing directly and effectively with domestic producers. This is why the Malari riots were focused on Japan and not foreign investment in general." Interview in Jakarta with Ali Budiardjo, 24 March 1989.

[30] This impression is based on a number of informal discussions in 1983, 1985, and 1989 with student leaders, many of whom were directly involved in the demonstrations leading up to and including the Malari.

[31] Indonesia's students were further excited because students in Bangkok had helped overthrow the Thanom-Praphat regime in October 1973.

healthy dose of intramilitary intrigue, the demonstrations quickly turned into riots as Jakarta's poor, ordinarily held in check by the army and police, seized the opportunity to act.[32] It is impossible to know how Suharto might have responded to the disturbances in Jakarta and other major cities on Java had he and his military advisers not been enjoying one of the more upbeat moments of the first oil boom. What is certain is that the sudden material abundance accompanying the boom presented Suharto with a wider range of options. He could, if he chose, offer a much more generous mixture of carrot and stick, rather than stick alone.

The urban poor taking part in the riots were dealt with in typical fashion: they were brutalized.[33] Students and other opposition figures, meanwhile, were treated somewhat better. A large number were arrested, and a few were tried and given jail sentences for being subversives. Top military officers who gave aid and comfort to the protestors in an attempt to strengthen their own position in the regime (and maybe even to push Suharto out) were dispatched even more gently. Some were forced to resign, while others accepted positions as ambassadors and promptly departed for distant lands where they could cause much less mischief. These actions were combined with policy changes intended to quiet Suharto's most vocal critics. Within a week of the Malari, President Suharto announced a hastily assembled package of regulations ostensibly designed to promote the interests of *pribumi* capitalists.[34] The changes received much attention in the media and proved effective in silencing critics who argued that policymakers were unresponsive to the country's *pribumi* investors.

[32] Nothing is more horrifying to Indonesia's social and political elites than the unleashing of the country's millions of urban and rural poor. Preventing such eruptions requires, at a minimum, a unified coercive apparatus and the cooperation of elite factions. In January 1974, neither condition was satisfied. A society's discourse on culture also plays an important role in maintaining social control and orderliness. For a thoughtful study of the emergence of this discourse in modern Indonesia, see Pemberton 1994.

[33] By nightfall on the first day of rioting, security forces in Jakarta had orders to shoot rioters on sight if necessary to restore order. During an attack on the Senen shopping complex, several people identified as "looters" were indeed shot. Private sources have told Daniel Lev that many nonelite individuals taking part in the riots were rounded up by Ali Murtopo's thugs and summarily executed. Personal discussion in Seattle, Washington, with Daniel Lev, March 1991.

[34] By 17 January a limited cabinet meeting had been called to formulate a response to the demonstrators. By 22 January the Council for Economic Stability met and announced decrees calling for a simpler lifestyle among the wealthy, promoting indigenous entrepreneurs, and prohibiting the import of built-up cars.

On the subject of Java.

A closer look at the changes shows that only in the most superficial way did they advance *pribumi* interests—indeed, being *pribumi*, although a necessary condition, was probably the least important factor in determining who would gain from these new policies.[35] Because the main effect of the new regulations was on the opportunities for officials to replace market forms of regulation with their own patrimonial discretion, an actor's access to and position within these structures was far more significant.[36] Suharto's January package stipulated that all new foreign investments would have to be as joint ventures with *pribumi* partners rather than with ethnic Chinese, which had been the dominant pattern. This practice had long been urged; it would now, the laws said, be enforced. When submitting a proposed investment for approval, foreign investors would be required to include a concrete plan for the eventual majority ownership by the *pribumi* side of the joint venture. Foreign investors would also be required to use Indonesia's proposed stock exchange to transfer shares more widely to salaried workers, not just to members of investing classes. Greater efforts would have to be made, moreover, to employ Indonesians and to train them if skilled personnel were not available. Incentives like tax holidays and import allowances were gradually reduced, and a variety of sectors previously open to foreign investors were restricted.[37]

As good as all this no doubt sounded, one problem was that most of the policy changes—even one law giving subsidized credit to Indonesians, provided they could come up with 25 percent of a venture's total equity themselves—did not address the policy needs of the country's relatively immobile, mostly small and medium *pribumi* capital controllers. The vast majority of Indonesia's indigenous entrepreneurs were in no position financially or otherwise to reap the benefits of these laws. This point was not overlooked in the advisory publications that were helping mobile investors interpret the meaning and concrete effect of the

[35] This discussion of what these policy changes really represented would not be particularly important were it not that the Suharto regime got considerable propaganda mileage out of claims that it adopted these policies to give significant advantages to the much beleaguered *pribumi*.

[36] This helps explain why, as I argue below, it was not *pribumi* in general who benefited from these regulations, but rather those who from a patronage perspective were of greatest use to key officials, who could use their signatures and phone calls to allocate investment opportunities.

[37] Business International 1975a:6–7.

new regulations. Referring to Suharto's January announcement, Business International stressed that although these rules created many difficulties for investors, appearances were worse than reality. "Indonesian Government policies are not always as definite and inflexible in practice as they may appear when looked at in print," Business International's analysts explained: "Indonesian officials are well aware of their own countrymen's lack of business skills and experience and realize that often the only practical course for a foreign investor is to have Chinese partners and employees—at least at this point in time. If any confirmation of this point is needed, it is seen in the considerable number of partnerships between Indonesian elite and Chinese, partnerships in which the latter often play the more active and responsible role."[38] The report concluded that although the president's decree "set the tone of subsequent changes in investment rules," the shortage of indigenous capital and skills and the absence of a stock exchange or other institutions capable of mobilizing capital meant that "the guidelines remain guidelines and cannot be implemented as the government would wish."[39]

Far more important than debates about intentions and motives regarding these policies is a clear assessment of their effect on the central tension in Indonesia's political economy between constraints rooted in capitalism and reflected in the policy demands of mobile investors for market-based policies and the efforts by patrimonial state officials to augment their discretionary control over access, opportunity, and resources as they tried to buttress their power base in Indonesia's extensive patron-client networks. The salient contribution of the new regulations

[38] Business International 1975a:6. For an analysis of how the Indonesian government backed down on its enforcement of the 51 percent transfer of foreign equity to Indonesians within ten years, see American Embassy 1975.

[39] Business International 1975a:7, 11. In the refreshingly blunt language characteristic of the publications designed to help investors choose among potential investment sites, the report added: "If there is any consolation for foreign investors who are plagued by the recent plethora of vexations and ill-conceived regulations affecting their operations it is this: Many officials realize the sheer impracticality of the various guidelines and regulations issued since early 1974 and consequently are not applying them harshly or inflexibly. They are well aware of the fatuity of rules about Indonesian equity participation when so few Indonesians have either the capital or the inclination to make such investments. In their franker moments officials advise foreign companies not to take the rules too much to heart. Companies 'need not drink the soup as hot as it is served,' is the advice offered by one official. Nevertheless, the ultimate intent of the 1974–75 changes in the investment rules is quite clear."

was that criteria other than whether one had adequate capital and market strength to enter a given sector and operate at a profit were suddenly far more crucial, and officials scattered throughout the bureaucracy would now sit and pore over stacks of paper to determine who would have the best opportunities and terms to invest. With the right contacts, or for the right fee, anything was possible. But being a prime candidate on market grounds was far less important than previously.

For the first time since the fall of Sukarno, patrimonial elites within the Indonesian state were responding to the constraints presented by mobile investors (in favor of markets) not just by setting up a sideshow (the second channel) but by challenging market-based allocation head-on. During the first boom, the results were mixed. In part, the factors that undermined the structural impact of the oil boom explain the weaknesses of this challenge. The economic ministers were especially successful in regaining control over policy once the Pertamina time bomb—set by the economic ministers themselves back in May 1973 when they succeeded in limiting Ibnu Sutowo (who walked into the trap) to short-term borrowing— finally went off.[40] A blunder or two notwithstanding, the ministers pushed through policy after policy in an attempt to maintain a competitive investment climate that could attract and retain mobile investors. The sudden "renegotiation" of production-sharing agreements with private oil companies in the middle 1970s, causing a sharp decline in exploration and liftings, was corrected by restoring a number of important incentives to the companies. The economic ministers also eased taxes in 1977, tried to respond to investors' complaints about bureaucratic red-tape by making the Investment Coordinating Board a "one-stop" service (which failed) in 1978, and in November of the same year pushed through a massive devaluation of the rupiah—their greatest and last achievement of the oil boom period. Robinson Pangaribuan argues that in the wake of the Malari and the Pertamina crash, Ibnu Sutowo and other figures close to Suharto were in disarray—giving the economic ministers even more political space to operate. In 1978, however, opponents of the economists regained much ground with the appointment of

[40] Rachmat Saleh explained how the economists undid their own restrictions on Sutowo: "We have converted Pertamina's short-term debts into medium- and long-term debts. That part of the problem is over." See Ensor 1979a. After blocking Ibnu Sutowo from borrowing medium and long, the economists turned around and refinanced Pertamina's short borrowing on precisely these terms.

Ali Murtopo and Daud Jusuf to the cabinet as minister of information and minister of education and culture, respectively.[41]

Mobile Capital Responds to Unresponsiveness

Even if the events surrounding the first boom ensured that a decisive victory was not handed to those opposing the economic ministers' market policies, the shift away from the responsiveness to mobile capital established after 1966 was strong enough to affect investors' behavior. In an attempt once again to use the fear among the country's most powerful decision makers that political destabilization would be precipitated by economic decline, in late 1976 the economic ministers commissioned a team of specialists from three of the world's premier consulting firms to assess the damage done to investor confidence and private investment rates by Indonesia's less responsive policy line begun in 1974.[42] In light of the fact that "both the absolute inflow of foreign private capital into Indonesia has fallen sharply in the last three years and the level of applications to the Investment Co-ordinating Board (BKPM) for foreign investment permits . . . is now significantly below the level reached in 1973," said the analysts' report, and given that "the fall in the number of foreign investment applications has been accompanied by an even greater fall in the number of domestic private investment applications," it was clear that mobile and immobile investors alike were responding in a predictable manner by withholding and relocating their investments. The consultants were charged with finding out precisely where investors were going, what their views were on Indonesia, and what policies needed most desperately to be changed.[43]

[41] Pangaribuan 1988:119. For a journalist's overview of this period, see *Business Week,* 17 December 1979:42–48.

[42] Loeb et al. 1977.

[43] Loeb et al. 1977:1. "We were also asked to suggest ways in which foreign investors might be encouraged." The consultants interviewed major companies in the United States, Japan, Western Europe, Hong Kong, Singapore, and Australia. Senior executives in charge of investment location decisions were queried. To ensure that a wide range of views and issues was covered, firms that had investments in Indonesia for a very long time, firms that had only recently invested, and firms that had contemplated investing but decided against it were included. The consultants also spoke to officials in Indonesia (mainly at BKPM) working on investment. Officials working in a similar capacity in Hong Kong, Malaysia, Singapore, the Philippines, and Thailand were consulted, as well as written materials on

Data on rates of investment clearly reveal that investors were sending unequivocal structural signals to policymakers that they were dissatisfied with the business climate after the first oil boom. Figure 3 shows changing levels of investment approvals for both foreign and domestic capital.[44] It should be noted first that a huge chasm separates "approved" and "implemented" levels of foreign and domestic investment in the private sector.[45] For the years 1968 to 1985, for instance, only $6.1 billion of the $13.6 billion in approved foreign loan and equity investment was realized. This realization rate of 45 percent for foreign investment is generally believed to be substantially higher than the rate for domestic investment.[46] Still, the picture of approved investments remains useful for two reasons: assuming that no great changes occurred in implementation rates over the entire period, trends in investor interest are visible; and it is levels of approved investments that are reported to the president and other ministers at monthly cabinet meetings.

Figure 3 reveals clearly that private sector investment was strong before the first oil boom, considerably weaker during the boom, and once policy changes in the postboom period began to bear fruit, noticeably stronger by the late 1980s.[47] This picture, as we have noted, is the

---

Ireland, Tunisia, and South Korea (these three being deemed highly successful in attracting investors from abroad).

[44] For comparison, approved investments are expressed in U.S. dollars and have been deflated to remove distortions from changes in currency values. Hill (1988) argued that domestic investment since 1967 had been considerably larger than foreign investment. Those providing President Suharto with his information do not appear to agree. Contradicting claims that a large amount of domestic capital had left Indonesia over the years, Suharto was reported to have said that only "about one third of the total private investment of Rp. 81 trillion during the period of 1967 through 1988 was made by local businessmen." See *Jakarta Post* 6, 260 (1989): 7.

[45] Until very recently, an investment was categorized as "foreign" if there was as little as 1 percent foreign participation. According to Hill's figures, of the $15.4 billion in total approved foreign investment between 1967 and 1985, 12 percent ($1.8 billion) was Indonesian equity. He does admit, however, that foreign investors frequently lent this money to Indonesian partners to enable the investors to meet requirements on Indonesian equity participation. See Hill 1988:36–37.

[46] Hill 1988:37. Also see *Jakarta Post* 6, 259 (1989): 7, which reports that Bank Indonesia's realized foreign investment rate of 44 percent is much lower than the Capital Investment Coordinating Board's inflated claim of 70 percent.

[47] The spike in 1983 was caused by a last-quarter rush to get investment approvals before the tax reform of 1984, which made deep cuts in tax holidays for new investments. An extraordinarily high percentage of these approvals did not materialize, and therefore the towering column for 1983 is an anomaly. This subject is discussed more thoroughly in the following chapter.

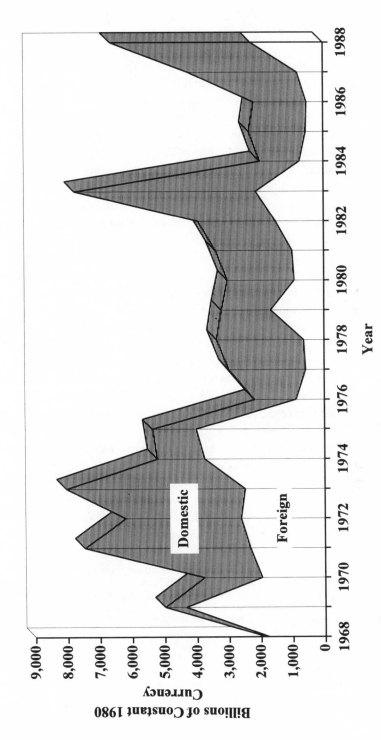

Figure 3. Approved private investment, 1968–1988. Data from Hill 1988:36; BKPM; Bank Indonesia.

reverse image of that showing the state's fluctuating position as the leader and follower in investment in Indonesia and parallels major shifts in state policy toward mobile private capital. The upper portion of the graph shows domestic investment; the lower portion shows foreign. Note in particular the surge in domestic investment (overwhelmingly ethnic Chinese) after 1968.

Data on realized investment are most reliable for capital entering Indonesia from abroad. Figure 4 provides still another angle on investors' responses to Indonesia's changing policy climate. Note first the steadily increasing levels of transnational investment from 1968 to 1972. By 1974 there was actually a disinvestment of capital, caused mainly by investors' skittish reaction to the policy changes begun in early 1974.[48] The extremely high peak for 1975 does not, as the picture might suggest, indicate a restoration of confidence in Indonesia's policies, but instead reflects two huge projects for which the negotiations had begun several years earlier.[49] The decline in interest from mobile foreign investors in subsequent years was almost as sharp as the incline leading up to the boom beginning in late 1973. Rather than Indonesia's massive wealth acting as a magnet for investors eager to take home a share of the country's new petroleum-boosted buying power, the policies associated with that wealth were more than enough to act as a net repellant to investors.[50]

Still another indicator of this point is available in the data on numbers of new investments approved following the first boom. For each of the years from 1971 to 1973, more than one hundred ventures were approved. In 1974 the number was ninety-two, and thereafter the figures dropped precipitously. For 1975 through 1977 approvals were forty-three, thirty-four, and twenty-nine projects. In 1978 the number of

[48] Hill (1988:38) concurs with this interpretation of the strong downturn.

[49] Fully 92 percent of all realized investment for 1975 is accounted for by $875 million from a Japanese consortium for the Asahan aluminum smelter in Sumatra and Shell Oil's $507 million investment in the Batubara coal project. Forty-one other projects approved in 1975 accounted for the remaining 8 percent. See Business International 1979b:54.

[50] The sad irony, in the view of one writer for *Asian Business,* was that growth figures for Indonesia's GDP—initially projected by the World Bank to be 6.5 percent per annum for the five-year period beginning in April 1979 and then adjusted upward to a heady 7.5 percent—were not drawing private capital to the country. Despite "this bullish performance, investors remain skeptical and major multinational corporations are still hesitant to involve themselves in Indonesia." The two main reasons cited were "over-regulation of the economy" and a "history of bureaucratic corruption." Castle 1980:55.

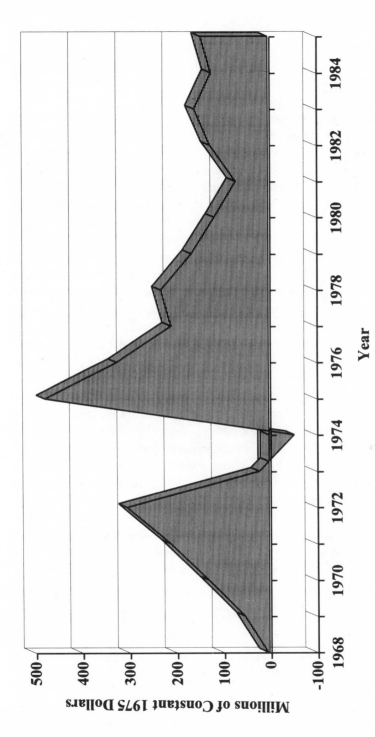

Figure 4. Realized foreign direct investment, 1968–1985. Data from Bank Indonesia.

projects inched up to thirty-seven, but the total amount approved was still barely a fraction, in real terms, of the levels invested before the onset of the oil bonanza.[51] Underscoring the obstacles to entry posed by the new regulation posture in Indonesia, the vast majority of these approvals, both in value and in number, represented expansions of existing operations.[52]

The consultants hired by the economic ministers gave their greatest attention to four factors deemed most responsible for the behavior of investors. All four concerned efforts by officials to exert greater control over the investment process. The first was the set of policies the government claimed was designed to promote *pribumi* entrepreneurs. Scolding those officials in Indonesia who wanted to play favorites with investors, the consultants pointed out that "one outstanding factor about Hong Kong," an ideal investment site, "is that no distinction is drawn by the government there between local and overseas companies." Hinting strongly that Indonesia's policymakers were badly mistaken to try to lead rather than follow the private sector, the report noted that Hong Kong's government "is concerned above all about the general investment climate and not the climate for some sectional interest and it sees its role as one of servant to the investor rather than his master."[53]

A second factor concerned the unpredictability of the Indonesian system, where policies change almost overnight and the specific wording of a regulation is far less important than the interpretation of the official who happens to be sitting across the table. "Many companies have complained, not merely of the existence of regulations," the analysts reported, "but of uncertainty over those regulations and arbitrariness in their application." They continued: "It is apparent that there is a wide margin for government discretion in most of the regulations affecting the foreign investor. Some foreign investors find considerable difficulty in divining the extent to which government regulations are negotiable."

[51] Business International 1979b:53–54, 17. Business International also noted that owing in part to investor "uncertainty about the direction of government policy, gross domestic capital formation growth slowed to only 6 percent in 1976 and just over 5 percent the following year. The average annual increases in the early 1970s were closer to 20 percent."

[52] It is surprising that the expansion rates of existing firms were not higher. Indonesia enjoyed the reputation of being the location for the highest returns on investment in the region. See tables 24 and 25 for comparative data on returns for the years 1967–1977 in Business International 1979b:59–60.

[53] Loeb et al. 1977:3.

Some of the executives interviewed said flexibility is a good thing, but for most it "merely increases confusion" and risk.[54]

A third factor, again putting Indonesia in a comparative light, concerned the operation of the main government institution handling investments. Hong Kong and Singapore had excellent bodies that worked tirelessly to smooth the way for investors. The Philippines was not bad, and Tunisia was better still. "In Indonesia," however, "the emphasis of the BKPM is not on smoothing the investor's path but on co-ordinating the interests of various government departments."[55] It was on these analysts' recommendations that BKPM was reformed late in 1977 and made a one-stop service. The improvement, it seems, was minimal.[56]

The fourth factor received considerable attention and is particularly relevant to the broader arguments in this book. Returning to Indonesia's new policy of picking and choosing among investors ostensibly on the basis of nationality and ethnicity, the analysts argued forcefully that Indonesia must recognize the fact of investor mobility: "Such socially oriented policies may be wholly admirable but most foreign investors, especially those involved in manufacturing as opposed to extractive industry, are able to make fairly sophisticated choices between Indonesia and other neighbouring countries as a site for their new investment."[57] Suggesting that Indonesia's posture of control over access "may have to be tempered by economic realities," they added, "Both in exploiting the country's natural resource wealth and in developing a manufacturing sector, account must be taken of the fact that Indonesia has to compete with the other countries. Indonesia may have an abundance of natural resources but so . . . do other countries throughout the world and, as far as manufacturing is concerned, the competition is much closer at

[54] Loeb et al. 1977:5.

[55] Loeb et al. 1977:4–5.

[56] The attempt in October 1977 to make the Capital Investment Coordinating Board (BKPM) a "one-stop" service followed the consultants' advice almost to the letter. The idea was to centralize the investment approval process, which until then had entailed running around to the ten ministries for permits and signatures. But problems persisted. "Although the revised regulations mean that it is no longer mandatory for companies to consult various ministries and government agencies other than BKPM, firms may find it is in their interest to make some contact with various ministries anyway. This means, however, that a company must now spend time following its application through the BKPM and more time calling on a number of ministries to promote good relations." Some investors claimed that the typical waiting period of twelve to fourteen months for approval had been shortened, but the target of three months remained out of reach. See Business International 1979b:74.

[57] Loeb et al. 1977:4.

hand."[58] The comment about "economic realities" forcing Indonesian officials to temper their penchant for being masters where investors would prefer they be servants gets to the heart of the matter of Indonesia's policies during this period. But it is also startlingly naive given that it was the new economic reality of the oil boom that permitted the roles of master and servant to be reversed and, by the way, was the main impetus for getting these high-priced consultants their contract with Indonesia's worried economic ministers. With 65 percent of total investment between 1974 and 1979 coming from the state, it was precisely the economic realities that ushered in the intemperance the consultants so skillfully diagnosed.[59]

Partly because the impact of the first boom on the structural power of capital controllers was moderated by factors that drained discretionary resources from the state almost as quickly as they flowed in, it was still possible to use reports like this one to persuade Suharto that antimarket and generally uncompetitive policies were hurting the country's ability to meet its investment needs, and that doing so on a sustained basis could have ominous political consequences. As a result, on balance the period following the first boom was still marked by significant policy successes for the economic ministers. The same cannot be said, however, of their efforts once the second oil boom hit. The determination shown by a broad base of clientelist officials close to Suharto to replace markets with their own more personal and wide-ranging discretion met with far more success by the late 1970s. The second oil boom insulated these state officials still further from the enormous leverage mobile investors typically exert over economic policy.

The Second Boom

There were no significant oil price hikes in 1974 and only minor ones between 1975 and 1978. During the entire period, however, the value of the U.S. dollar, the main currency in the oil trade, continued the decline it had begun even before the onset of the first oil boom. The real revenues of oil-exporting countries were seriously affected by this trend—so much so that the Bank of International Settlements reported in February

[58] Loeb et al. 1977:20.
[59] Business International 1979b:52.

1978 that by the third quarter of 1977, oil-exporting countries as a whole were net borrowers of new funds from the international banking system, for the first time since 1973. In an attempt to counter this deterioration, more serious efforts began within OPEC to increase the price of crude. An OPEC conference in December 1978 concluded with an agreement to push prices up a gentle 15 percent by October of the following year. This modest agenda was accelerated by events in Iran. The dictatorship there was quickly unraveling even as the OPEC ministers were putting the finishing touches on their December agreement.[60] By mid-January 1979 the shah of Iran had been overthrown and the global oil market had suddenly become extremely volatile. By June the average official price of a barrel of crude had soared some 40 percent to $18, while the spot price was nearly twice this amount. Toward the end of 1979, Saudi Arabian marker crude was at $26, and the spot price had reached $45. Prices continued to rise well into 1981, when they peaked at $41 a barrel. Between the last quarter of 1978 and the beginning of 1981, the price of oil had more than tripled. But in contrast with the first boom, this time the base price being multiplied was much higher.

Figure 5 provides still another angle on the structural impact of these price changes within Indonesia. The graph shows, in constant 1980 rupiah, absolute amounts of unallocated government surplus for each year.[61] The relative size of the second boom, its more sustained character, and the suddenness with which discretionary funds plummeted in 1986 back to their pre-1974 levels are all plainly evident. In sharp contrast with the surge occurring late in 1973, this second boom was not enveloped by resource-draining crises that could match the rice shortage of 1972–1973 and the collapse of Pertamina. This boom handed tremendous and unbridled structural power to the Indonesian state while simultaneously undercutting the structural power of institutional and private capital controllers. Again, the central questions at the time were, Into whose hands would these resources fall, and to what ends would the potential power they contained be put?

The rest of this chapter focuses on policy changes and institutional

[60] Whatever Iran's bargaining position on production cutbacks may have been, it was moot because oil exports from that country had already been stopped completely in December owing to domestic disarray.

[61] Recall that figure 5 showed each of these amounts as a percentage of the previous year's entire development budget.

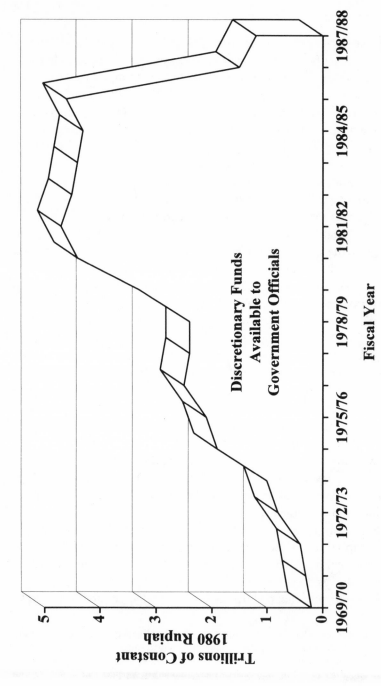

Figure 5. Impact of oil windfalls on discretionary government resources, 1969–1988. Data from Indonesian Ministry of Finance.

innovations in the wake of the second oil boom. As we will see, though consistent with attempts made after 1973 to replace market-based regulation of Indonesia's economic system with control by officials, the initiatives begun in 1979 went much further and met with much more success. So powerful did the officials spearheading the Indonesian state's departure from its preboom policy of responding to mobile investors become that, though in late 1982 there were already signs that the country might once again need to attract mobile private capital, it was not until 1988 that these officials and the pocket of tremendous power they had created within the state were finally closed down completely. What follows is the story of Tim Keppres 10, or Team 10, a body established by Presidential Decree 10 in 1980 to control procurements by the Indonesian government.

Team 10: The Setting

The full impact of the second oil boom was hardly being felt yet when there were signs that the economic ministers were losing ground as they struggled to maintain market-based economic policies. In their discussion of new "racial policies" in investment, Business International's analysts maintained in early 1979 that the "stagnant state of Indonesia's extractive industries, especially oil," boded well for the private sector and predicted that such policies would likely be postponed. "Because of the important role slated for private investment in Repelita III [the Third Five-Year Plan], such a postponement is vital if Chinese and foreign investment is not to be impaired."[62] One year later, when the government issued its latest "Investment Priority List" (DSP) closing still more areas to foreign investment, analysts at Business Asia in charge of assessing changes in Indonesia's business climate were less sanguine. "The new

[62] Business International 1979a:52. Still unaware that a second boom was taking shape, Bank Indonesia analysts argued that officials would have little choice but to turn to the private sector, especially transnational investors. "But it will have to take steps to improve the investment climate if it wants to attract substantial sums, since its policy toward foreign investment in the past few years has been increasingly restrictive." Rachmat Saleh, then governor of Bank Indonesia, was asked, "Do you expect the role of the capital inflows to change over the next five-year period?" He responded that "though private foreign capital is most welcome, we would like to be more selective than in the past in providing incentives to make investment in Indonesia extra attractive." See Ensor 1979a:17.

DSP confirms recent statements by government officials that additional incentives to encourage investment will not be introduced," they reported. "The government feels that incentives currently being offered—such as two- to six-year tax holidays and investment allowances—are sufficient to attract investors."[63] In other words, state officials were not feeling nearly as constrained by pressures to be responsive to mobile capital controllers.

For veteran observers, there was an alarming sense of déjà vu. "There are disturbing signs," warned *Business Week,* "that the military government of President Suharto may once again miss the opportunity, as it did after the 1973–74 price runup, of converting the new oil windfall into a springboard for sustained economic development"—meaning based primarily on private investment.[64] Referring to the painful devaluation pushed through by the economic ministers in November 1978, Eric Hayden, speaking from the Tokyo office of Bank of America, said: "Nine months ago the day of reckoning was here for Indonesia. The price of oil turned things around for the near term," he added, "but long term, the structural problems are as deep and serious as ever."[65] Indonesia would probably be able to attract private capital for its major energy-related projects (especially from customers eager to ensure a steady supply of fossil fuels, like Japan), but covering the 30 percent share of a total investment target of $7.6 billion slated for private investors in the Third Five-Year Plan was another matter. "It is just not in the cards," Hayden opined. "Indonesia will not be the recipient of a massive inflow of foreign investment."[66]

Dour commentaries like these would multiply as the second oil boom pressed on. Although the mood of investors sank with every new policy announcement after 1979, nothing caused more distress for the champions of free markets than a set of policies begun harmlessly enough in early 1979 with Presidential Decree 14, designed, like similar laws before it, mainly as a sop for small and medium *pribumi* investors hurt very badly by the November 1978 devaluation.[67] Within a year Team 10 had

[63] *Business Asia,* 11 April 1980, 113. And this was only the beginning. Between April 1981 and March 1982, the number of areas open to foreign investment decreased from 402 to 296. See Business International 1982:92, and *Business Asia,* 24 April 1981, 133.

[64] *Business Week,* 17 December 1979, 42.

[65] *Business Week,* 17 December 1979, 43.

[66] *Business Week,* 17 December 1979, 43.

[67] Most of the trouble for *pribumi* came not from the devaluation, but from mobile capital's anticipation of and reaction to it. Fearing a devaluation (and in part accelerating

been born—perhaps the most powerful and notorious nonmilitary government body to exist in Indonesia since Ibnu Sutowo's heyday at Pertamina.[68]

Unusual Origins

Given Team 10's reputation as the locus of far-reaching government control and an enclave for kickbacks to officials and contracts for everyone from backers of the Suharto regime to the president's children, it is surprising to discover that the idea for this centralized government procurement unit was the brainchild of Professor Widjoyo Nitisastro—one of the most prominent and influential economic ministers. Back in 1972 BAPPENAS had blazed the trail for Team 10 by organizing a seminar funded by the United Nations Development Program to discuss problems typically associated with government procurement—waste, inefficiency, ministries working at cross-purposes, and the like.[69] Before Team 10 there was only macrocontrol of government purchases and spending, conducted by the economic ministers in BAPPENAS and the Ministry of

its eventuality), investors controlling liquid assets transferred their money out of the country on a very large scale. As a result, access to credit within Indonesia for immobile investors (especially medium and small entrepreneurs) was severely curtailed. The devaluation itself probably had only a slight effect on small and medium entrepreneurs, since few of them were engaged in manufacturing and fewer still used imported inputs in their plants. Among large and mobile investors in Indonesia, the Japanese complained the loudest, because many of them had raised yen capital for their operations back in Japan. Suddenly, servicing their commercial debt cut much more deeply into rupiah profits.

[68] Iman Taufik, one of the select group of *pribumi* investors to have been launched with the help of special laws like Decree 14, had this to say: "The slogan at the time was *menjadi tuan di rumah sendiri* [become head of your own household]. Special promotion was given to *pribumi*. We made a seminar right away in KADIN [Indonesian Chamber of Commerce]. Another important piece of legislation was Presidential Decree 10 of 1980. This was the real kick off of *pribumi*zation." Interview in Jakarta with Iman Taufik, 1 April 1989. Boy Kuntjoro-Jakti, who represented the Department of Trade on Team 10, said that Decree 14 was beneficial to small entrepreneurs, whereas Team 10 helped the big players— in other words, those huddled around the president, the State Secretariat, and linked at the top to GOLKAR, the government party. Interview in Jakarta with Boy Kuntjoro-Jakti, 6 December 1989.

[69] Business International 1975b:72. Academics cross-dressing as consultants (no doubt fresh from their success in cleaning up waste and mismanagement in Washington, D.C.) were brought in from Georgetown University Law School, presumably to beef up the seminar's credentials. This report warned that "potential suppliers should be aware that procedures may change as the authorities search for new and better ways of handling state buying." These prophetic words were followed, unfortunately, by an observation the editors would later regret: "Any inconveniences resulting from fluctuating methods and new institutions, however, appear to be well worth enduring."

Finance. The DUP/DIP and DUK/DIK schemes,[70] together with a "postaudit" procedure conducted by an agency based in the Ministry of Finance, were the main instruments for maintaining this limited control.

So that the contrast with procurement procedures under Team 10 is sharp, it is worthwhile to digress briefly and sketch how the DIP/DIK system works.[71] BAPPENAS draws up a proposed development budget based on government priorities contained in the current five-year plan. These spending priorities are divided along *sectoral* lines. In January of each year the actual government budget, drawn up by the Ministry of Finance and still apportioned along sectoral lines, is submitted to parliament by the president and promptly passed without amendment.[72] Meanwhile, during the months prior to the budget's passage, all government bodies, from local to ministerial, busily prepare and submit their DUPs—project proposals. Note that these proposals are drawn up along *departmental and regional* lines. BAPPENAS gathers all the DUPs together, divides them into "technical assistance" and "project" categories, and publishes what is called the "Bluebook," which has two volumes corresponding to the departmental and regional categories. The Bluebook is distributed to creditor country embassies, the World Bank,

[70] DUP and DIP refer to *Daftar Usulan Proyek* (Proposed Project List) and *Daftar Isian Proyek* (Filled Project List), while DUK and DIK refer to *Daftar Usulan Kegiatan* (Proposed Activity List) and *Daftar Isian Kegiatan* (Filled Activity List). The system of handling government procurements is said to have been imported from Pakistan via Dick Patten of the Harvard Institute for International Development (HIID), the core foreign consulting group for the Ministry of Finance since the early days of the New Order (when it was called the Harvard Development Advisory Service, HDAS).

[71] For a business perspective on how the government handles procurements, see Business International 1981. Note also that what are described here are only the procedures associated with on-budget spending by departments and ministries. There is a still murkier, off-budget side to government spending that even the Ministry of Finance knows very little about. According to Bakir Hasan, secretary general of the Department of Trade and a figure known to be close to Sudharmono, "Every department of the government has its official budgetary resources and its nonbudget resources. The Department of Trade has an official budget of about Rp 40 billion. Our nonbudget resources are only an additional Rp 4 billion. But this is nothing compared with, say, Forestry. Of course, there are no records of the size of these nonbudget resources. Even the Ministry of Finance doesn't know the figures." Can the Ministry of Finance compel other ministries in the government to report these off-budget budgets? "They're trying," Hasan admitted, "but it's not easy. Strong officials with close ties to the president can just ignore the finance minister's requests for data. Then what?" Interview in Jakarta with Bakir Hasan, 23 March 1989.

[72] The proposed budget is referred to as the RAPBN (*Rencana Anggaran Penerimaan dan Belanja Negara*), while the actual budget is the APBN (same as above but without the first word, which means "planned"). The budget is passed in time for Indonesia's fiscal year, which starts on 1 April.

and the ADB (various entrepreneurs also try to get copies so they can begin to angle for contracts).

The creditor countries then "shop" for projects they want to fund.[73] "The Bluebook is supposed to reflect the priorities originally set forth in the Indonesian government budget," explained Eugene Galbraith, who worked for USAID, "but this rarely happens. Instead, it tends to reflect the desires of those who pay."[74] The circle is finally closed when various DUPs are selected for funding by the creditor countries. DUPs in the Bluebook that get approved become DIPs, which are legal contracts representing a commitment among foreign creditors, the Indonesian government, and representatives in the foreign and domestic private sector. Agung Laksono, a member of parliament and a former leader of HIPMI (*Himpunan Pengusaha Muda Indonesia,* or Young Entrepreneurs Association of Indonesia), explains how the process works for companies in his group. "First the various ministries draw up a list of their projects and what they'll need. Take my field, communications, for example. The Ministry of Information makes up a list of their projects and the equipment needed. It's all pulled together by BAPPENAS into what's called the Bluebook. Then we send it to the IGGI [now CGI] donor countries and they see what they can supply on the list. When the time comes to give the soft loans, agreements are drawn up regarding what we must purchase from each country with the loans. In my case, I buy broadcasting and navigation equipment from England and the Netherlands with the soft loans they supply through IGGI." Laksono is the "sole agent" for the equipment, and all purchases in Indonesia from the foreign companies he represents must go through him. He supplies only the government, and none of the imported equipment is subject to the tariffs private importers must pay for similar goods.[75] DUKs and DIKs work in a similar way, though no loop involving foreign funding is

---

[73] The coordination of this entire process is remarkably bad. Creditor countries shop through the Bluebook in June, three months *after* the beginning of the fiscal year for which the DUPs were submitted.

[74] Indeed, it appears that creditor countries play a big role in writing the proposals that find their way into the Bluebook from which they will eventually shop. "You can tell by the English," Galbraith added. Interview in Jakarta with Eugene Galbraith, 22 November 1989.

[75] Interview in Jakarta with Agung Laksono, 13 March 1989. Each DIP is assigned one project head ("*pimpro*" or *pimpinan proyek*) and one treasurer. These are the only two people permitted to draw down the project funds that have been deposited in the Central Bank. Both parties must sign each draft.

involved (mainly because foreign creditors have tried hard not to fund so-called routine government expenditures).[76]

It is evident from this brief digression that control over levels—and the general direction—of government spending is shared by the economic ministers and foreign officials representing the aid agencies of their governments (who in turn are linked politically and structurally to firms and investors back home). Once DIPs are approved and turned back to the various government bodies that put them forth as DUPs in the first place, yet another stage in the control and distribution process begins: private sector bidding and the awarding of projects.[77] Before the introduction of Team 10, this occurred in a highly decentralized manner.[78] Only after projects were under way would the central government have one more stab at regulating government spending by conducting postaudits.[79]

[76] Note that the state's two hundred or so companies also are involved in procurement for their operation. "At least 142 government companies are spread throughout 11 government departments, and only a few appear in departmental budgets. Most operate in a fairly independent fashion, making purchases from their own cash flows." Those selling to these state firms usually make contact with them directly and avoid going through respective parent departments. "Government involvement in these cases is limited to officials overseeing progress, much like the board of directors of a private company, without taking an active role in actual management." See Business International 1981:183.

[77] In addition to those with political connections, large firms appear to have enjoyed significant advantages in winning tenders. One reason is that, as with most contracts with large bureaucracies, there is a substantial delay between the time goods and services are supplied and when they are paid for. Small firms with tight cash flow often encounter difficulties in such circumstances. For those companies requiring payment up front, the government was willing to pay only 20 percent of the total amount outstanding in advance. Says Business International: "At least one foreign supplier—Toyota of Japan—has used this bureaucratic delay to secure a competitive edge over other potential suppliers. From the early stages of its presence in Indonesia, Toyota has offered to deliver vehicles immediately upon approval of the DIP/DIK without waiting for the SPMU [government promissory note] to be processed, thus outmaneuvering other firms with more limited financial resources." Business International 1975b:74—75.

[78] On the discretion enjoyed by government offices around Indonesia, Business International explained the system this way to its customers seeking to sell to the government: "Under the DIP/DIK system, the Finance Ministry must approve the proposed purchases, but it does so mainly with regard to the timing of spending and the amount involved—all in an effort to adjust government buying to the general spending profile outlined by the Finance Ministry. Beyond that, the buying units have considerable freedom to choose among sources, specifications, and brands, particularly for such general items as office equipment." Business International 1975b:73.

[79] There were other guidelines of a general nature to assist in controlling procurements. Presidential Decree 28 of 1972 stipulated, for example, that purchases over Rp 1 million had to be made through an open or limited tender. Business International 1981:201.

Although this system hemorrhaged fairly massively, it is difficult to say precisely why the economic ministers decided to risk jeopardizing even this limited role markets played in allocation by joining with top officials at the State Secretariat (SEKNEG) to erect a bureaucratic unit like Team 10—that had so much potential for advancing the power of patrimonial officials close to Suharto. Pangaribuan, underscoring the importance of factional competition within the Suharto regime, argues that given the constellation of forces arrayed against the economists, making a pact with the least objectionable group at the time— Sudharmono and his supporters based at SEKNEG—was the best option available, especially in view of the way the oil boom was draining their power to direct economic policy.[80]

A second explanation, supported by comments and observations from a variety of quarters, is that the economic ministers were afraid the second oil boom would trigger another period of high inflation, and that ways had to be found to retard the upward slide in the money supply as petrodollars were translated into rupiah purchasing power at home. The ministers seem to have been fully aware that creating a body like Team 10 would put at least some drag on the implementing of government projects.[81] A final and very compelling explanation is that on seeing that Suharto was tilting toward Sudharmono, SEKNEG, and GOLKAR as the next base from which to maintain and expand his political base and

[80] See Pangaribuan 1988. Pangaribuan suggests that both the economic ministers and the Sudharmono group were eager to see Suharto's presidential assistants (his *asisten pribadi,* or *aspri*), led by General Ali Murtopo, pushed aside. The *aspri,* though damaged politically by the Malari and materially by the fall of a key financier, Ibnu Sutowo, were still clinging to the tremendous power they had wielded since the early days of the New Order. The economic ministers were especially determined to detonate Ali Murtopo's power base because the latter almost succeeded in convincing Suharto that the ministers had worked closely with the cabal of generals and other opposition figures involved in the Malari intrigue. Ali Murtopo's gang was one of several groups surrounding (and, to be sure, working closely with) the president seeking to steal control over government surplus money away from the economic ministers.

[81] Team 10's own final report indicates that this "braking" function was among the reasons for creating the unit in the first place. "Initially, the team's activities were directed toward utilizing the SIAP [government surplus] and excess foreign exchange [from oil] to purchase equipment that was not yet produced domestically—and in so doing to dampen the inflationary impact of a sharp increase in the money supply." See the team's final report, Sekretariat Negara 1988:4. This report, consisting of a main volume and six appendixes towering more than a meter high, is written in a very defensive manner, clearly reflecting the many criticisms leveled against Team 10 during its eight years of existence. See also Sacerdoti (1980:52–54) for a concurring view on the economic ministers' motives.

wealth, the economists had few choices but to go along, especially with a second oil boom taking shape.[82]

A Breach Birth?

Whatever longer-range planning went into the creation of the Government Procurement Team, it was the rather sudden availability of Rp 884 billion (about $1.4 billion) in *unspent* government surplus in the last quarter of FY 1979–1980 that was its proximate cause.[83] Although the economic ministers served as midwives in the birth of the team, there were several signs that from the start they were not in a position of significant control. First, the team was based at SEKNEG rather than at the Ministry of Finance or BAPPENAS, where key aspects of government procurement had been managed until 1980. Also, despite the inclusion of Minister Sumarlin, an influential member from the economists' camp, on the team as vice chair, Suharto put State Secretary Sudharmono in charge and, in early 1983, elevated Ginanjar Kartasasmita, a Sudharmono protégé, to vice chair to manage the team's daily activities.[84] Moreover, most of the team's members were from SEKNEG, and its top officials answered directly to the president rather than to Finance or even

[82] It is well known that Suharto chooses ministers who will not challenge him. On this subject, a very bitter Ibnu Sutowo (who claims he and Armed Forces Commander Benny Murdani were both pushed out because they dared speak up to Suharto) said this: "Everyone, without exception, does the bidding of Suharto, and he is suspicious of anyone who acts without his permission. He can't take criticism. He wants people to follow his line 100 percent. But with what consequences for the country? Just look around. You never hear a minister make a major pronouncement without its being noted that he just emerged from a meeting with Suharto, or that it was the president's wish that it be so. Suharto has no interest in creative and independent actions. Look at the people around him now. They're all like this [smiling and bowing, with hands folded over the pubic area]. Even when they know big mistakes are being made, they remain silent and agree. No one has any guts." Interview in Jakarta with Ibnu Sutowo, 7 March 1989.

[83] This pool of money consisted of Rp 520 billion and the equivalent of about $582 million in foreign exchange. A "Crash Program" was begun to speed the implementation of some of the projects already outlined in the Third Five-Year Plan. "To guarantee the most efficient use of the substantial Crash Program funds, so that the program can be carried out with the least cost and with the greatest benefit for the country, a team was needed which could work in a coordinated fashion, quick and effective. Hence, the formation of the 'Presidential Decree 10 Team.'" KEPPRES 10/1980 was signed by Suharto on 23 January 1980. Sekretariat Negara 1988:3–4.

[84] Presidential Decree 17 of 1983, dated 26 March 1983. Although the same decree added an assistant from the coordinating minister for economics' office to the team's roster, this hardly offset the power shift in favor of the SEKNEG group on the team.

the coordinating minister for economy, finance, and industry. And finally, despite the team's initial mandate to spend the Crash Program funds mostly abroad—a stipulation the economic ministers included to achieve their anti-inflationary objectives—several of Team 10's patronage-minded officials immediately began looking for ways to spend as much money as possible at home.[85]

These were only the first indications for the economic ministers that the alliance (with SEKNEG) and its progeny (Team 10) would prove disastrous for maintaining whatever gains had been made in market-based regulation of access to opportunities for production and commerce in Indonesia. Established as a temporary body with its Crash Program mandate, just two months later Team 10 was transformed into a permanent fixture in the Suharto government. "Seeing the results which had been achieved," wrote Sudharmono in the team's final report, Suharto issued Presidential Decree 14A of 1980, breathing new life into the team and empowering it to control government purchases of goods and services valued at Rp 500 million or more (at the time, equivalent to about $800,000). Although Sudharmono and others on Team 10 insisted repeatedly that they played only a coordinating role in government spending, the team's interventions went far beyond mere coordination. Team 10 controlled aspects of land acquisition for projects, granted permits for and oversaw tenders, as well as empowering a variety of technical teams and institutions (some private) to study projects and proposing purchases of equipment from a variety of different angles.

Over the next five years the team's power would be extended vertically through the state apparatus and horizontally across the archipelago. The vertical spread of power began within half a year of Team 10's becoming a permanent institution at SEKNEG. At first Team 10 was charged with overseeing major purchases by ministries and nondepartmental government bodies (called *lembaga*). But in July 1980 Suharto issued Presidential Decree 42, extending the team's power to encompass all state companies—including the biggest prize of all, Pertamina. Before this

[85] "It turned out," said the team's final report, "that some of the goods that were believed to be produced only abroad were in fact already produced domestically, or at least had the potential to be produced at home. Of all the funds spent (Rp 400 billion), roughly half (Rp 200 billion) went to purchase goods produced domestically." Sekretariat Negara 1988:4–5. Goods purchased at home included ships, small earth stations to monitor the weather, planes, double-decker buses, diesels, equipment for water purification, communication instruments, various cables and pipes, and kilowatt-hour meters.

rule, relatively few foreign companies had been affected. But suddenly the inclusion of numerous big-ticket expenditures in the oil sector—such as exploration, well development, platform expansion, and new supply services—meant that Team 10 would examine and approve all purchases over $800,000 by production-sharing contractors.

The next two initiatives enlarged the team's (and the central government's) power horizontally. Presidential Decrees 18 and 20, both issued in May 1981, were intended to give Team 10 the right to force provincial governments to follow the same tendering procedures that had been adopted by the central government—especially in how lists of "qualified bidders" were drawn up and how closely provincial governments had to stick to these lists in making awards. Decree 20 was aimed at tightening the team's control and supervision of development policies in the provinces by providing for the establishment in each province of a group called the Coordination Team for the Control and Supervision of Development in Regions. The regional teams were empowered to instruct and advise local authorities on "weak economic group" (a euphemism for *pribumi*) projects, ostensibly to minimize irregularities among local officials involved in them. The regional teams were also able to conduct studies and investigations as they deemed necessary in overseeing local development projects and were required to report periodically to Team 10 based in Jakarta.[86]

Expanding Team 10's vertical and horizontal power still further, Suharto linked this body to its controversial policies on "countertrade" and requirements that all imports be transported on Indonesian ships, both announced early in 1982;[87] purchases over Rp 500 million by state banks, provincial, and regency governments would, as of late March 1983, also fall under Team 10's control.[88] A year later Team 10's grip was tightened even more when Presidential Decree 29 of 1984 ordered that the threshold for the team's control over contracts awarded *without bidding* be lowered from Rp 500 million to Rp 200 million. The same

---

[86] *East Asian Executive Reports*, 3 (15 July 1981): 7.

[87] The countertrade policy, requiring that all firms awarded government contracts purchase and sell abroad an equivalent value of Indonesian commodities drawn from an official list, was decided in a cabinet meeting on 31 December 1981 and formally linked to Team 10 through SEKNEG note R-079/TPPBPP/1/1982, dated 21 January 1982. Presidential Decree 18 of 1982, dated 12 April 1982, concerned requirements on using Indonesian bottoms for all imports, as well as Team 10's role in helping enforce the rule.

[88] Presidential Decree 17 of 1983.

decree also empowered Team 10 to exercise still more control over "prequalification" processes that determined which firms, down to the provincial level, would get on key lists so they would be allowed to bid for projects. On the same day, another decree was issued requiring every ministry and department (the armed forces were explicitly excluded) to set up its own mini Team 10, chaired by ministers or department heads, to handle bidding below the main Team 10's Rp 500 million threshold. Each of these mini teams was required, as one might expect, to answer to Team 10 at SEKNEG.[89]

A tremendous blow was dealt to the BAPPENAS and Finance Ministry system of controlling foreign aid spending through DUPs and DIPs when a regulation was issued in November 1984 requiring Team 10 approval of all procurements involving the use of foreign credits.[90] Interestingly, this rule was issued by the coordinating minister for economy, finance, and industry.[91] Less surprising, perhaps, is that the last institutional holdout was the armed forces. It was not until 1985 that a presidential decree was issued giving Team 10 control over ABRI and HANKAM procurements.[92]

Thus far the emphasis has been on Team 10's origins and metastasis. As this process unfolded, the concentration of power within the team

[89] Presidential Decree 30 of 1984, dated 21 April 1984. Procurements of between Rp 20 and 200 million could be made by direct award without bidding. Amounts up to Rp 500 million had to involve bidding at the ministry or department level—overseen in part by the main Team 10. And all amounts over Rp 500 million, of course, would be handled directly by Team 10. The Department of Interior, meanwhile, would oversee all regional bidding processes for procurements valued between Rp 200 million and 500 million, again below Team 10's threshold. (Recall, however, that Team 10 would be involved in any direct awards worth Rp 200 or more at the provincial or regency levels.)

[90] See MENKO Ekuin circular S.095/M.EKUIN/1984, dated 13 November 1984.

[91] There are only two possible explanations for this very unusual turn of events. Either the economic ministers welcomed Team 10's intervention into all contracts involving foreign assistance—which is difficult to imagine—or President Suharto simply directed the economic ministers to write the law and, once again, they did as they were told.

[92] Presidential Decree 40 of 1985. ABRI stands for *Angkatan Bersenjata Republik Indonesia* (Armed Forces of the Republic of Indonesia), and HANKAM stands for *Departemen Pertahanan Keamanan* (Department for Security Maintenance). Decree 40 also gave a representative from HANKAM a rotating seat on Team 10. Bank Indonesia's seat was also rotating. Team 10's final report notes that secret procurements by ABRI and HANKAM were overseen by a technical team, then handed up to Ginanjar as head of the daily working team for his perusal, and finally passed on to Sudharmono, in his capacity as chair of Team 10, for final approval. All other armed forces procurements were handled together with the rest of the government's purchases. See Sekretariat Negara 1988:18.

was achieved as discretionary control over massive state resources from the oil boom was taken away from the economic ministers and other officials arrayed both vertically and horizontally within the system. The next section explores the nature of this power in greater detail.

New Terms of Access and the Patronage Dimension

The resources that passed through Team 10's approval process are mind boggling. According to the team's final report, during the eight years of operation it awarded a staggering Rp 52 trillion worth of government procurements.[93] To put this number in some perspective, consider that the *total discretionary government surplus* for development spending from 1980 to 1988 came to just Rp 43 trillion.[94] Even if another Rp 3 trillion in "program" aid, over which there was considerable government discretion, is included, the total unallocated funds for the period come to only Rp 46 trillion. In other words, Team 10 controlled all domestic discretionary funds during the time it was in operation and reached beyond these by yet another Rp 6 trillion (most likely money controlled by creditor countries for projects they were funding).

To look at the number Rp 52 trillion from still another angle, consider that total approved domestic investment (ethnic Chinese and other) during the same period was Rp 36.2 trillion, of which probably only 40 percent, or Rp 14.5 trillion, was actually invested.[95] Total realized foreign investment during the same period was even less. It is no wonder Indonesian officials could frequently be heard crowing proudly (during the oil boom, that is) that the state was the "engine of development." The resources the state was releasing into the economy easily overshadowed those supplied by the private sector. Indeed, for private firms the return on investment could be boosted substantially by linking one's own private resources to those being awarded for projects by the state.

Those drafting Team 10's final report went out of their way to downplay the clientelist aspects of their operation. Taking at face value

[93] Sekretariat Negara 1988:24.

[94] Total domestic government receipts were Rp 121 trillion, of which fully Rp 78 trillion went for routine expenditures. Figures are from the Ministry of Finance.

[95] Figures are from Bank Indonesia. Only one-fourth of the total amount invested in 1988 is used in this calculation because Team 10 closed shop at the end of the first quarter of 1988.

both the text of the report and various statements over the years by Sudharmono and Ginanjar, the message these officials wanted to transmit was that they cared most about plugging leaks in the government's procurement procedures and, as always, giving a boost to *pribumi* producers and suppliers of the goods and services the government was purchasing. The *pribumi* issue has already been discussed; the matter of waste can be dispensed with in short order. Team 10's final report indicates that the money saved by cutting government waste amounted to just 4 percent of all awards made-—a figure that was probably offset by the on-budget costs alone of keeping all of Team 10's many tentacles in constant motion for eight years.[96] The report never mentions how much it cost to operate the Team 10 system. A high official in the Ministry of Finance admitted that at first Team 10 accomplished some good for the government. "But then SEKNEG took over," he added grimly. "Even typewriters were getting purchased centrally. In some cases the delays were years. Sudharmono used this operation to supply contracts to the president's children. He's very dirty." Trying to distance the economists from Team 10 and the patronage game everyone came to associate with it, the official added, "Doing this was Sudharmono's idea, not Widjoyo's."[97]

Team 10 was excellently suited to become an instrument for building, expanding, and maintaining highly centralized patronage structures. First, the legislation setting up the team, and Sudharmono's own subsequent implementing regulations, provided for numerous procedures to be followed and criteria to be assessed for each bid or direct award. Each stage in this process presented another opportunity for discretionary control by the officials involved. And so that the rules themselves did not complicate the patronage game too severely, they were written so as to allow maximum flexibility to decision makers. In the words of one observer trying to make sense of a fairly straightforward regulation stipulating which projects had to be open for public bids, "the exceptions for direct assignments [by officials] are extensive and threaten to swallow the rule."[98]

Officials enjoyed many opportunities to exercise control and demand

---

[96] Sekretariat Negara 1988:24.

[97] Widjoyo Nitisastro was the most influential economic minister during the New Order. Confidential interview in Jakarta, 29 August 1989.

[98] Gingerich 1982:7.

upeti from firms and investors lucky enough to get lucrative government contracts.[99] The initial stage was prequalification—the process for determining which firms would get on lists of qualified bidders. Team 10 worked hard to manage this process down to the regency level.[100] The next stage was the evaluation of bids and the awarding of contracts. These two stages were typically spread over months, sometimes years, allowing plenty of time to "consult" with contractors on their bids and negotiate the terms of the *upeti*—the key element of the bidding game from the perspective of officials. Were any unforeseen political problems or material needs to arise, those associated with Team 10 still had one more opportunity to flex their patronage muscles. "Spot checks" could be made as the team "deemed necessary" to evaluate projects and ensure their proper implementation—in other words, a catchall provision legitimizing the sorts of ongoing relations essential to stable patron-client ties.[101]

The standard practice, according to one investors who admitted having a long and profitable association with Team 10, was to inflate project costs to allow investors to share legally dispersed public funds with the Team 10 officials in charge of awarding tenders. If the project really costs Rp 300 million, said the investor, who spoke to the press on condition that he not be identified, one would bid Rp 500 million "so there's extra money to be divided up." As for the danger of other bidders making a public stink about losing, the "age-old system" was employed. "For instance," said the Team 10 crony, "you have five firms bidding for a project. Company A has a tie to official X, and so naturally A will win. The project bid is jacked up nicely so that there is no complaining among the four losers—as they each receive a share from the difference between the real cost of the project and the amount tendered."[102]

---

[99] The term means "tribute paid by subjects." Pangaribuan (1988:160) used the word to describe the kickback system described to him in interviews with insiders familiar with how Team 10 operated.

[100] The lists were called DRM for *Daftar Rekanan Mampu* (literally, List of Qualified Companions). Not only did Team 10 want to have a say in which firms got on these lists, it also did what it could to prevent provincial and regency governments from picking unlisted contractors (one of the key provisions in Presidential Decree 18 of 1981). Firms refusing to play the patronage game would be excluded from the DRM and effectively cut off from the oil bonanza.

[101] Sekretariat Negara 1988:20.

[102] All quotations in this paragraph are from *Kompas,* 31 March 1988, 1. In the end, this entrepreneur admitted that having fewer hands in the till would probably be beneficial

The evidence that Team 10 was an instrument for deepening patronage structures is overwhelming. Beneficiaries were selected for their political and personal proximity to powerful officials in the palace and at SEKNEG, for their utility in securing support in geographical areas or among social groups where the Suharto regime felt insecure, and for the personal ties of trust that bind different factions jostling for power in Jakarta and in the provinces. The period of Team 10's operation coincided, for instance, with a massive drive to build support for GOLKAR, a quasi party that has functioned as Suharto's election machine since the early years of his rule. In addition to his position as chair of Team 10, Sudharmono was also made chair of GOLKAR in 1983. His dual role was no coincidence. According to Iman Taufik, a *pribumi* investor with extensive knowledge of Team 10's structure and operation, "It was decreed that all purchases by the Indonesian government had to be approved through Sudharmono's office. One reason was to minimize non-GOLKAR members' access to projects [*pribumi* or not]. It's true this was done. For seven years Suharto agreed to this practice."[103]

KADIN, the Indonesian chamber of commerce, was also used both in Jakarta and in the provinces. KADIN's local branches played a central role in helping officials draft the all-important bidding lists determining which firms qualified as "economically weak." Although it is certain that with all the resources Team 10 had to spread around benefits would inevitably be enjoyed fairly widely, it is also true that medium and smaller firms most frequently attached themselves to Team 10's largesse by operating as subcontractors to the big players linked at the apex of the system to Suharto, SEKNEG, Team 10, KADIN headquarters, and GOLKAR headquarters. In effect, the patronage structure in the state was replicated in a parallel structure in the Indonesian private sector. For years complaints could be heard *from pribumi entrepreneurs* that there were irregularities with Team 10's procedures, and that big players close to Sudharmono were benefiting most.[104] One report said: "Several sources told *Tempo* that Team 10 succeeded in plugging the holes in the

---

to the economy and country. "When you have a team," he lamented, "the leaks in the system are more plentiful because there are a lot more people asking for a share of the spoils."

[103] Interview in Jakarta with Iman Taufik, 1 April 1989.

[104] Once Team 10 had been dismantled, some of the names of the biggest recipients in the private sector finally surfaced in the press. See, for instance, *Tempo*, 31 March 1988, 91–92.

state budget in the early period. And then, they watched TPPBPP [Team 10] grow to become a sort of superwarlord, making selected firms their favorites for tenders." One official who worked on the team (and asked not to be identified by the press) admitted that it was not uncommon for the procurement body to award contracts to well-connected firms whose bids were 15 percent above their competitors'. "Heck, there were still companies that complained," the official was quoted as saying. "'They wanted 30 percent,' said the official with a laugh."[105]

There are still other indications that many of the old tricks associated with previous regulations ostensibly designed to promote the interests of *pribumi* entrepreneurs had been dusted off by clients eager to skim whatever they could from Team 10. Presidential Decree 14A of 1980, for instance, gave important advantages to "economically weak" firms, defined by how much capital was invested in the firm. "The major loophole here," an alert reporter noted, "is that any large *pribumi* firm could in theory create a subsidiary at slightly less than maximum asset value and thus qualify as economically weak. A number of politically-connected *pribumi* companies which have thrived on government contracts in the past have already done this."[106] Before long, small and medium *pribumi* companies all over the archipelago were overwhelmed as big operators from Jakarta fanned out to set up front companies so that they could qualify on paper to be included on bidding lists. "Since the passage of Keppres 14A," noted one report, "thousands of 'economically weak' firms have sprung up. Many have merely acted as brokers, passing on work to third parties for a commission."[107] All of this prompted a reprimand from Widjoyo Nitisastro. "The weak economic group must not only make demands," he warned, "but must also fulfill and carry out the regulations made by the government." He noted that "some members of the weak economic groups still prefer to pass on their work and responsibility to groups that are already economically strong

---

[105] *Tempo*, 2 April 1988, 88. Also see Pangaribuan 1988:160.

[106] The reporter added that a loophole of this kind "undermines the decree's main purpose." Sacerdoti 1980:52. It might have been more accurate to say it undermined the *stated* purpose.

[107] *East Asian Executive Reports* 3 (15 July 1981): 7. This is of course the familiar "Ali-Baba" scheme practiced by *pribumi* for decades. To be sure, all these firms were legitimately incorporated. But anyone examining data showing sharp increases in the number of indigenous firms during this period would be mistaken to conclude that some sort of major transformation was under way.

in the country. Apparently they are already satisfied in receiving commissions, because they are not real entrepreneurs."[108] A presidential decree was issued to dampen some of the criticism.[109] It forbade those who were awarded contracts as weak *pribumi* to pass their contracts along to others. Anyone discovered doing this would be permanently barred from bidding lists all over the country. But this was not the end of the story. Partly to extend control over the regional governments and partly to keep the door open wide for the same big players in the capital, the law also empowered Team 10 to exercise more control over the criteria for establishing the bidding lists in the regions. Ostensibly, Team 10 sought to "unify" the entire bidding process all over the country by establishing different categories of firms depending on their size, proven performance record, and so on. Firms in category A—Team 10's business partners based in Jakarta—would be permitted to bid on projects anywhere in the country, whereas all lower categories (down to C3) had to limit their bids to ever narrower local contracts.[110] In short, a patrimonial logic can be found behind nearly every regulation associated with Team 10.

In discussing the contributions of this chapter from the perspective of the broader arguments of the book, it is important to recall that the central issue has less to do with the influences and leverage that operated during the oil boom period than with those that did not—and to recall why. That is, we can learn as much—if not more—about the structural dimensions of investors' power within capitalism when that power is severely undermined as when it acts to present strong constraints on the options policymakers feel it is safe to consider. The material presented in this chapter not only traces shifts in the Indonesian state's policies toward private capital controllers—especially mobile ones—but links those shifts to changes in the pattern of access to and control over critical resources needed to meet the country's overall investment needs.

Several points discussed in the body of the chapter deserve additional

[108] *East Asian Executive Reports* 3 (15 July 1981): 7.

[109] Presidential Decree 18 of 1981, dated 5 May 1981. Decree 20, issued on the same day, was the one setting up coordination teams at the local level, answerable to Team 10 in Jakarta, to help enforce central control over these important processes.

[110] Decree 18 of 1981 started this categorization. It was refined and strengthened in subsequent legislation—especially Decree 29 of 1984 and one of Team 10/SEKNEG's last major regulations, 3457/TPPBPP/XII/85. See Sekretariat Negara 1988:29.

emphasis here. First, there is clear evidence both from the investment activity of capital controllers and from the observations of various analysts and reporters that the period from roughly 1974 to 1982 represented a decline in the responsiveness and competitiveness of Indonesia's investment climate from the perspective of mobile capital controllers. Paralleling this decline, though certainly not causing it, was a marked diminution both in the power of the economic ministers within the state and in their ability to maintain control over the terms of access to opportunities for investment and profit in Indonesia. Although they struggled steadily to keep intact those market mechanisms they had successfully installed before the boom, the role of markets was nevertheless eroded— slowly at first and more rapidly by the end of the 1970s. In its place there arose an even deeper and more extensive system of patronage and official discretion than existed at the height of Ibnu Sutowo's reign at Pertamina.

Two related forces converged to undermine the power base of the economic ministers. Just as the Indonesian state's access to massive replacement resources blocked the effectiveness of the structural power of both mobile and immobile investors, so it robbed the economic ministers of the prime basis of their leverage in winning policy battles with President Suharto. Backed by neither a major political party nor the armed forces, the economic ministers (a collection of university professors, really) derived their power over economic policy from the need Suharto perceived to meet the country's ongoing *private* investment needs, and the fact that these officials had proved themselves adept at doing precisely this. The economic ministers alone, through the signals they send both directly and through policies to capital controllers, could serve as the nexus between private investors and the material needs of the Indonesian jurisdiction. When the need for the resources investors privately command began to wane, so too did Suharto's sense of urgency regarding the policies the economic ministers advised him to adopt or maintain.

The second and related dimension was that the tremendous replacement resources that became available to policymakers in the Indonesian state flowed not into the hands of the economic ministers, but instead into the grip of actors occupying the office next to that of President Suharto himself. Even had other antimarket policies not accompanied such a development, the dramatically expanded discretion of officials to allocate these resources according to a clientelist logic that benefited

Suharto and his supporters *by itself* severely undermined the economic ministers' attempts to maintain market-based forms of allocation, and by extension to maintain a basic element in Indonesia's competitive position with other jurisdictions. The point is not that patronage did not exist before the birth of Team 10: it certainly did at the more disaggregated levels at which procurement occurred previously. What Team 10 did was centralize the process, drawing patronage power upward and into the center, and elevate to the level of *formal* national policy a pattern of tight micromanagement of opportunity and success throughout the archipelago that had not existed previously.

Although fundamental changes in the state's access to resources helps account for changes in the intensity and effectiveness of investors' structural leverage—especially the capacity to raise the political costs perceived by policymakers of not adopting market-oriented, competitive policies—these changes in no way determine the course of subsequent policy. In the absence of other major forces in Indonesia's political economy, it is entirely conceivable that even without being structurally constrained to pursue market policies of the sort mobile investors find advantageous, Indonesia could have stayed on the same course begun back in the late 1960s. Put differently, a consideration of the structural power of capital controllers is most helpful in predicting the character or direction of a country's policies when the impact of this structural power is high. When the structural leverage of investors is effectively blocked, as during the oil boom in Indonesia, one can account for the direction of policy changes only by looking at contextual factors that vary widely from jurisdiction to jurisdiction. In Indonesia there has been a fundamental tension *within* the ranks of capital controllers and *between* market-supporting actors and those whose interests lie squarely in the country's patron-client relations over the role that market allocation of investment opportunities should play.

CAPITAL'S POWER RESTORED, 1982 TO THE PRESENT

Although Team 10 proved able to hang on until a new cabinet was installed in 1988, the oil boom that made this body and its policies possible had already begun to evaporate by the end of 1982. The slide in oil prices was gradual at first, but by 1986 a steep drop returned the real cost of a barrel of oil to its pre-1973 level. The impact of the oil bust on the struggle between proponents of market-based and clientelist forms of allocation was as pronounced as the effect of the oil boom itself. The major difference was that the relevant structural forces were now working in the opposite direction. The pendulum of influence had swung back in favor of private investors—and with a vengeance, for by the early 1980s the mobility of capital was vastly wider and more rapid than before the first oil price hikes in 1973. A public relations firm working for Indonesia's economic ministers, and advising them specifically on how to send the clearest and most favorable signals to mobile investors about the competitive advantages of Indonesia's investment climate, offered this view in 1985: "Competition to attract foreign industrial investment has never been keener. Even the most developed economies are seeking foreign investment to develop weaker industrial sectors and less prosperous regions. Developing countries are being forced to pursue foreign investors actively with well-planned investment objectives and strategies. The strategies that governments employ to obtain a growing share of the global investment pool will be key to the outcome."[1] Significantly, even some *pribumi* members of Indonesia's capitalist class had

[1] Hill and Knowlton, Inc. 1985:3.

begun to enjoy the mobility that was formerly the preserve of transnational and ethnic Chinese investors. This development, as we will see, had important implications for the balance of power between those favoring and opposing predominantly market-regulated access and entry in Indonesia.

Despite important differences between the conditions existing before and after the oil boom in Indonesia, a fundamental feature common to both periods and largely absent during the oil boom itself was real constraints on policymakers to create and maintain a competitive and responsive investment climate as the means of ensuring an adequate supply and rate of overall investment for society. The state's own replacement resources based on windfall profits from fossil fuels had permitted policymakers to assume a much more indifferent attitude toward the policy demands of mobile capital controllers because the decline in private investment did not damage the economy. The shrinking of the state's replacement resources in the 1980s restored the potency of mobile actors' structural leverage. And once again policymakers eager to prevent major social disruptions rooted in investment declines and crises found themselves paying much more attention to the effect of various policies on the locational and reinvestment strategies of those who privately disposed of crucial investment resources. In short, the country had returned to the pattern of resource control that predominates under capitalism in most countries most of the time.

The central point of this chapter is that Indonesia's "era of deregulation,"[2] embarked on soon after the oil boom ended, is linked directly to the reinvigoration of the structural power of investors. I present this argument by juxtaposing policymakers' insulation from and indifference to criticisms from important capital controllers about Team 10 and related policies of personal control by officials during the boom with the entire sweep of "deregulation" (including the ultimate demise of Team 10) ushered in once the boom years had passed. In particular, I examine the keen sensitivity policymakers showed to the interests and behavior of

[2] I use the term "deregulation" here in part because it is used so widely when states change their policies in favor of market-oriented allocation of opportunity and benefits. A much more accurate term would be "reregulation," since what was taking place in Indonesia was not a removal of regulation (sheer chaos), but rather regulation according to market criteria instead of criteria set by officials in government ministries. Rather than confuse everyone with a new term, I will put "deregulation" in quotation marks to underscore the point that there was a change in (rather than an absence of) regulation.

mobile investors before and during the introduction of major reforms in taxation—one of the first major initiatives in the economic ministers' "deregulatory" thrust.

Indonesia's major tax reform in 1984, and the highly controversial issue of eliminating tax holidays, is especially interesting because on its face it appears to signify an unresponsive state (this time at the hands of the economic ministers), but in fact it convincingly demonstrates the opposite. At the same time, it underscores nicely a fundamental conflict that exists between pressures on policymakers to address the state's revenue needs and the society's investment needs at the same time. The problem, of course, is that as officials improve their ability to collect a share of the social surplus as taxes, the success itself represents a disincentive to investors, who would like to pay the lowest taxes possible. The chapter closes with a brief section on major *pribumi* entrepreneurs and their influence on the ability of the economic ministers to advance their agenda of eliminating the discretion of officials over access and allocation in the economy and replacing it with a system regulated by markets.

Capital Controllers React to Team 10

As the previous chapter showed, there were clear winners and losers among investors when Team 10 was introduced. Persons in close political proximity to key members of the Suharto regime enjoyed significant nonmarket advantages and made handsome profits in the process. A few mobile investors did their best to play the risky patronage game being run from the State Secretariat. But as the data on declining private investment rates showed, many others postponed their investment plans, departed for more secure locations, or never came to Indonesia in the first place. Beginning almost immediately after the policy changes in 1974, the economic ministers could be heard reassuring investors that restrictive rules would be implemented "realistically" and "flexibly." Business publications and other analysts joined them in the view that Indonesia would have a hard time following the new regulations to the letter. Many investors were persuaded. But when J. B. Sumarlin responded in July 1981 to a reporter's question about the marked shift toward even more government control after the second oil boom by saying, "It's really not as bad as it sounds," few of the investors still around to listen were convinced.[3] When it came to Team 10, pessimism prevailed among mobile capital controllers. After an initial period of "vast confusion" about what Team 10 would be and do, the reality was clear. Said one agency that watches developments in Indonesia's business climate: "Diplomats and businessmen—and Indonesian officials—are agreed that the government is taking the [Team 10] campaign seriously."[4]

Private investors usually avoid open criticism of Indonesia's policies. Because it is the hallmark of the Suharto regime to make surgical strikes on those it considers troublemakers, individual firms and their executives (foreign or domestic, *pribumi* or ethnic Chinese) are loath to criticize policies publicly. Especially for those already investing, and thus somewhat less mobile, efforts to voice dissatisfaction are made through associations. A good example of this was seen in the middle 1980s, when the gap separating the price of a barrel of oil on world markets and the (higher) price the Indonesian government used to assess taxes on production-sharing contractors became intolerable for the oil companies. Rather than lobby officials publicly or privately, the International Petroleum Association in Jakarta petitioned the government and, after cutbacks in new exploration and liftings backed up these protests, the government responded favorably.[5] The Japanese, who occupied the archipelago during the Second World War and were a magnet for student criticism during the demonstrations and riots in 1974, tend to be the least vocal of all. It is all the more surprising, therefore, that figures representing Japanese investors took the extraordinary step of adding public protest of Indonesia's policies to the structural signals already

---

[3] Briggs 1981:121. The occasional article reporting on meetings between investors' organizations and Indonesian officials during the oil boom years always reflected the Indonesians' awareness that their policies were increasingly unresponsive but could rarely report any news of concrete efforts to change the situation. See, for instance, *Straits Times,* 17 April 1980.

[4] *East Asian Executive Reports* 3, (15 March 1981): 9.

[5] Interview in Jakarta with John Frannea, senior vice president at Mobil Oil Indonesia, 31 March 1989. When oil companies apply this kind of pressure, it does not mean they are hurting in some absolute sense, only that they are reaping more profits elsewhere. By 1989, when I spoke to the president and general manager of Mobil Oil Indonesia, he said this: "We make *big* money here. Real big money. The Indonesians aren't hard-core capitalists like, say, the Nigerians, but they don't seem to mind obscene profits." Interview in Jakarta with H. K. Acord, 13 June 1989.

contained in declining rates of new investment. In 1982 and 1983 the Japanese focused their criticism on Indonesia's countertrade policy, whose implementation was overseen by Team 10. Suddenly headlines like "Japanese Want Jakarta Policy Changed" and "Indonesia's Cargo Stipulation Straining Ties with Japan" were appearing regularly.[6] As late as July 1984 there were still signs that the Indonesian government was reluctant to yield on its unresponsive policies.[7]

Other investors, determined (either because their investments were sunk or because the opportunities for profits were so great) to find ways around the restrictions and difficulties introduced when officials at SEKNEG began exerting enormous control over Indonesia's economy, began to explore the loopholes in Team 10's system of choosing winners for lucrative government projects. Most of the ingenuity came from the oil sector, which was increasingly hard hit as Team 10's reach extended to ever smaller state procurements.[8] One method of circumventing Team 10 control was for certain officials to join with selected companies and write project proposals (DUPs) that were so technically specific that only one company could possibly win the bid.[9] This scheme backfired, however, as Team 10 upgraded its own Technical Group (hiring still larger numbers of Indonesian consultants and academics) and challenged the narrowness of the specifications in the project proposal—adding still longer delays to the approval process.[10] Another somewhat more effective ploy was to avoid purchases altogether for government-linked projects and lease machines and material instead. One report noted that not until 1982 did "leasing of heavy equipment start in earnest" in Indonesia. Previously there had been "little inclination" by bankers to

[6] See, for instance, *FEER*, 27 August 1982; *Straits Times*, 23 October 1982 and 28 February 1983.

[7] "Jakarta appears intent" on carrying out its Team 10 policies, said one report, "even though they are discouraging prospective foreign investors." Citing a "general hardening of the government's approach in investment negotiations" reaching back to the oil boom years, the report noted that even big players accustomed to getting their way around the globe were being treated with astonishing indifference. "IBM, for instance, was recently told to make an early decision or lose its opportunity at an investment project," one business journal reported. *East Asian Executive Reports* 6 (15 July 1984): 6.

[8] In 1980, when Team 10 was first established, the Rp 500 million floor above which the team would control procurements was equal to about $800,000. After the 1983 devaluation, Rp 500 million was only $500,000, and after the 1986 devaluation the team was vetting all government purchases of $300,000 and above.

[9] Discussion in Jakarta with Stephen Parker, an economist with USAID, 26 July 1990.

[10] Sekretariat Negara 1988:28.

compete for this sort of financing. Suddenly, however, the incentives were strong indeed.[11]

These reactions of "voice," withdrawal, and relocation from private investors were joined by unusually severe criticism of Indonesia's deteriorating investment climate from the World Bank and USAID. In February and March 1980, a World Bank mission consisting of seven consultants visited Indonesia and produced a six-hundred-page report[12] that "ignited the most intense controversy" anyone had seen between an international agency and the Indonesian government since the days when Sukarno ejected the World Bank and other suppliers of institutional capital from the country in the 1960s.[13] The report was slated to be presented at the annual meeting of the IGGI in the summer of 1980, but Indonesian officials vehemently insisted it be struck from the agenda. According to the *Far Eastern Economic Review,* the draft version it had obtained said that Indonesia was "a bureaucratic mess" and that its business regulations and licensing procedures were "counterproductive and lead to corruption."[14] Despite at least two major rewrites and heated negotiations spanning almost a year, the Indonesians remained stridently opposed to the report. Indonesian officials simply "refused to accept it," a minister told the *Review.*[15] In the end, the World Bank blinked first—perhaps realizing that the country's oil revenues greatly diminished the bank's structural leverage and fearing that a decade and a half of good relations with Indonesia might be jeopardized if it pushed too hard in such circumstances. Said the World Bank's top official in Jakarta, "They didn't need our money and they didn't listen to what we said."[16]

[11] Baxter 1984:14.

[12] World Bank 1980. This document is a revised version of the report circulated in September 1980.

[13] See *FEER* 112 (29 May 1981): 44–48. So charged was the atmosphere surrounding this World Bank report that when the bank discovered that the *Far Eastern Economic Review* had received (via *Counterspy* magazine, based in Washington, D.C.) a copy of the sole leaked version of the report, immediate efforts were made to contain any damage press coverage might cause. The *Review* decided to devote its cover story to the subject. I received my copy of this article from the office of the governor of Bank Indonesia (complete with the minister's underlining, exclamation points, and checkmarks in the margins). Although the *Review* is widely distributed in Southeast Asia, this photocopy was nevertheless stamped *terbatas* (confidential) in large black letters.

[14] *FEER* 112 (29 May 29, 1981): 1.

[15] *FEER* 112 (29 May 1981): 46.

[16] Interview in Jakarta with Atilla Sönmez, 3 January 1990.

The thorough and blunt tone of the report was surprising given the awareness among World Bank officials in Jakarta that Indonesians do not countenance being criticized directly, and certainly not in public. Indeed, it usually takes the skills of a Cold War Kremlinologist to divine the bank's criticisms of Indonesian policy in its annual report for Indonesia's consortium of creditor countries. (The IMF's annual report tends to be much less circumspect.) Explaining the World Bank's soft touch in Indonesia, Atilla Sönmez, the top World Bank official in Jakarta in the late 1980s, said solemnly, "Indonesia will always choose hardship over indignity."[17] Another bank official explained how the Jakarta mission has adapted its ordinary procedures to permit Indonesian officials their public dignity. "More so than in any other place, we play a policy-making role in Indonesia. But the actual paper trail doesn't even come close to reflecting what we do here. Recently one of our own World Bank teams came through to assess the effectiveness of our operations. They were frustrated by how hard it was to piece together the story of our role here. Countless technical notes are produced by our staff members for the Indonesian government. A minister will call up and we'll talk about something, and he'll ask for a note on it. We understand the sensitivity of our position here, so the note that gets produced is never circulated, nor are copies of it kept in any central location. We don't even send a copy to the Washington office. Each staffer has his or her own files. So much of what we do is on a personal level." Bank officials are very proud of the way they have learned to handle Indonesian sensibilities and still get the desired results. "One of our biggest problems over the years has been to convince those back in Washington that normal operating procedures must be flexible enough to accommodate conditions such as those found in Indonesia. The approach the bank uses here is very specific to this place. The Indonesians are unwilling to be told what to do. Therefore our standard loan format, which clearly states the policy conditions for the loan, 1, 2, 3, 4, 5, and which is used in many parts of the world, is impossible here. We use what I call 'implicit conditionality.' In other countries we are right up together with the government. The current objectives of the bank get implemented as the loans are put forth. In Indonesia there's a lag. We let the government ride out in front. We slowly and steadily push a set of policies, and in time they adopt them.

[17] Interview in Jakarta with Atilla Sönmez, 3 January 1990.

They lead and we follow. It's a very time-consuming process, which is why our staff is so huge here, but it works. The end result is the same, even if on paper it looks different. Sometimes the bank people in Washington don't like this method of operation. They want to see the conditions of each loan set out clearly as the money is being approved. But the standard paperwork for Indonesia usually says something like, 'In view of the good progress being made on X, Y, and Z, and in view of anticipated changes in A, B, and C, we recommend the following loans.' This throws them off a little."[18]

The central criticism of the 1980 World Bank report was that the controls imposed by officials on investment, trade, and finance—adopted in what the report referred to repeatedly as an "*ad hoc manner*"—not only were preventing the country's economy from reaching its potential, but worse, were actively working against the government's own stated goals of rapid job creation and the creation of a freestanding class of *pribumi* entrepreneurs. "Laws and regulations are couched in broad terms and, frequently, in ways that are ambiguous," the World Bank charged. "In such situations, illegal payments become common features of the regulatory system and such payments are often made either for the proper execution or for the adjustment of the rules."[19] Put less delicately, the system was designed to give numerous opportunities for patronage to officials at the expense of a more impersonal system of market allocation. The report added that small and immobile *pribumi* firms, which the myriad regulations were said to promote and defend, were in fact one of the groups most disadvantaged by such practices. This was especially the case in tax collecting and port clearing procedures. A system based on direct fees to officials for services "tends to reward those who are capable of making such payments by erecting barriers for potential entrants who are not familiar with the various detailed procedures that must be followed to conduct business in Indonesia. Consequently, skills such as dealing efficiently with the bureaucracy carry a premium, and the relatively smaller, inexperienced *pribumi* firms with fewer resources are, in practice, discriminated against."[20] Of course, as we saw in the previous chapter, not every *pribumi* entrepreneur faced this discrimination. Those associated per-

[18] Confidential interview in Jakarta with a senior World Bank official, 14 June 1989.
[19] World Bank 1980:vi.
[20] World Bank 1980:vi.

sonally or institutionally (or even genetically) with the officials conducting traffic in Indonesia's economy benefited nicely from this same systematic discrimination.

Aiming its guns at the financial sector, the World Bank wrote that
policies designed to give subsidized credit to small *pribumi* operators
actually ended up helping their larger and better-connected competitors.
Because "financially viable projects from *pribumi* entrepreneurs are
scarce," the state banks that are supposed to supply *pribumi* with credit
below commercial rates "often deposit their excess funds in off-shore
markets such as Singapore, and some of these funds are subsequently
recycled into the country through off-shore capital markets with a higher
cost and a foreign exchange risk by non-*pribumi* and joint-venture
firms."[21] Noting the severe drop in the country's ability to attract and
retain private capital since 1974, the bank, speaking on behalf of individual investors far too vulnerable to voice their own complaints, leveled
a terse attack on the determination of some policymakers to control
access to profits and opportunity in Indonesia. "Prior to 1974," the
report said, "the Government had adopted essentially 'open-door' policies, but in the post-1974 period, these policies became increasingly
restrictionist." As a result, realized foreign investment peaked in 1974. If
the Asahan smelter in Sumatra is discounted, total approved investments
took a precipitous drop from $4 billion for the five years spanning
1970–1974 to less than $0.9 billion for the subsequent five years span-
ning 1975–1979.[22] The bank noted, quite correctly, that restrictions
imposed by officials had a weaker impact on firms already established
and operating, hurting instead those seeking to enter the system: "Established foreign and joint venture firms have learned to operate very prof-
itably within the system. Nevertheless, the disincentives associated with
such a system have acted as a very serious impediment to the inflow of
new private foreign investment. Many potential new entrants, encouraged by the Government's public relations abroad, are taken aback and
disillusioned by the amorphous barriers erected in their paths by these
regulations. It is not surprising, therefore, that most of the recorded
private foreign investment since 1974 has been due to the expansion of
existing firms rather than to the entry of new enterprises."[23]

[21] World Bank 1980:ix.
[22] World Bank 1980:x. These are nominal figures, whereas those used in the graphs in
the previous chapter were deflated.
[23] World Bank 1980:x; emphasis in original. On the same subject, Sadli had this to add:

Indonesia must, the bank's consultants added, seek fewer, not better, controls if it is to attract more capital from mobile sources. The World Bank's most fundamental policy recommendation (among the twenty-nine specific reforms it "suggested") was that a "Deregulation Commission" be established immediately so that Indonesia could transform itself from "an administratively determined allocation system to a price-based one."[24] Significantly, the report nowhere mentioned the rather weak interest in or commitment to a system of price-based allocation among the clientelist officials exercising the greatest influence over policy at the time. To give its criticisms additional force, the bank applied a bit of structural pressure by recommending in 1980 that the IGGI supply the same amount of foreign assistance as it had the previous year. This was the first year since the IGGI was formed that its annual commitments were not increased in absolute terms.

Indonesian officials across the board reacted strongly to these charges. Even some economic ministers were among those expressing outrage, feeling that the bank was not sensitive enough to the difficulties they faced in trying to maintain market-based policies in the midst of an oil boom, the windfalls from which had been commandeered by officials not only working closely with the president but operating very much with the entire current of the country's patrimonial history. The economists criticized the writers of the report, saying they were "naive about the cultural and social [meaning clientelist and feudal] constraints on any government in Jakarta."[25] The *Review* reporter who broke the World Bank report story noted, however, that privately the economic ministers were "pleased to see the World Bank report take pot-shots at

---

"A lot of changes toward investors came during the oil boom. There was nothing like DSP [the book-length Investment Priority List that micromanaged investment opportunities] before the oil boom. We wanted investment everywhere and anywhere we could get it. But it's important to remember that the ones who got hurt were those who weren't already 'in.' The new regulations were basically barriers to entry. The oil years were boom times, and no one was complaining. The Chinese [Indonesians] did especially well. The 'conglomerates' everyone's talking about now had their seeds sown during the years just following Malari." Interview in Jakarta with Mohammad Sadli, 6 November 1989.

[24] Always giving Indonesia's officials the benefit of the doubt, the report said that its various ad hoc policies had created a highly biased structure of industrial incentives that, "however unintentional, has become inimical to the realization of some of the very objectives that the Government is attempting to realize"—especially job creation and the promotion of *pribumi*. World Bank 1980:22.

[25] *FEER* 112 (29 May 1981): 1. The *Review*'s reporter added, "The basis for government policy is not capitalist industrial efficiency [via market allocation], but an almost feudal protection of industrial concerns."

some of the sacred cows that browse among them."[26] One admitted, tongue-in-cheek, according to the *Review,* that "some of the Bank's recommendations are warranted—we would like to take them up. I only wish they would not stop there. . . . How about some advice on how to implement them?"[27]

The USAID mission in Jakarta produced its own assessment of government policies.[28] More exploratory in nature, the USAID report sought to analyze where Indonesian policies seemed to be heading, and with what impact. Like the World Bank study, the USAID report found that an enormous gulf separated stated policy objectives and actual results. Placing the greatest stress on the matter of job creation, the report said that "the employment impact of the government's present industrial plan illustrates how completely inadequate the plans are in addressing the Third [Five-Year] Plan job target of about 600,000 new jobs per year."[29] Moreover, the report echoed other critics who had noted a rather disconcerting predilection among Indonesian officials for micromanaging the economy.[30]

Not fully appreciating the intimate connection between patronage politics under Team 10 and how access and entry to the economy were being controlled, the USAID analysts, still grappling with sluggish job creation, tried to suggest that the two could be separated, somehow permitting officials like Ginanjar and Sudharmono to allocate massive

[26] *FEER* 112 (29 May 1981): 45.

[27] *FEER* 112 (29 May 1981): 48.

[28] USAID 1982. In October 1981 President Ronald Reagan issued a directive to agencies like USAID to incorporate more of what he called "the magic of the marketplace" into U.S. foreign assistance programs. Indonesia and Thailand were targeted as the first two countries where the approach would be applied. Unlike the World Bank report, the USAID study was intended more as an internal document suggesting where the agency might have the greatest success in changing Indonesian policies than as an instrument to criticize policymakers and how they operated. See *Straits Times,* 2 November 1981.

[29] Relying on data from the World Bank, the USAID report continued: "If, for example, real manufacturing value-added continues to grow at 12 [%] per year as it has, the World Bank estimates that 117,000 jobs will be created each year, the equivalent of only 6% of the annual increase in the Indonesian labor force of about two million people. The BKPM has made a similar estimate, based on investment approvals. At the end of ten years, industrial growth could employ about 12% of new entrants. This is a hopelessly inadequate contribution from industry." USAID 1982:44.

[30] After summarizing the various categories, priorities, objectives, and procedures for complying with the government's ever more comprehensive Investment Priority List (DSP), one observer noted that in the final analysis it was individual officials who would decide— "on an individual basis at the time an application for approval to conduct business in Indonesia is made"—which incentives firms would receive, if any. Brasier 1981:3.

resources according to their priorities but still, as it were, "get the prices right" so that the private sector could flourish. "The issue is not one of diverting public funds from large to small firms though that may be desirable in some areas, but of directing prices and regulations so that private sector investment can help balance the structure of Indonesia's industry, improve its overall competitiveness and thereby increase its job creating potential. Market environment is the issue."[31] One passage several pages later seemed to hint that perhaps all the often-cited ironies everyone finds in Indonesian policies—that they frequently accomplish almost the exact opposite of their stated purpose—were neither ironic nor mysterious.[32] "Investors voice frequent complaints about the constraints to private investment in Indonesia," said the USAID report, and yet "many of these 'constraints' reflect either explicit public purpose or are the long term consequence of public policy." Underscoring just how much ground had been lost since the days of market-oriented policies in the late 1960s, USAID argued that "the (now older) New Order government plays a much larger role in ensuring domestic stability, in allocating resources, and in the redistribution of income than did the Sukarno government (or the New Order government itself in its early years)."[33] Backing away from so politically sensitive an assessment, however, the USAID analysts retreated into the safety of arguments based on state weaknesses and competing ideologies, suggesting that "this litany of 'constraints'" is "a definition both of underdevelopment and of weak institutional capability and also of the government's economic philosophy."[34] Putting USAID's assessment another way, if Indonesia were simply more developed, if its institutions were more capable, and if the country's guiding philosophy were the right one, officials would not

[31] USAID 1982:45. At least the last sentence is rooted in reality. During their visit to Indonesia in late 1981, as Team 10 was growing stronger, USAID's consultants found a decidedly unresponsive attitude toward mobile capital prevailing. "The government expects investors to adjust to its restructuring goals or to leave," the report grimly noted.

[32] "There is an increased awareness in some circles that the national pricing and regulatory structure is not pulling in a labor-using direction. Behind the tensions of this economy lie the irony of huge profits in a few extractive and consumer sectors and a far from optimal level of processing and manufacturing activity, *a level consequent to the government's struggle to reshape opportunity.*" USAID 1982:29; my emphasis.

[33] USAID 1982:47.

[34] USAID 1982:56. Such pseudoanalysis surfaces again when we are told elsewhere that the Indonesian government "finds a laissez faire attitude to social and economic change unpalatable."

have submitted every conceivable aspect of the country's economy to their political control.

Only in passing did the USAID report touch on the most important reason behind the ineffectiveness of the pressures and restrictions coming from private investors and institutional capital controllers like the World Bank. Noting a clear "reduction in their [the Indonesians'] willingness to yield to western influence," the report added that "the test of competition, domestic or foreign, will not be given ample scope to guide efficiency and, thereby, industrial adjustment to new opportunities." The people at USAID were at a complete loss for how to deal effectively with the Indonesians toward the end of the oil boom. The report turned in circles as even the idea of upgrading officials in key places like BKPM (perpetuating the naive notion that they were behaving as they were because they were backward or unprofessional) was rejected for fear that, in present circumstances anyway, officials with better skills would only exercise official discretion more effectively. At one point the report said in horror, "The BKPM had plans to establish a DSP licensing system for all BRO firms which would have meant regulation by type and location for all firms as small as ten to twenty employees. Despite the government's having backed off of this degree of regulation, this proposal is symptomatic of the government's philosophy towards the market."[35] Twenty or so pages later, in a section exploring possible ways for USAID to have the influence it wanted in Indonesia, the matter of offering consultants and training to BKPM to "strengthen the BKPM's investment analyses and therein to identify opportunities for U.S. companies" was followed by this caution: "There are risks here, however. BKPM may use an improved analytical capacity to implement its plans to extend industrial regulations and licensing to small firms as described earlier. Should this be the case, AID support for BKPM might be inappropriate." To say the least. Referring specifically to the role the state's own replacement resources played in weakening the leverage of all actors—inside and outside the Indonesian state—who were pushing for market-oriented policies, the report admitted that "the government has the domestic resources to support inefficient and uncompetitive industries [and] firms, for now." Unaware that an oil bust would begin to take shape not long after their report was published, the USAID analysts were

---

[35] USAID 1982:50–51. BRO firms are those incorporated (mostly by domestic investors) without going through BKPM—meaning investors forgo any incentives such as tax holidays and import duty drawbacks.

pessimistic. They concluded, "There is little prospect for significant economic liberalization in the post [1982–83] election period."[36]

The rest of this chapter focuses on the effect the decline in oil windfalls had on the leverage of different actors, as well as on the direction of Indonesian policy as the country entered the 1980s. In presenting an interpretive account of the efforts of the economic ministers to restore the competitiveness of their country's investment climate, I will use the fate of Team 10 and the controversies surrounding tax reform to illustrate the ways power relations changed in the wake of the state's diminishing access to replacement investment resources. To give readers a sense of the broader sweep of Indonesia's "era of deregulation," however, I first offer an overview of the main policy initiatives.

Deregulasi

Once the price of oil began to slip, the economic ministers wasted no time in presenting to President Suharto their case that the windfall oil profits the country had been enjoying would not last, and that particularly in light of the country's heavy debt-servicing burden, it was critical to improve the competitiveness of the country's investment climate so that investment rates in all sectors, but especially for nonoil exports, could be boosted and potential political problems arising from investment and production shortfalls could be deflected. To repeat the observations of a USAID economist who both watched and participated as the economic ministers pulled the country into its "era of deregulation," "The reforms have come from a few minds, accomplished by horror-story analysis presented to non-economists."[37] Unlike his response during the oil boom period, however, Suharto proved to be much more attentive to the investment processes and political consequences the economic ministers laid out before him.

In a truly ironic twist, the blueprint for the country's return to market-based policies was none other than the World Bank report that had been so thoroughly rejected only two years before. When asked if the decline in oil prices after 1982 marked a change in the way the bank and its policy prescriptions were received among Indonesia's officials, a senior member of the bank's Jakarta mission said, "That's definitely the case.

---

[36] USAID 1982:25–26.
[37] Discussion with Stephen Parker of USAID, 7 September 1989.

When the bottom fell out of the oil market, many people in the World Bank said, 'Ah, finally, some sanity again. Now we can get some policies in place!'"[38]

Only a brief sketch of the concrete steps taken to restore the country's competitiveness will be presented here.[39] A deeper analysis of the power dynamics involved, however, is given in the case material presented below. Key initiatives include the following:

Financial reform (1983). This major banking "deregulation" was intended to mobilize much larger pools of private capital. Greater competition in banking (e.g., in setting interest rates) was introduced.

Tax reform (1984). Discussed in much greater detail below, this package of policies streamlined tax collection procedures (reducing opportunities for predation by tax collectors), simplified the tax structure, and introduced self-assessment. Tax holidays for investors were eliminated in exchange for an overall reduction in tax rates.

Tariff rebate for exporters (1985). Tariffs paid on imported inputs into products that were subsequently exported would be completely refunded.

Customs service replaced (1985). The Indonesian government's own hopelessly corrupt customs officials were replaced by the private Swiss firm SGS, which was contracted to oversee all imports valued at more than $5,000. Customs officials would no longer inspect exported goods unless requested to do so in writing by the (new) director general of customs.

Trade and investment reform (1986). A further loosening of restriction and tariffs on those who import inputs for the goods they export. This package greatly insulated exporters from the high costs of domestic production. The package also included "several modifications of the regulatory framework governing foreign investment designed to make Indonesia more attractive to investors."[40] These modifications include a relaxation of the DSP; a lowering of the minimum foreign investment to below the old $1 million floor; expanded ability to reinvest in one's own or any other venture without having to get officials' approval first; an easing of joint-venture requirements; revisions of the thirty-year limit on foreign investment licenses; a reclassification of which companies are foreign and domestic and thus which ones qualify for special domestic incentives.

Trade reform (1986). Reduced licensing restrictions on 329 categories of imports; lowered duties on hundreds of product groups.

[38] Confidential interview in Jakarta at the World Bank, 14 June 1989.
[39] For a fuller description, see Shinn 1989.
[40] Ministry of Finance 1989:7.

Trade reform (1987). Further reduction of import restrictions on 548 items accounting for 37 percent of all items and 60 percent of total import value previously restricted. Tariffs were also reduced.

Trade and investment reform (1987). Further relaxation of import and export restrictions; extensive adjustments in tariff rates; time requirements on equity transfer to domestic joint-venture partners relaxed; wider opportunities for near-total foreign ownership; more access to subsidized state bank credit for joint ventures whose majority partner is Indonesian; capital markets invigorated to mobilize more private resources.

Financial, monetary, and banking reform (1988). Wider opportunities for foreign and domestic banks (and nonbanks) to open branch offices around the archipelago; better mechanisms for swap and money market activities; requirements that state companies deposit their resources only in state banks relaxed.

Trade, industry, agriculture, and sea communication reform (1988). Still further easing of restrictions on imports, especially in agriculture, and reductions of tariffs; shipping "deregulated."

Capital market and financial reform (1988). Private stock exchange established; stock exchanges opened in various cities; insurance "deregulation."

Financial, monetary, and banking reform (1989). Follow-up to the 1988 package. Eased laws on bank mergers; legal lending limits increased; opened possibilities for banks to enter rural areas.

It is abundantly clear even from this schematic presentation of Indonesia's "deregulation" packages that the economic ministers began to exercise far more influence over the direction of policy once the structural pressures to create and maintain a more competitive investment and production environment became more palpable. Although far too powerful to be undone in a single blow, Team 10 was also affected by having a shrinking oil surplus to allocate and by pressures from the economic ministers to shut down one of the country's most concentrated centers of patrimonial, antimarket influence.

The Demise of Team 10

Criticism of Team 10 and its role in blocking higher rates of investment in the private sector became loud beginning in 1984.[41] By that time no one, least of all President Suharto, believed the oil market would

[41] See *Kompas,* 21 July 1984, 1.

bounce back. Partly to do damage to Team 10's legitimizing propaganda, and partly to reassure ethnic Chinese investors whose capital policymakers wanted to see invested at increasing rates, the head of the armed forces announced in March 1984 that it was no longer acceptable for public officials to make racist references to *pribumi* and non-*pribumi* Indonesians.[42] Rather than refer to nationality or race, references would instead be based on market dominance and size—hence "economically weak" groups and "conglomerates." By the early 1980s, some conglomerates were owned by Indonesians that were not ethnic Chinese.

The year 1986 was crucial for Team 10. The pressures on Indonesian policymakers intensified considerably as the price of oil plunged to levels not seen since the early 1980s. The last significant expansion of Team 10's power occurred in 1985. In 1986, by contrast, events were moving in the opposite direction. That year restrictions imposed by Team 10 were eased for importing equipment to be used in all projects funded by foreign credit.[43] The following year Team 10 lost considerable control over the oil and gas sector when the government decided to allow foreign oil operators that had not yet discovered hydrocarbons in Indonesia to make equipment purchases without the team's prior approval.[44] New entrants had been particularly vulnerable to Team 10 manipulation. By the time the final blow came—on 1 April 1988, at the hands of the then vastly more influential economic ministers—President Suharto had, in a manner reminiscent of his treatment of Ibnu Sutowo, clearly pulled back his support for the Sudharmono-Ginanjar operation he had helped launch in 1979, and from which he had gained considerable personal and political benefit.[45] The economists met at the Ministry of Finance,

---

[42] Awanohara 1984:26–27. Recall that there was considerable antagonism between the armed forces and SEKNEG. The SEKNEG–Team 10–GOLKAR axis cut many military figures out of state resources and challenged their hegemony over the country's politics. Sudharmono, who was a military man but was a lawyer rather than a soldier, was hated by the leaders of the armed forces. The announcement on acceptable terminology also struck at Ginanjar Kartasasmita, junior minister for the promotion of domestic production, who made frequent references to *pribumi* interests in his capacity as a junior minister and as a leading figure in Team 10—a body that attracted public support by claiming to help *pribumi*.

[43] U.S. Department of Commerce 1986:18.

[44] *Platt's Oilgram News* 65, (30 September 1987): 2.

[45] Presidential Decree 6 of 1988 (dated 28 March) was announced to revoke various laws and regulations pertaining to government procurement, including those establishing and empowering Team 10. Presidential Instruction 1 of 1988 (also dated 28 March) was the replacement legislation. See *Kompas,* 31 March 1988, 1.

signifying the decisive shift of power over government procurement away from SEKNEG (where Team 10's formation was announced), and formulated the laws that replaced Team 10's system. Underscoring the fundamental change from a centralized-patronage system back to a scattered-market system, the *team* of officials micromanaging all government purchases (and by extension, a significant share of the Indonesian economy) was supplanted by a set of impersonal procurement *guidelines* that the separate ministries, departments, and state firms would be required to follow in awarding contracts.[46] Abolition of the team had been "expected for some time," according to one business publication, but it took until 1988 because the president himself was deeply involved in the entire operation.[47] Said an officer in the armed forces faction of parliament, "It was a real scam, and we had to work hard to close it down."

In the final cadences of a mostly self-serving final report for Team 10, Sudharmono was careful to thank and to share blame with President Suharto for all that the team was and did. He was grateful to the president, "who gave his leadership and guidance whenever it was needed— so much so that the Team was able to work with calm, smoothness, and filled with a full sense of responsibility as it made each and every decision."[48] The last two sentences of Sudharmono's report contain a typically unconvincing "apology" to the rest of the government and the private sector for any mistakes that were made and repeat that everything the team did was in the service of the nation and, through the president, an expression of the will of the people. Team 10 was an important source of money for the president's "*Bantuan Presiden*" (BANPRES), his personal slush fund for various projects. Unlike INPRES (*Instruksi Presiden*) spending, which goes through various govern-

---

[46] Presidential Decree 1 of 1988 established the following decision-making hierarchy for government procurements. Contracts worth Rp 500 million or less would be awarded by an office head or a project leader. Contracts worth between Rp 500 million (Team 10's former threshold) and Rp 1 billion would be awarded by a director general or an official of equivalent rank. Contracts worth between Rp 1 billion and Rp 3 billion would be under the control of ministers or officials of equivalent rank. Those over Rp 3 billion could be awarded by a minister or an official of equivalent rank, though the coordinating minister for economic, financial, and industrial affairs and development supervision (the *menko ekuin*, as he is called) reserved the right to review procurements of this magnitude. See Nelson 1988:20.

[47] Boatman 1988:6.

[48] Sekretariat Negara 1988:52.

ment agencies like BAPPENAS and the Ministry of Finance, BANPRES
money is spent by the president himself as he pleases. The SEKNEG
money was used for this, and that is why it lasted as long as it did.[49]

Background on Indonesian Taxation

In response to a series of questions probing the early years of revenue
collection under Suharto, a retired official from Indonesia's Central
Bank recounted an experience he had in 1967. A mission from the World
Bank, saying it wanted to meet only with the leaders at the very top,
came to Jakarta in search of some basic information about the government's fiscal condition. Partly to impress and partly to buttress their own
confidence, the Indonesians packed a conference room to overflowing
with what they told the World Bank representatives were top officials
and experts from the Central Bank. As it turned out, both parties left the
meeting somewhat bewildered, though for quite different reasons. According to my respondent, the World Bank mission was shocked to see
how many leaders Indonesia had at the very top, while the Indonesians
were astonished to discover that they had rallied a small army of officials
to answer just two simple questions. "The first was 'How many people
in Indonesia pay taxes?' We answered, between ten and twenty thousand. They then asked if our national budget is approved by parliament.
We responded, 'What budget?' "[50] The story was an entertaining way of
saying that the New Order state, as we saw in the chapter on the preboom period, started out in fiscal terms from virtually nothing.

The Balanced Budget Law of 1968 solved one of these problems,[51] but
more than a decade into the tax reform era, the taxpayer registry remained astonishingly small. And the efficient collection of revenues from
those who are registered (80 percent of all taxpayers on the rolls are
concentrated on Java) continues to elude the Ministry of Finance, which
oversees the Directorate General for Taxes. Revenues from agriculture,
the sector employing the largest number of people in the country, and

[49] Confidential interview in Jakarta with a middle-level officer in the armed forces
faction of Parliament, 18 September 1989.
[50] Interview in Jakarta with J. A. Sereh, 6 February 1989. From 1970 to 1976, Sereh
was one of six managing directors that served under the governor of the Central Bank.
[51] The 1968 law, described briefly in the previous chapter, ensured that government
deficits could be only as big as the annual injection of foreign borrowing.

taxes on land contribute a very small share of total receipts—even if individual smallholding farmers find the chunk taken from them each year onerous.[52]

At times to an extraordinary degree, the state in Indonesia has been fiscally insulated from the broader population.[53] With respect to the ordinary citizen, this insulation has allowed the state to remain aloof. It has asked for very little over the years, and one avenue through which citizens might demand more from the state with some legitimacy and punch (through tax evasion and tax strikes) has been completely absent. Not surprisingly, there are signs that this is beginning to change as the state, through the 1984 tax reform, is digging ever deeper into domestic pockets. The Indonesian parliament, for instance, has always approved the president's budget without amendments or changes of any kind. And so it went with the 1989–1990 budget. But this time around the approval was accompanied by some unusual critical commentary from some unusual sources. The GOLKAR faction in parliament (Suharto's own party) and the ABRI faction, which has supported the president since he came to power, cautioned that "the government's all-out tax campaign should also be offset with improved services to taxpayers." They added that "the people should also be informed about how the tax receipts are spent."[54] Although this is still a long way from suggesting that the people should have a say in deciding, even in a general way, how their tax receipts are spent, it is nevertheless a basis of accountability that had not existed previously. As an editorial that same day bluntly stated: "The political repercussions of budgetary wastage and losses are much graver now than those in the 1970s when most of the government revenues were derived from oil and natural gas and not from the people's pockets."[55]

[52] The value-added tax introduced in April 1985 places an especially heavy burden on farmers, since the 10 percent VAT applies to a number of farm inputs (particularly fertilizers) but does not apply to the farmers' produce (with the result that farmers pay taxes on more than just the value they add).

[53] According to Anderson (1983:479), this is hardly new. Stressing how much of what we notice in the structure and operation of the modern Indonesian state is in fact inherited and adapted from colonial times, he points out that the Dutch colonial state's finances came "largely from its own monopolistic operations and an efficient exploitation of local human and natural resources." For an indication of major sources of revenue for the years covered in this book, see figure 4.

[54] *Jakarta Post*, 1 March 1989, 1.

[55] *Jakarta Post*, editorial, 1 March 1989, 4. Though the point is well taken, the editor

To argue that the Indonesian state has been fiscally insulated does not imply that the revenues it does collect, even from "itself," have been pulled in without a struggle. By far the biggest problem for the Indonesian state (or parts of it, anyway) over the years has been prying resources out of Pertamina's hands and getting them deposited in the state treasury. From the earliest days of the New Order, it was extremely difficult to bring what were legally state funds under the control of the Ministry of Finance and the Central Bank. To the suggestion that a tug-of-war over this issue was taking place between Pertamina and the economic ministries and departments, J. B. Sumarlin (formerly the minister of finance) replied: "I don't know if 'tug-of-war' is quite the right way to put it, but let's say there was another pool of ideas about how to run the country. The people in Pertamina played a direct role in collecting oil revenues, and they had their own ideas about spending it. The basic problem was that the Pertamina chief [Ibnu Sutowo] could use the funds without first turning them over to the treasury. This was our biggest source of trouble. They spent the money on all kinds of things having nothing to do with the oil industry, like a steel mill, hotels, and so on."[56]

Even today Finance's ability to extract the state's revenues from Pertamina is more tenuous than many realize. A well-positioned official in Finance explained the problem this way: "In theory, Pertamina is supposed to be an arm of the government that handles the oil and gas sector on behalf of the government. But in reality it doesn't quite work that way. There is a single person in the Ministry of Finance, the director general for oil receipts and taxes, who has direct contact with Pertamina. No one else can say for sure what is going on there. Pertamina has two basic sources of money: its own oil operations, which are very small, and the money that flows in from production-sharing agreements with oil companies. Usually Pertamina receives its share in cash, though when the price of oil is very high the company likes to be paid in barrels so it can market the oil itself. From Indonesia's total oil production, first the oil companies deduct a share to cover their costs. Of the remaining amount, Pertamina gets 85 percent and the companies get 15 percent (though there are some old contracts with slightly different terms). Then

---

has exaggerated for effect. Although data do not permit an accurate estimate of the share of total government receipts coming from "the people," it is certainly no more than one-fifth. Still, this is a huge increase compared with the oil boom years and before.

[56] Interview in Jakarta with J. B. Sumarlin, 5 July 1989.

Pertamina is supposed to deduct its operating costs, which are small, and in theory the rest is supposed to be turned over to the treasury. What actually happens is another story. The only source of information we in the Ministry of Finance have about Pertamina's receipts comes from Pertamina itself. There are so many different kinds of contracts, and the whole thing is such a tangled mess, that a thick book of materials exists just to get a rough estimate of Pertamina's revenues. The director general for oil receipts and taxes handles all this for the Ministry of Finance. All we can do is try to do our own analysis to see if Pertamina's claims for costs are accurate. Once, we received their estimated costs and did some analysis of them. We concluded, conservatively, that they were inflated by 30 percent. So we went to [a very powerful official in the Ministry of Finance] and showed him, and he took it to the minister. A letter was drafted and presented to Pertamina through the director general. And then the negotiations began. Apart from this, we're limited. There is the possibility of analyzing Pertamina's oil export claims against oil import claims of purchasing countries. We only export to about ten countries, so it's not too hard. I once did some thumbnail calculations and, indeed, the official data on total imports from client countries came to a lot more barrels than Pertamina claimed to us it sold abroad."[57]

Pertamina, even among state enterprises, is a special and complicated case. Other businesses and individuals pay taxes in a relatively more transparent and orderly fashion, especially since more simplified procedures were introduced in 1984. The method of payment for all taxpayers, corporate or individual, is essentially the same. The money itself is handed over to one of the many Government Treasury Offices (KPN) scattered around the country. These, in turn, deposit the money at Bank Indonesia. Taxpayers take their KPN receipts to a tax office, and they are tallied by the Directorate General for Taxes. The figures produced by the directorate can lag three or four months behind actual collections, which is much too long for a state to wait—particularly one with the levels of deficit financing typical in Indonesia. With the advent of computerization, the Ministry of Finance and the Central Bank can monitor aggregate state finances daily because the many KPNs around the country

[57] Confidential interview in Jakarta with an official at the Ministry of Finance, 15 November 1989. According to another observer, "Singapore does not publish trade statistics with Indonesia because of expected discrepancies between Singapore and Indonesian figures, caused by the volume of smuggling between the two states." Davies 1983:7.

count their receipts and close their books every day, much like a commercial bank. The information is passed on to the Directorate General for Budgeting in the Ministry of Finance using fax machines, modems, and telexes.

Tax Reform: The Internal Battle

Loyal critics of the government argue that the oil boom years represented a lost opportunity to implement difficult changes at a time when they could be cushioned by windfall oil revenues. According to a respected economist at the University of Indonesia who often consults for the government, the hard choices on taxes were postponed: "From 1974 to 1982 the ministers were proud of the fact that the SARA [domestic receipts minus routine expenditures] were so high that not enough ways could be found to spend it all. During this period there was no effort made at all to raise government revenues outside of the oil and gas sectors. When the oil market collapsed, suddenly the government was trying to raise revenues everywhere."[58] The problem, as we have seen, was that the policy recommendations of the economic ministers were ignored or blocked during periods when the structural power of capital controllers was weak or when economic crises were absent.

Although many in the government acted as if they believed the oil bonanza would go on indefinitely, it appears that not everyone shared this view. Ali Wardhana, reputed to be one of the longest-serving ministers of finance in recent world history, began planning for the end of the boom at least as early as 1979. Said one Finance official who participated from the start, "We had all the big names working on our tax reform policies: Dew, Musgrave, and so on. We had about thirty [foreign] professors in all on the team."[59] If preparations for tax reform

[58] Interview in Jakarta with Mohammad Arsjad Anwar, dean of the economics faculty, University of Indonesia, 24 August 1989. This criticism was echoed by a high government official then at the center of the tax effort. "During the oil boom we made no serious effort to collect taxes." Interview in Jakarta with Hamonangan Hutabarat, of the Research and Development Center, Ministry of Finance, 2 November 1989.

[59] Confidential interview in Jakarta with an official at the Ministry of Finance, 11 July 1989. At first only a handful of Indonesians took part. "The problem was," the official continued, "not many people could follow the discussions. The minister of finance [Wardhana] decided we needed more capable staff. About twenty or thirty people were sent abroad in the late 1970s and early 1980s in preparation for the tax reform package put forth after the end of the oil boom. Now we have more than one hundred M.A.'s and

were begun during the oil boom, putting the policies in place would have to wait until structural factors were more favorable to the economic ministers. As Sumarlin explained, "We were already at work on the tax reform package five years before 1984. We just had to wait for the right time to push it into place. I'm not saying that no tax reform would have been attempted without the collapse of the oil market. But there's no doubt that the collapse made our job of switching to the collection of revenues from sources other than oil much easier. The new tax system ended up being our savior in 1986. It dampened the effect of the revenue crisis caused by the fall in oil prices."[60]

Because tax reform entailed restructuring the procedures and channels of revenue collection, it encountered strong resistance throughout the state apparatus. Officials directly involved in collecting taxes, for instance, were especially unenthusiastic about any changes that would undermine their capacity to siphon off public resources for their own patrimonial and personal uses. Once again, as an economist at USAID explained, timing was crucial.

> The problem has been to grab the opportunities for putting the changes into place. There have been key crisis points where it has been possible to push changes through. Tax reform is a good example. Since the end of the 1970s, Ali [Wardhana] has worked on this. In fact, Malcolm Gillis [an American consultant to the Indonesian government for more than twenty years] was pushing it since before then. But the Tax Office, and all the vested interests associated with it, fought him tooth and nail. Only with the financial collapse of the government sector in 1983 was he finally able to gain some ground.[61]

Because of the tangle of rules and regulations, and because there existed no workable framework for internal oversight and auditing, the opportunities for individual discretion, and of course the skimming of resources that tends to accompany such power, were widespread in the tax offices. One tax reformer's observations sum up the situation nicely:

> As Indonesia entered the early 1980s, the tax system was a complete mess. We had a dense forest of overlapping regulations that no one really under-

---

Ph.D.'s, mostly educated in the U.S."

[60] Interview in Jakarta with J. B. Sumarlin, 5 July 1989. The large increases in indirect tax receipts after 1985 occurred mainly because the VAT was applied to petroleum and tobacco products.

[61] Interview in Bukittinggi with Stephen Parker of USAID in Jakarta, 29 June 1989.

stood. It could take years to figure out which laws were in effect and which ones had been superseded. This put businessmen and individual taxpayers at the mercy of tax officials. You could never feel confident that you had fulfilled all the requirements because if someone wanted to cause trouble for you, he could always find a rule or regulation you had not followed. The result was that businessmen needed to develop personal links with individual officials to ensure that all went well. And since all the laws were open to widely varying interpretation, it was a good idea to focus on a single individual and develop the relationship over a long period of time. There was no other way to be safe. Of course, you had to pay a lot to this person to be certain he'd take good care of you.[62]

Useful as this explanation may be, it is flawed insofar as it places the entire blame on the tax collectors. This was hardly the case. Taxpayers, particularly in the corporate world, were quite willing to negotiate with tax collectors so they could keep a larger share of their profits. According to a top Ministry of Finance official, "We're not meeting our tax revenue targets because business doesn't want to pay and the collecting administration is corrupt. If the tax assessment is 100 million rupiah, for instance, the tax officer cuts it back to 50 million and takes an additional 10 for himself. The total is still reduced by 40 percent, which is substantial, and both sides are happy."[63]

At a certain level, then, tax reform was a technical matter of changes in modes of revenue collection from private taxpayers, both corporate and individual. The nexus between state and taxpayer needed to be changed. This was achieved through simplification and depersonalization. "What we did with the tax overhaul," explained one of the main tax reformers, "was to abolish, in a single stroke, the whole tangle of regulations that made personalized service necessary. Now we have just three taxes: an income tax, with clear tax brackets, a value-added tax, and a land and building tax. The exemptions and depreciation schedules are easy to understand."[64] Computers also helped.

[62] Interview in Jakarta with Hutabarat, 2 November 1989. Underscoring the challenge to the system of patronage contained in the economists' tax reform package, he added, "The strongest resistance to tax reform, as it turns out, came from the tax officials themselves. They had the most to lose from the depersonalization and simplification of the system. It was the same with customs. Before we could go ahead with tax deregulation, we had to replace the director general of taxes. Without this move, we could achieve nothing."

[63] Confidential interview in Jakarta, 29 August 1989.

[64] Interview in Jakarta with Hutabarat, 2 November 1989.

We introduced the computerized registration of taxpayers. In 1982, we began reregistering all companies in Indonesia. Upon registration, we key in all the data on the firm and issue a single taxpayer ID number. Previously, firms could have three or four such numbers, and it made tracking their activity very difficult. Before this new law, we had ten different kinds of taxes. Now we have just three. The most important result of these changes is that there is now no need for taxpayers, business or individuals, to have a lot of personal contact with tax officials. Forms are submitted and entered into the computer, and the required taxes are paid. We work on the self-assessment system. We leave it up to firms to report their earnings. But we have the software to cross-check the returns for a grouping of firms. This allows us to spot irregularities that we can target for audit.[65]

The tax collectors were effectively bypassed. When things go properly, tax returns are submitted, checked for completeness, stamped, and passed on to data entry personnel who know little or nothing about tax assessment. Taxpayers, in theory, should no longer have the opportunity (or misfortune, as the case may be) to sit face-to-face with collectors.[66]

Stephen Parker took the point one step further in noting that policy changes like tax reform are difficult to push through from above. "Getting the policy changes in place is one thing," he pointed out, "but getting them implemented is another entirely. A decision maker with a crew of advisers can write up a decree. But what about having the staff on hand who can—or is even willing to—carry out what you want? A good example is tax reform. The people on top pushed through the changes. But what about all the thousands of people who daily go about the business of bringing in the revenues? They weren't consulted and didn't like the changes at all. You can't bring SGS in to do your revenue collection as well. That's why macropolicy is so far ahead of micro. Ali Wardhana could do a devaluation all by himself. But the tax department has fought the Ministry of Finance."[67]

[65] Interview in Jakarta with Hutabarat, 2 November 1989.

[66] How far these changes have gone is hard to judge. What is clear is that the tax officials at all levels of government, the only civil servants in recent years to receive significant wage increases, resent having to adjust to much simpler lifestyles.

[67] SGS is the Swiss-based Société Générale de Surveillance hired by the government in April 1985 to take over the job of inspecting goods imported into Indonesia. The state's own customs branch was impossibly corrupt. Not only were these government duties shifted to a foreign private firm, but the actual work was shifted abroad to provide maximum insulation. SGS examines Indonesian imports at their port of origin and issues an LKP (report), which becomes the basis for assessing import duties and taxes. Interview in Bukittinggi with Stephen Parker of USAID in Jakarta, 29 June 1989.

Tax Reform and the Private Sector

It is impossible to provide an accurate count of all the individuals and institutions around the globe—from the Harvard Law School and Harvard Institute for International Development (HIID), to Erasmus University in the Netherlands, to the various ministries and consulting firms in Jakarta—that have played a role in designing this grand policy change for Indonesia. It would be even more difficult to estimate the number of studies and reports that were generated in the process. But it is certain that a great deal of time and effort was spent carefully assessing the effect of the tax changes on the calculus of private capital controllers. Specifically, the planners and decision makers were intensely concerned with how mobile investors would react. How did taxes rank among all the factors investors considered when choosing when and where to invest? Would investment levels flatten or sink if tax holidays were abolished? What were tax policies like in neighboring, competing states? Were they offering a better tax deal, and might new investors choose more "inviting" locales like Thailand, Malaysia, or Singapore that would allow them to keep a greater share of their surplus? In short, the policymakers were once again responding to the structural power of capital controllers to exercise full discretion over the resources Indonesia wanted and, the policymakers (including President Suharto) were convinced, needed to attract and retain.

It should be underscored that from the beginning of the oil bust there was a tension between the need to encourage higher investment rates from the private sector and the need to replace oil receipts by drawing a greater share of government revenues directly from these same investors. In his 1986 Independence Day address, and in the midst of the most catastrophic drop in oil prices Indonesia had yet endured, President Suharto stated the obvious: "We cannot rely on oil earnings alone, because this would create long-term uncertainties in our national development strategy."[68] The state-run engine of development and growth had run out of gas, and an effort was under way, according to the president, "to shift our reliance primarily to the nonoil/gas sector for our state and foreign exchange earnings." To keep both the state and the economy afloat, Suharto stressed his "continuing attempts to create a more attrac-

---

[68] "President of Indonesia Responds to Economic Challenges," PR Newswire, 15 August 1986. All of Suharto's comments in this paragraph are drawn from this article.

tive climate for foreign companies to participate in our development by investing their capital and by other forms of cooperation."

This tension was certainly manifested in the tax reform package. The challenge was to pull in sufficient revenues without pushing away investors who could, if they chose, invest in another country or simply withhold their resources and delay a new investment or expansion. The result was a tax package that in the long run was highly responsive to capital's interests and demands but in the short run—perhaps the only run that matters when crises loom—was decidedly antagonistic to private investors because tax incentives were being abolished.[69] The state's brief was that it was trading an admittedly unattractive disincentive to business for a far more attractive incentive—a streamlined, less corrupt tax regime with lower taxes overall.

It is striking, given the paltry sums the private sector in Indonesia has contributed to total revenues (never more than 5 percent in any given year), that it was this societal actor more than any other that commanded the attention of Indonesian policymakers and gave them pause as they wrote their tax reform laws. In fiscal terms, the state was almost as insulated from corporate taxpayers as it was from private citizens. The difference between the way makers of tax policy treated investors and every other social group—farmers, ordinary laborers, the urban intelligentsia—had to do with the simple fact that the investment function for the society was squarely in the hands of those privately controlling capital. Keenly aware of this, those considering major changes in the country's tax regime first had to study the logic and motives of investors. Based on responses to questionnaires, the factors relevant to investment decisions were ranked. The next step was to compare Indonesia's overall climate for investment—but particularly tax incentives—with the cli-

[69] The main tax incentives previously applicable to licensed projects included the following: (1) Tax holidays. Investors in priority industries qualified for a basic two-year exemption from corporate tax that could be extended for up to six years provided certain other requirements were met. (2) Dividend taxes. Shareholders receiving dividends were exempted from dividend tax for the period of the company's tax holiday as long as these dividends were exempted from tax in the shareholder's home country. (3) Investment allowances. An investment allowance was granted for second-priority ventures that might not qualify for full corporate tax exemptions. The allowance was a deduction from taxable profits of 20 percent of the amount invested spread over four years at 5 percent annually. (4) Carry-forward losses. Any losses incurred could be carried forward for four successive years. Losses incurred during the first six years after establishment of the company could be carried forward indefinitely. See Harink 1984:8.

mates in countries that compete with Indonesia for capital (such as Thailand, Malaysia, and the Philippines).[70] A Finance official who has been at the center of tax reform since the beginning articulated the conclusions of the government's studies best. Visibly agitated by my suggestion that Indonesia's decision to eliminate tax holidays had been risky, he began:

> Why do investors invest in Indonesia? There are basically three important reasons: natural resources, low labor costs for labor-intensive industries, and a sizable market. Now if investors can only get certain natural resources here, why should we give them incentives? The same goes for labor costs. Where are they going to go in ASEAN besides here for low labor costs? Bangladesh? Sri Lanka? The African countries? These are all very unstable places. What about Thailand? Well, first, wages there are high, and they cannot handle the investments they already have. The country's single port is overcrowded. It can take weeks to get a container to port, and then still more time to wait to get it loaded. Malaysia? They have a labor shortage. They have Indonesians coming in working on their plantations. The Philippines? They have political troubles, a small labor force, and higher wages than we do. They also don't have the natural resources. Indonesia, on the other hand, has lots of resources, a large market, and cheap labor. We have 2.5 million new high school graduates coming on line per year over the

[70] In an IMF-sponsored seminar assessing, among other things, Indonesia's tax reform, Dono Iskandar, a senior official at the Ministry of Finance, made the following comments: "The problem regarding tax holiday for investor can be debated intensively, but anyway when the government decided not to give any more tax holiday for new investments, especially for foreign investments, it was based on a study made by consultants on what are the factor affecting the investment decisions of foreign companies. The study was done in ASEAN, in Indonesia, and in several neighboring countries. They tried to find out what was actually the major factor affecting the decision. They find that tax holiday is about number 7 or 6, not the most important factor. In fact, the most important factor was the political stability and the other is less red tape and frequent changes of the regulations. For instance, the DSP (List of Priority) from BKPM, which changes frequently, almost every year, will create uncertainties to foreign investors. Other things being equal, of course the tax holiday will be useful also to promote further investment. But since this is not the major factor, then the government considered to create better investment climate first by streamlining the procedures, regulations, etc. This is more important or more attractive than the tax holiday itself. If you compare Indonesia with other Asian countries, such as Korea, Taiwan, and Malaysia, we have more restrictions and requirements imposed on foreign investment than those countries. For instance, they have to transfer to Indonesian side or partners in 15 years, whereas in Korea there is no limit, or at least 30 years. If you are the investor, you will think it is better to go to Korea than to Indonesia. And there are still many other examples and considerations." Bank Indonesia 1988. Note in particular here that the concern about tax holidays was focused on the most mobile of all companies to be affected by the new tax system.

next several years. They will keep the wage rate depressed in Indonesia for probably the next five to ten years. So what do we have to give extra incentives for? It's our competitors who face the pressure to make concessions to draw investors.[71]

Armed with these conclusions, based on studies carried out mainly by foreign consultants, the tax reformers based in the Ministry of Finance decided it would be prudent and safe to proceed with the highly controversial policy of cutting tax holidays.

Indonesia's parliament (the DPR), a body that has not exercised its powers of legislative initiative since Suharto came to power, expressed its concern over the negative impact of ending tax incentives. But as Finance Minister Sumarlin explained:

> We studied that tax holiday matter carefully. Although there were objections in the DPR, we were able to win because they could not refute our arguments. We made three basic points. First, the tax holidays were being abused. When a company's holiday was ending, it would set up a new company so it could continue the holiday. Second, since the taxes we proposed were on profits, companies that experienced losses for the first two or three years basically enjoyed a tax holiday anyway. And we had provisions to allow businesses to carry forward their losses. And third, with the reform of the system from fifty-eight different tax rates to just three, the overall rates for business were lower.[72]

Repeating the argument voiced by virtually every Indonesian official associated with tax reform, the minister said that the government had "surveyed the business community on taxes and found that tax holidays were not their prime consideration in choosing to invest [in Indonesia]. What was far more important were things like a stable environment, consistency of policies, a stable economy, a free exchange system. Confidence was the key."[73] One might counter the force of Sumarlin's argument by pointing out that the "prime considerations" he mentioned would have to be in place for *any* investment site to be considered seriously, and that in fact it is additional "sweeteners" like tax holidays that give a country a competitive edge in attracting investors. Several officials intimately involved with tax reform confirmed that several stud-

[71] Interview in Jakarta with Hutabarat, 2 November 1989.
[72] Interview in Jakarta with J. B. Sumarlin, 5 July 1989.
[73] Interview in Jakarta with J. B. Sumarlin, 5 July 1989.

ies were conducted by the Indonesian government (particularly through consultants with HIID) to ascertain the hierarchy of motives for investing in Indonesia. "Tax holidays were down around seventh or eighth," said a USAID economist, dismissing my suggestion that potential investors are lost when tax incentives are cut.[74]

Tax reform began on 1 January 1984. The initial reactions from business were mixed. According to one veteran reporter writing just after major parts of the tax reform package were announced, "The business community has given a warm welcome to the new tax system, particularly because the system it will replace is amazingly complex and cumbersome."[75] Put more bluntly, the changes greatly reduced the risks associated with confronting predatory tax collectors.[76] This was the good news. But the same reporter also sounded a note of caution on eliminating tax incentives: "There are fears that the abolition of tax holidays for projects, both domestic and foreign, licensed through the Capital Investment Coordinating Board (BKPM) will send potential investors scurrying to other countries in the region."[77]

By mid-1984, caution had given way to widespread alarm. The greatest concern was sparked when Suhartoyo, chairman of the Investment Coordinating Board, announced that there had not been a single new foreign investment approval during the first quarter of 1984.[78] During the same period in 1983, by contrast, eleven projects worth $1.2 billion had been approved. Domestic investments had also plunged, from forty-seven projects worth Rp 185 billion in the first quarter of 1983 to just seven worth Rp 22 billion for the same period in 1984. According to a reporter for the *Financial Times* of London, Suhartoyo "was one of those to blame the tax laws [for the country's investment problems]. He said that investors were adopting a wait-and-see attitude."[79]

[74] Interview in Bukittinggi with Stephen Parker, 29 June 1989.

[75] Astbury 1984:59.

[76] One of the officials in charge of tax reform at the Ministry of Finance explained: "Businessmen like the simplification of regulations, and they support the steps taken by the government. . . . What makes them happy is to know all the money is going into the treasury, and not into the pockets of officials." Interview in Jakarta with Hutabarat, 2 November 1989.

[77] Astbury 1984:59.

[78] Suhartoyo, like most other chairmen of BKPM before and after him, was not close to the economic ministers but was instead allied with powerful figures close to Suharto, such as Sudharmono and Ginanjar.

[79] Cooke 1984:7.

It was during this investment crisis that Sudharmono, Ginanjar, and others associated with Team 10 found themselves under fire for the first time since the team was established. The possibility that the team's restrictive role in all aspects of Indonesia's economy, but especially trade and investment, was responsible for the poor investment showing in the first quarter of 1984 was raised on the front page of Indonesia's most widely read newspaper, *Kompas*.[80] When reporters tracked down Sudharmono to ask if he knew why investment levels had dropped so low, he could only say, "Once we've learned the reasons, steps must be taken to push so that investment levels in this country can be increased again."[81]

Ginanjar, trying to deflect reporters' attention away from SEKNEG and its activities, claimed that "the decline in investments in Indonesia was not because of domestic factors, but rather was global in character."[82] *Kompas* added, however, that this was little more than Ginanjar's opinion and that he lacked data and analysis to support his views. More surprising still, the article went on to quote Priasmoro Prawiroardjo, managing director of PT Indoconsult (a tool of the economic ministers, especially Widjoyo and Wardhana), who directly contradicted Ginanjar by saying that the drop in investment levels certainly was caused by domestic factors.[83] The most direct attack on SEKNEG and Team 10 was delivered by Mohammad Sadli. Seizing the opportunity of an alarming downturn in private investment to apply direct public pressure to the economic ministers' opponents, Sadli joined others in contradicting Ginanjar's attempt to shift the blame abroad. The *Kompas* article reported that, "according to Prof. Sadli, the interest on behalf of both foreign and domestic investors is still quite great. But it is blocked by 'pebbles' [*kerikil-kerikil*] which appear small, but are in fact major obstacles. And it is precisely on the domestic front that these pebbles are thrown in investors' way."[84] There can be little doubt that Sadli's refer-

[80] *Kompas,* 21 July 1984, 1.

[81] *Kompas,* 21 July 1984, 1.

[82] *Kompas,* 21 July 1984:1. In his *Financial Times* statement, Suhartoyo may also have tried intentionally to direct the focus of investors and others toward the tax issue and away from the operation being run by his powerful patrons at SEKNEG.

[83] Perhaps to soften his challenge to Team 10's powerful officials, he directed his subsequent comments to the issues surrounding the new tax reform, arguing that a five-year transition period should be used to reduce the outrage and shock at having tax holidays removed. *Kompas,* 21 July 1984, 1.

[84] *Kompas,* 21 July 1984, 1.

ence to pebbles was a metaphor for the various controls that Team 10 was exerting over procurement, investment, and trade.

The *Kompas* article appears to have provided investors, all of whom were *pribumi*, with a rare chance to express openly a number of issues concerning the business climate in Indonesia that had long frustrated them. Tanri Abeng, head of the Indonesian Management Association and president of a joint-venture company, supplied several observations. Covering the entire spectrum of investors' concerns and possible explanations for sluggish investment figures in Indonesia, Abeng began with the issue of the country's competitiveness with other states as an investment site: "The attractiveness of Indonesia for foreign investors is no longer as strong as it used to be. The government's schemes and facilities offered are no longer appropriate for today. And even more so if they are cut back. Competition with neighboring countries to attract foreign capital is getting worse."[85] With Indonesia's responsiveness to investors at a low, said Abeng, "the time has come for the government to reassess various policies in its effort to attract foreign capital. . . . If necessary, research comparing the various incentives offered by other developing countries trying to attract capital should be conducted. Incentives currently being offered by Indonesia are not that attractive when compared to those offered in neighboring countries." Addressing the options mobile investors faced, Abeng added: "If they find Indonesia's incentives lacking, they'll pack up and move to another country."

Abeng said that the elimination of tax holidays was only one of several obstacles to investment, and probably not the greatest, since with overall lower rates and higher depreciation, firms were better off. Without specifically mentioning Team 10 and BKPM, he stressed that "the thing which really obstructs investment is the convoluted and time-wasting bureaucratic system to get permission to invest. Even with improvements that have been made, Indonesia still cannot compete with neighboring states." Abeng rounded off his critique by saying that the government's frequent flip-flops on policy were on balance a disincentive,[86]

[85] This quotation and all other comments made by Tanri Abeng below are from *Kompas*, 21 July 1984, 1.

[86] Drawing on Abeng's analysis, the *Kompas* reporter wrote: "Actually, Indonesian officials are enormously pragmatic—meaning they are willing to amend or replace a policy if business judges it mistaken. But this pragmatic approach is not an attractive feature as only a limited number of entrepreneurs are able to engage officials in dialogue." Quoting Abeng directly: "Every government policy should be thought out more fully so that it can

that the country's political stability was not a major draw for investors because there was no sign that major political upheavals were imminent in any of the states competing with Indonesia for capital, and that the country's cheap labor was a mixed blessing because depressed wages translate directly into a weak market for consumer goods. "No matter how vigorously BKPM tries to sell the idea of investing in Indonesia," Abeng said, summing up his position, "it will be a waste of time and effort so long as the incentives here do not balance those offered elsewhere."

Returning to the events surrounding the investment crisis, although efforts were made to play down its impact, it remained, in one business reporter's view, "nevertheless embarrassing, especially as Indonesian missions are visiting numerous foreign capitals to woo investors and so much is pinned on the new five-year plan introduced earlier this year."[87] By October 1984 the situation had not improved much. The *Financial Times* reported that the Indonesian government was "clearly anxious to reverse this sharp decline."[88] Suhartoyo, whose position as head of the Investment Coordinating Board was now seriously in jeopardy, was quoted as saying, "I am extremely worried about the slowdown. Our combined foreign and domestic investment target for 1984 approvals is $8bn, but by the end of September we had only managed to achieve $2bn." J. B. Sumarlin, then minister for national development, was steady in his faith (publicly anyway) that all the high-priced studies and analyses done under the aegis of the Ministry of Finance had provided accurate assessments of investors' preferences and likely responses. Clinging to the view that the long-term benefits of the tax package would eventually overshadow the current tempest over tax holidays, he said he "did not expect the adverse impact of the tax reforms to continue."

In what may have been a ploy to buy precious time, Sutanto, director general for taxes in the Ministry of Finance, told a meeting of investors in London in late October that the Indonesian government was prepared

---

be implemented properly and it is not necessary to communicate with business to make all kinds of changes." See *Kompas,* 21 July 1984:7.

[87] Cooke 1984:7. Note that, as before the oil boom, investment levels in the private sector were once again being related explicitly to pressures policymakers were feeling to meet at least minimum investment requirements for society.

[88] All quotations in this paragraph and the next are from Cowper 1984:7.

to "make some adjustments fair to all parties," though he declined to say what the adjustments would be or when they would be implemented. So loud was the outcry from all investors over the value-added tax, a key component of the 1984 package, that the government had already announced it would postpone its introduction for at least eighteen months.

The controversy continued into 1985. The *Asian Wall Street Journal*, widely read by officials and mobile investors alike, reported that overall investment (including domestic) dropped by 70 percent between 1983 and 1984.[89] The pressure was still on later in the year. In September a bulletin on taxes serving the foreign investment community in Jakarta included the following closing observations:

> In a recent speech to 500 foreign business people, Ginandjar Kartasasmita, Indonesia's Chairman of BKPM, the agency with responsibility for promoting investment, admitted it has been tough going so far. Investment in Indonesia is at the lowest it has been in many years, with a drop of foreign capital investment from $2.9 billion to $1.1 billion between 1983 and 1984. Not an auspicious beginning. While this decrease is due to many factors, the government knows that it needs to promote private investments by foreign investors. . . . The government has begun to face this problem by cutting back on red tape and attempting to eliminate corruption. But it may need to provide more tax incentives for foreign investment.[90]

[89] Pura 1985. In the same article it is evident from the comments of Ali Wardhana, who was finance minister at the time, that immobile investors were also adding to the investment decline by withholding new investments. Explaining why this slowdown among some domestic investors was occurring, Wardhana remarked that "first, they haven't studied the new tax reforms or compared them with the old system and, second, there are also others . . . who have practically been able to avoid paying tax at all. With the new system they're going to get caught, and that scares them." The impact of the value-added tax, finally implemented in 1985, was far more important to local entrepreneurs, who are deeply involved in consumer and service sectors. See *Jakarta Post,* 26 February 1985.

[90] Hammer, Elliot, and Shah 1985:366. Note, by the way, that in addition to his being the junior minister for the promotion of domestic goods and the day-to-day head of Team 10, Suharto also handed Ginanjar the top position at BKPM, formerly held by the hapless Suhartoyo. The foreign press in particular noted that giving Ginanjar the top spot at the Investment Coordinating Board was rather like asking the fox to guard the chicken coop. Cooke (1985:6) wrote that "Mr. Kartasasmita dismisses claims that he is too nationalistic or too protectionist. [He] denies there is any conflict between his various posts and emphasises the link the Indonesian Government sees between investment and the promotion of domestic products. He says that by overseeing both contracts and investments, he hopes to rationalise the system."

By far the most thorough and penetrating critique of the state's policy and strategy had appeared several months earlier, in August 1984. Vincent Harink, writing in *East Asian Executive Reports,* pointed out in a straightforward manner the salient issues that Indonesian policymakers and private investors needed to consider and resolve.[91] After reviewing the country's investment needs and underscoring the state's declining capacity to satisfy them, Harink observed, "Indonesia is faced with keen competition from other Asian countries still offering tax incentives, and some foreign businessmen have indicated that they are also concerned about the Indonesian government's slow progress in implementing simpler regulatory requirements." In a direct response to officials in Finance who claimed that the short-term downside of the tax reform package was far outweighed by the longer-term upside (not to mention all the other often-cited reasons investors invest in Indonesia), he wrote:

This may be true—but it is apparent from the figures for the first half of 1984 that tax incentives are important, particularly in the short term until the new tax law is fully implemented. The new tax law offers as the main attraction for investors the lowering of the maximum tax rate from 45 percent to 35 percent. It is argued that since the tax holiday is only enjoyed in the first few years of operation, when investors generally suffer losses and therefore do not pay tax anyway, the lowering of the maximum tax rate will be of more benefit in the long run. The figures and calculations presented by the Ministry of Finance appear to support the view that in the longer run it is more beneficial to investors to have lower tax rates than tax incentives such as the tax holiday. But it would appear that a large number of potential investors still consider the tax holiday a very important incentive, particularly since they continue to receive such an incentive in other parts of Asia. The attraction of a tax holiday may be more psychological in nature; but, in economic terms, such a psychological factor is not to be minimized. In the final analysis, it may well determine the decision on whether to invest or not.[92]

[91] Harink 1984:8. All of Harink's comments are from this article.

[92] Harink was not the only one to attack the Finance "line" on trade-offs in the long and short term. Astbury, a veteran observer of the business scene in Indonesia, argued that the assertion "that foreign investors 'are drawn here not by investment incentives but by the country's political stability, its large domestic market and the abundance of natural resources' is seen by some as little more than a rationalization. Investment incentives are important, or the government would not have been touting them since 1967." Astbury 1984:59.

Reversing the state's own arguments about why the elimination of tax holidays should not matter to investors, Harink suggested a rationale for reinstating the holidays:

> If investors consider tax incentives such as tax holidays important, and if most investors, as it is argued, incur losses in the first few years anyway, then it may be sensible to reintroduce a tax holiday as it is unlikely to cost the government a great deal in lost tax revenues. *In any case, reduced tax receipts would be preferable, particularly in the longer term, to a continued low level of investment.*[93]

A. R. Suhud, a former minister who was himself a successful entrepreneur before joining the government, and who often battled the economic ministers over policies toward the private sector, claims that neither the economists nor the consultants they hire for their policy studies fully understand how business is done or how investment decisions are made. Pressed to bring in more tax receipts from business and individuals as the money from oil dried up, the economic ministers were convinced that they had to make a principled stand on making business pay for all the services it receives in Indonesia. " 'Why all the facilities and incentives, like tax holidays?' they would ask me," Suhud explained. "But I argued that things like tax holidays were nice 'sweeteners' or 'sales gimmicks' that psychologically were very important to investors—if for no other reason than it helped executives sell the investment to their own stockholders—but not very costly to Indonesia because most companies didn't make a taxable profit in their first few years of operation anyway. They [the economists] ignored me. When I would speak out on things like this, and on unnecessarily high levels of foreign borrowing, for instance, they would react negatively."[94]

By 1987, three years into the tax reform period, and armed with better data on how the private sector was responding to the new tax regime (and all the other reforms discussed above to restore competitiveness to the country's economy), it appeared that the Finance people were right and that the investment slump, for both mobile and immobile investors,

[93] My emphasis.
[94] Interview in Jakarta with A. R. Suhud, 13 December 1989.

had passed.[95] The booming rates of new investment gave government officials more confidence and allowed them at times to react less pliantly to investors who embarrassed them by publicly criticizing aspects of the country's investment climate that were still unsatisfactory in the eyes of mobile capital controllers. When in 1987 a prominent Japanese business leader suggested yet again that Indonesia ought to consider backing down on its tax holiday position to prevent Japanese investors from taking their capital elsewhere, Ginanjar responded by saying, "If Japanese businessmen prefer increasing their investments in Thailand and Malaysia, it's alright [sic] for us because more investments in those countries will help bolster their economics [sic] and will consequently strengthen the regional resilience of ASEAN." This comment might have provoked a chuckle or two. But what followed was almost certainly taken very seriously. Firing a warning shot across the private sector's bow, he added that if the claim by prominent Japanese businessmen that they wanted to take their investments to other ASEAN countries was true, then "it is simply their right to do so because the Indonesian government will not try at all costs to woo foreign investors."[96]

As recently as late 1989, one could still hear representatives from the private sector calling for tax relief. Officials in BKPM, charged with raising the levels of private investment in Indonesia, continue to complain that investments are constantly being lost to competitor states that still offer tax holidays. Although it is difficult to know how much higher the investment and expansion rates in the private sector would be if the tax holidays were brought back, the record levels already achieved through the broader "deregulatory" policies put forth since 1983 appear

[95] Generous levels of foreign aid played a crucial role in allowing Indonesia to ride out the storm over tax holidays. Record levels of foreign loans were pumped into the economy, in large part as direct and untied cash injections, to close the gap. Official assistance for the five years between 1982–1983 and 1986–1987 totaled almost as much as the previous fifteen years combined.

[96] Both quotations are from *Jakarta Post*, 2 February 1987. The public posturing evident in Ginanjar's statement is not always a good indicator of how a policymaker will act when faced with difficult choices. In 1989, as minister of mines and energy, he led the fight against the Ministry of Finance over value-added taxes on oil companies, particularly on their exploration efforts. In the face of privately expressed warnings that oil companies would react to the new taxes by cutting back exploration and production, he campaigned hard in favor of more incentives to encourage the oil companies to find and bring up more oil—Indonesia being one of the OPEC countries that typically fails to meet its share of world production quotas. Examples like this abound, particularly for Ginanjar.

to have strengthened the resolve of the people in the Ministry of Finance responsible for pushing this policy through. Said one official, "We have lots of investments coming in now that are relocations of firms from the NICs who lost their GSP [Generalized System of Preferences] status. Why should we give special treatment to them if it's already in their interest to come here? What extra bait do you need to give?"[97]

Tax Reform and State Responsiveness to Capital

If we believe Harink's arguments, tax policy is an important element of a country's business climate. It is certainly among the factors that are assessed as investors make investment decisions. If investors are internationally mobile, tax regimes in different countries are evaluated comparatively to determine their impact on a firm's bottom line. What is curious about the case presented here is that at first blush it appears that the entire tax reform package, but especially the tax holiday element, was rather *unresponsive* to capital precisely when, according to the structural power arguments in this book, theory would predict the opposite. On closer inspection it turned out that the economic ministers were trying to balance the tension inherent in attempting simultaneously to satisfy the revenue needs of the state and the investment needs of society under conditions where direct state access to resources sufficient enough to accomplish both objectives was vanishing rapidly.

It is clear from the story that the power of mobile capital was substantial and was recognized by decision makers. Before taking any action, the state studied (so that it could predict) the reactions of the private sector. Not a few of the architects of tax reform admitted that the entire 1984 tax package was designed with the objective very much in mind of making Indonesia a more attractive investment site. The economic ministers were willing to eliminate tax holidays only after they had seen report after report showing that they were a low priority for capital and would not trigger an investment crisis at a time when the state was

[97] Interview in Jakarta with Hutabarat, 2 November 1989. In February 1990 investors from Taiwan announced that they planned to move hundreds of small and medium-sized factories to Indonesia. In addition to this $2 billion investment, they also expressed interest in investing $2 billion in industrial estates. Were both these amounts to be implemented, they would represent more than twice Taiwan's total investment in Indonesia between 1967 and 1987. See *Indonesian Observer,* 1 February 1990, 6.

vulnerable. In other words, the stubborn position taken on tax incentives was an indication not of state indifference to capital, but rather of a very keen sensitivity that led the economists to suspect that the culprit behind the poor investment figures was more likely the "pebbles" of Team 10 than their own fiscal reforms.

Even if it is true that the economic ministers firmly believed their tax reform policies were not causing the apparent problem with private sector investment, why did they not, as Harink suggested, restore the tax incentives? The fiscal impact, it seems, would have been negligible. There are several plausible reasons. First, knowing that opposition to the tax reform would come from *all* directions (including from within the state), the ministers appear to have adopted the strategy that the only way to avoid backing down and undermining the reform initiative was to dig in their heels and maintain the integrity of the entire initial package as designed. The VAT, which already had a delayed implementation date in the original package, was the only deviation. But despite a considerable uproar, the economists allowed only a postponement of the VAT, not a policy change. Second, tax reform was among the first attempts the economic ministers made to regain the sort of preboom hegemony over economic policy that they once enjoyed. Having waited so long for an opening, they were especially determined to be neither thwarted in their efforts nor embarrassed publicly by collapsing under the enormous pressures to restore tax holidays. And finally, the ministers did not want to appear too soft on business when they were trying to squeeze larger revenues out of private citizens. Also, from Sumarlin's comments in parliament, it is clear that because of abuses (the starting of new companies when tax holidays ran out), he believed the revenue losses were far greater than Harink suggested in his analysis.

The evidence that policymakers were being supremely sensitive to mobile capital is seen in their efforts not only to anticipate investors' reactions, but also to monitor them once the policies were in place. Levels of new investment served as a kind of structural barometer that told officials how their policies were being received. If it is true that mobile investors "vote with their feet," then highly favorable policies are signaled by an inward flood of investments and policies viewed as antagonistic or hostile are marked by movements in the opposite direction. Two questions are still unresolved from the discussion above. Was the investment collapse at the center of the 1984 controversy real? And was investor behavior linked, as many people believed, to the tax holiday issue?

On one hand, the drop in approved investment levels in 1984 looks much less severe if 1982 is used as the base year of comparison instead of 1983. Figure 6, which provides a slightly closer view of trends already seen in figure 3, illustrates the point nicely. There was a surge in investment applications in the closing months of 1983 as investors, uncertain about the tax changes and aware that holidays would be cut, tried to turn the situation to their best advantage. It is hardly surprising that compared with a surge year like 1983—the basis for computing all the shocking statistics and percentages quoted in the media—1984 looked anemic. Figure 6 indicates that approved foreign investment levels were just as flat during the three years after 1983 as during the three years before. Domestic approvals did dip slightly below their 1982 levels after the 1983 spike, but they recovered and increased earlier and faster than their foreign counterparts. Note also that investment activity in subsequent years increased fairly dramatically despite no reversal of the state's tax incentive position. This fact alone renders strong claims of a causal link at least suspect.

Yet there are good reasons to insist that the behavior of investors was linked to changes in tax policy. First, in the course of his investment-based critique of Indonesia's tax incentive stance, Harink pointed out that of the $3 billion in new investments that received *provisional* approval late in 1983 (these projects accounting for the spike), almost all were canceled by investors once it became clear that the tax incentives did not in fact apply when final approval was given in early 1984. Second, although it is indisputable that investment rates increased sharply once other aspects of Indonesia's policy changes favoring allocation by markets were in place, it is entirely possible that investment rates would have been even higher had Indonesia not been losing investments to competitor states, as many observers in BKPM, AMCHAM, and other agencies believe was occurring (and continues). Finally, even if with data available today we can show that no serious investment crisis actually occurred, what really matters for explaining the actions of policymakers is their perception of reality and the space for choice it appeared to contain. It is investment approvals that are tracked and reported monthly to the president. Data on approvals, supplied by Suhartoyo, showed that the reaction of business was a near-total invest-

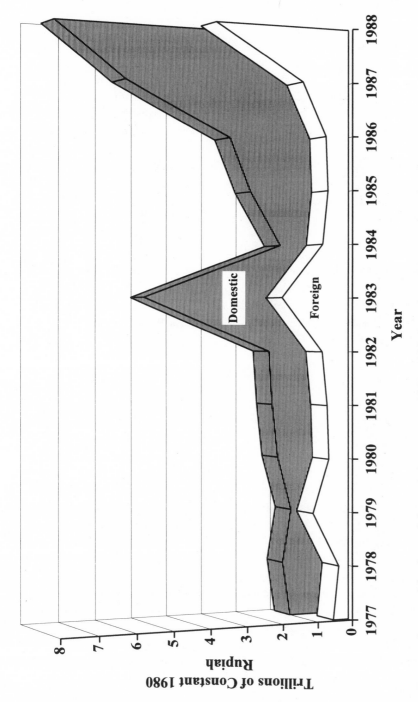

Figure 6. Approved foreign and domestic investments, 1977–1988. Data from BKPM and Bank Indonesia.

ment strike in the first quarter of 1984, picking up only slightly in subsequent months. In a meeting with Suharto in August 1984, the BKPM chairman was instructed to remove the obstacles to investment.[98] The president, at least, showed signs he was rattled.

It would be safe to argue that concern among top decision-makers was real and fairly widespread when investments plummeted in 1984. The economic ministers, despite all their reservations, might have restored tax holidays to reverse this economically destabilizing trend had massive stopgap resources from Indonesia's creditors not saved the day. Between 1983 and 1985, annual injections of aid were about $3.5 billion, compared with a $1.5 to $2 billion range during the three previous years. Once investments had become bullish again, the economists were relieved that they had stood their ground against the opposition *voiced* by mobile investors. That they stood their ground, however, reflected not independence from private capital controllers, but rather a certain empirically based confidence among officials that on this issue, anyway, investors' bark was worse (or at least more sustained) than their bite.

The *Pribumi* Factor in the Postboom Era

What of the role major *pribumi* capitalists played once the oil boom ended? We saw that early in 1984 the initiative to stop references to *pribumi* and non-*pribumi* Indonesians was backed by very powerful figures in the armed forces. Although this move certainly had its coercive dimension, it was directed not so much at the upper reaches of the *pribumi* investing class as at the middle and lower strata. This section will develop that claim by assessing important changes that occurred in the wake of the oil boom.

As previous sections have argued, it is extremely difficult to characterize the effect of oil boom era policies on *pribumi*. With data either inaccurate or unavailable, the size, character, and political-economic role of Indonesia's indigenous entrepreneurs can at present be evaluated best through the observations of academics, consultants, business leaders, and officials who have day-to-day contact with business. Everyone agrees that a thin stratum of major *pribumi* entrepreneurs exists. There

[98] Harink 1984:8.

is also considerable agreement on the size of this class, ranging from fifty big players to a few hundred.[99] For a country of nearly 200 million people in 1995, this group represents only a tiny fraction of a percent.[100] Observers generally agree, also, on how these capitalists came into being. Links to the state—or more specifically, state spending on projects— paved the way. Sadli provides a crisp snapshot of *pribumi* entreprenuers at the end of the 1980s:

> The existing group of *pribumi* entrepreneurs very much reflects the way they developed out of links to the government. If you look, you'll notice that they have no foothold in production, industry, or trade. The *pribumi* businessmen are all lumped together in the services—especially engineering and construction. This is hardly surprising. They all got their start through government contracts to build infrastructure during the latter years of the oil boom. Law 10 of 1980 was extremely important in their development. Without it you wouldn't have your Arionos and your Imans [two important *pribumi* investors]. It's also interesting to note that the strongest body within KADIN and KADINDA is the Construction Association. Every other group is weak.[101]

Iman Taufik himself agrees fully, adding that the postboom years, when the state budget collapsed, were very hard on *pribumi* firms. "A lot of *pribumi* businesses were started by piggybacking on these policies from 1979 forward and from Sudharmono's operations at SEKNEG. We had about 30,000 contractors going there for a while, all being fed from

---

[99] Christianto Wibisono, whose consulting firm produces profiles of the Indonesian business scene costing between $500 and $2,500 *per report,* says that according to his extensive database (among the best, though still constructed from highly unreliable and partial figures), "the process of creating a major and freestanding *pribumi* entrepreneurial class has begun, but it has not progressed very far." Not counting former officials who merely front for foreign or ethnic Chinese capital, Wibisono adds, "I would say that of the top two hundred big *pribumi* companies, maybe fifty are really run by *pribumi* entrepreneurs." Interview in Jakarta with Christianto Wibisono, 7 February 1989. Also see Robinson 1986, MacIntyre 1991, and McVey 1992.

[100] One government official widely viewed to be a protégé of Sudharmono stressed that although *pribumi* had made gains, others had moved faster still. "Looking back from 1965 to 1970 to now, so-called *pribumi* have made great progress in absolute terms. The number of big *pribumi* businessmen has increased. But the [ethnic] Chinese have moved even faster, so that in relative terms we are weaker than before." Interview in Jakarta with Bakir Hasan, secretary general at the Ministry of Trade, 23 March 1989.

[101] KADINDA is the regional version of the national Chamber of Commerce (KADIN). Interview in Jakarta with Mohammad Sadli, 19 September 1989.

government projects. Suddenly, when the oil prices fell, this number dropped to 10,000." [102]

It is important to point out that although 30,000 sounds like a large number of firms, the vast majority were very small and worked as subcontractors for the big players linked politically to Team 10 and other government agencies and officials. Many others were simply paper companies used to rig the bidding processes. "It works like this," explained a former government official familiar with bidding on construction projects. "You have a list of, say, ten firms bidding on a project. One, two, and three are real companies, and in most instances they've already worked a deal out among themselves as to which firm will submit the winning bid and how much the losers will receive for playing along. These companies take turns winning and paying the others off. Companies four through ten, meanwhile, actually belong to firms one, two, and three but exist only on paper and are included either to make it appear as if the tender is hotly contested or to win bids through different company names to hide the fact that the same companies are getting all the projects." [103]

Perhaps the most important question centers on the potential for political independence for these investors born of the state. Can the umbilical cord be severed? Are there any indications that anyone wants to sever it? And how did these major *pribumi* players respond to the pressures toward more market-based forms of regulation after the oil boom passed—and with what results? One place to start might be the matter of mobility. According to the dean of the economics faculty at the University of Indonesia, "The biggest investors in Indonesia, whatever their race, enjoy pretty much the same levels of mobility for their investments. . . . The [ethnic] Chinese probably have some advantages given the networks in the region [Southeast Asia]. In the area of finance capital, of course, there are few differences. Almost anyone can shift their resources around the globe these days without any serious trouble. This is probably the main reason interest rates are kept so high here." [104]

---

[102] Interview in Jakarta with Iman Taufik, 1 April 1989.

[103] Confidential discussion in Jakarta with a former government official, 22 June 1989.

[104] Referring to the ways capital mobility forces countries to compete with each other, he added: "We need to match the interest rates in the main financial centers of the world, plus tack on an additional percentage equal to the expected decline in the value of the rupiah over the course of the year. If the government keeps interest high and the rate of exchange reasonable, the money stays in the country. Given how this works, it's clear the

Although Arsjad is correct in noting that the most liquid forms of capital are equally mobile, he glosses over the fact that, as Sadli pointed out, *pribumi* are most heavily concentrated in services linked to state spending. If we emphasize not just where one locates one's liquid capital but where one locates one's firm for production or the provision of services, *pribumi* as a group will be at a disadvantage as long as their "market" for customers is mostly limited to the Indonesian state. A longtime observer of the Indonesian business scene put it this way: "If foreign investors apply pressure, the government will change. Not much pressure for real change comes from *pribumi* investors mainly because they're all tied up with the government. Backed by the IMF and the World Bank, foreign investors are powerful. All they have to do is move to Thailand or Malaysia. The options for Indonesian firms are greatly reduced because so many of them are directly involved in government contracts."[105]

By the late 1980s there were early indications that the lines separating groups along racial and sectoral lines were blurring as *pribumi* began to move out of their narrow service base into other areas. One consultant who worked for the economic ministers through HIID, and later as a private specialist on investment in Indonesia, offered these impressions of the behavior of major *pribumi* investors: "There definitely has been change. One very good sign is how many Indonesian investors are diversifying their businesses. The old pattern was to have just one or two lines of business operating behind strong NTB [nontariff barrier] protection—a license or what-have-you. This is less common today, and it represents a significant change. Also, many *pribumi* businessmen, who raised rent seeking to a highly refined art here, are making a more serious effort to join with Chinese as real partners."[106] Perhaps one of the strongest indications that a new role is emerging for this thin layer of *pribumi* investors can be seen in their reaction (or lack of one) to the new

---

devastating impact devaluations have on the confidence of those caught off guard." Interview in Jakarta with Mohammad Arsjad Anwar, 24 August 1989.

[105] Confidential interview in Jakarta, 13 April 1989. Even this has begun to change in recent years. Yusuf Kalla and his relative Achmad Kalla of the Kalla Group (launched by Team 10) said in a newspaper interview—just as Team 10 was being abolished—that they were not terribly concerned if there were big changes in tendering and other business opportunities from the state for *pribumi*. "Their business was directed not only at the domestic market," the reporter wrote, but "they had also exported asphalt and construction equipment valued at $1 million." *Tempo*, 31 March 1988, 92.

[106] Interview in Jakarta with James Van Zorge, 23 July 1990.

policy trajectory pushed by the economic ministers with the onset of the oil bust.

One of the most important developments to take place as Indonesia entered the politically and economically difficult years after 1982 was the unwillingness of major *pribumi* investors to use their considerable size, influence, and connections to battle against the systematic dismantling of the very policies and institutions that gave them their start. When the head of the armed forces put a stop in 1984 to the manipulation of the *pribumi* issue for political and economic ends, not only did the big *pribumi* entrepreneurs not oppose the move, they seemed to go out of their way to embrace it publicly. Almost immediately, the leaders of HIPPI, the *Himpunan Pengusaha Pribumi Indonesia,* changed the second *P* in their group's name to *Putera,* transforming the organization from the Association of *Indigenous* Indonesian Entrepreneurs to the Business Association of the *Sons* of Indonesia. The same reaction was not shared, however, by the smaller and middle players in the organization. Well into the 1990s the middle and lower strata of HIPPI were still arguing angrily that *pribumi* is a valid word and cause, and that if the group did not defend their interests in the face of more market-based forms of regulation, who would?[107]

Why did the major *pribumi* capitalists not oppose the removal of protections? There were two reasons. First, they were perceptive enough

---

[107] I had the opportunity to attend the weekend-long 1989 national meeting of HIPPI, where members (large and small) from around the country were brought in to be wined and dined and supplied with a controlled environment within which to vent their frustrations. HIPPI leaders sat on a platform at the front of the room, pencils in hand, taking notes on the vitriolic statements coming from the organization's rank and file. After listening patiently, the group's leaders would usually crack a joke to relieve some of the tension in the room. They also nodded their heads and assured those who complained that their businesses were going under by the hundreds and thousands because of "deregulation" that their needs and interests had been duly noted and would be included in the official report to the ministers and the president (one of HIPPI's leading members is the president's half-brother). When I commented to one of HIPPI's leaders that this was one of the first times I had witnessed such an open—albeit behind closed doors and out of reach of the media—display of anger and dissatisfaction (government ministers and even HIPPI's own leaders had aspersions cast on their character), he replied: "This is good for them. They express themselves and leave Jakarta feeling good that they've met government officials and businessmen they've seen in magazines and newspapers, and that they've had a role in shaping government policy. They show everyone the pictures when they get back to their own cities and towns." The terms in Indonesian for this process are *musyawarah dan mufakat,* meaning "discussion and consensus." The rank and file discuss, and the leaders come to a consensus.

to see that the oil boom days were over and that the policies that gave them their boost were sure to be challenged. They could fight, but the battle would be hard and the chances of winning grew slimmer with each slip in the price of a barrel of crude. Second, now that they themselves were big players in the Indonesian economy, their perspective on how opportunity should be regulated was very different. Though they were still *pribumi,* they now had much more in common with larger and more mobile foreign and ethnic Chinese investors than with the small and middle investors making up the rest of the still struggling *pribumi* group. For the first time among indigenous Indonesians, *pribumi* status and immobility crosscut rather than coincided. The point is that these important indigenous actors were allowing a major change in policy without putting up a major fuss. This is not to suggest that *pribumi* investors were opposed to seeking special access and favors whenever the chance arose. "Formally, in public, they don't oppose deregulation," Arsjad explained. "But in practice it's another matter. They still scramble like crazy to get special access to government projects, and so on. The names of the powerful are still used to influence and intimidate."[108] Thus, they support market-regulated access *as government policy* but do everything they can *as individuals* to gain an advantage over their competitors. In other words, they act like every other capitalist in the world.

The cooperation of Indonesia's big *pribumi* investors had a significant impact on the success of the economic ministers in rapidly restoring market forms of regulation to the economy. At precisely the moment when the economists were once again being called on to rescue the country from the clutches of a fiscal, investment, and thus political disaster, any attempt to use the *pribumi* weapon had been doubly blocked. First, leading *pribumi* investors had broken ranks and joined with mobile capital and the economic ministers. And second, those claiming that *pribumi* still needed protection could easily be shouted down by pointing to the indisputable presence of prominent indigenous entrepreneurs.[109] By their very existence these investors demonstrated that the impossible was possible and, more important still, lent credence to the argument that failure to succeed in business had more to do with

[108] Interview in Jakarta with Mohammad Arsjad Anwar, dean of the economics faculty, University of Indonesia, 24 August 1989.

[109] From what I witnessed at the 1989 HIPPI meeting, even the big *pribumi* players made this argument—pointing to themselves.

individual, personal factors (drive, ingenuity, etc.) than with biases in the system—political or economic. There were, to be sure, limits to this line of argument, since most people are convinced that *pribumi* who have made it big did so mainly because they were politically connected. On the other hand, because concrete evidence is in far shorter supply than spicy rumors, it is difficult to trace every *pribumi* success to connections or to show that these connections persist and account for the continued viability of a firm that may only have been launched by state patronage. If only because of human pride in one's heritage, doubts can easily be seeded that certainly not *every* indigenous Indonesian who has "made it" had his or her hand held by a powerful official.

Because the basic themes in this are by now completely familiar, it is unnecessary to emphasize again the importance of shifts in the patterns of resource control and access in Indonesia in accounting for changes in the influence of the economic ministers and in the course of policy as the country entered the postboom phase. It was not the fact of structural influence among investors that changed, but rather its intensity and potency. Two issues are brought out quite clearly in this chapter. The first concerns the unmistakable evidence of greater transnational mobility of investors in this third and most recent phase. Reflected in the comments of capital controllers, business climate analysts, and policymakers themselves, perhaps no consideration was mentioned more frequently in the debates surrounding "deregulation" than the vastly greater pressures that existed in the 1980s to maintain an investment climate that could compete with other jurisdictions. This was obviously a major concern when the economic ministers commissioned a study of the investment calculations of mobile actors before introducing the tax reform package (sans tax holidays), as well as during the investment crisis that gripped policymakers in 1984 and 1985.

Also significant is that increases in mobility not only are occurring horizontally across a wider geographic spread, but are also incorporating a wider vertical segment of capital controllers. The elevation of key *pribumi* investors to a higher degree of mobility represents only Indonesia's experience. Similar developments are occurring in many other countries. The important analytical issue this raises concerns how these actors should be categorized. The arguments of this chapter suggest that much more than nationality and ethnicity, relative mobility shapes the interests that lie behind the policies for protection or openness that different capital controllers promote.

The second issue centers on the contradictions inherent in trying simultaneously to meet the revenue requirements of the state and the investment needs of the society. The juxtaposition of boom and postboom periods is useful on this point. During the boom, an arrangement highly unusual under capitalism existed in that it was abundant state revenues that financed investment for the society. After the boom the situation was reversed. As the Indonesian state tried to reform its tax system to draw more resources from the nonoil private sector, the effort was interpreted by investors, as taxes generally are, as a disincentive to investment. For mobile investors and policymakers alike, as a result, the benchmark for assessing a given tax regime has much less to do with matters of tax incidence or justice or even the state's desperate need for revenue than with the tax regimes put in place by policymakers in competing jurisdictions.

CAPITAL MOBILITY: APPLICATIONS AND COMPARISONS

Everyone who writes about countries that experience resource booms seems to notice that government officials tend to rely less on markets and try harder (and with greater success) to direct the economy in ways that follow some developmental or political logic.[1] These renegade officials are said to be "interventionist," their policies "heterodox." Conspicuously absent from such studies is an explanation of the policy shifts themselves, other than to make the fairly uninteresting point that abundant resources allow rulers the luxury of putting off the "tough choices" typically imposed by scarcity. In addition to being circular, this reasoning takes markets, private property, and scarcity (from the state's perspective, anyway) as the norm from which everything else diverges. It also ignores power and the ways that shifts in control over resources confer leverage to some as they withdraw it from others.

The structural-materialist perspective informing this work is concerned with tracing how the critical resources that populations and their leaders rely on are controlled, how and why control over resources translates into power, and the ways power relations throughout the system change when fundamental shifts occur in the pattern of control over investment resources. The patterns predominating under market capitalism, and especially the ways they are changing, do not serve merely as a backdrop to political analysis but instead form the focal point of the book. The central actors in the Indonesian story were capital controllers (both private and official) and a fairly small set of policy-

---

[1] For instance, Gelb and Associates 1988 and Neary and van Wijnbergen 1986.

makers at the apex of the state. What mattered most was not the nationality of capital controllers (foreign or domestic), but instead the relative mobility of the resources they commanded. Both their power and their policy interests were linked to how readily their resources could be supplied to the Indonesian system for investment and production and, more important, how easily their resources could be withdrawn or relocated to other locations.

To capture one of the central tensions in the country's political economy during the last three decades, officials within the Indonesian state were divided into two opposing groups. One faction comprised the economic ministers. Sometimes referred to as the "technocrats" or the "Berkeley Mafia," this group lacked an independent power base and thus was ascendant within the state only when President Suharto turned to them in times of economic crisis or when the system's investment needs could not be satisfied by the state itself. They pushed hard for market reforms in Indonesia partly because of training and faith, but mostly because those who controlled the needed resources were able to demand a favorable climate as a condition for supplying their capital. Arrayed against the economic ministers was the rest of the cabinet, with President Suharto swinging uneasily between the two factions—though siding with the market-unfriendly faction for a variety of social and political reasons whenever structural conditions allowed.

Indonesia's political economy since 1965 was divided into three periods, with the middle period—usually described as highly statist—coinciding with the oil boom from late 1973 through 1982. A major objective was to show that the profound shifts in economic policy across these three phases reflected a redistribution of the power rooted in the control over capital. It is not merely that tough choices could be postponed, but rather that the power balance ordinarily operating in capitalist systems like Indonesia was disrupted. Direct state access to abundant replacement resources during the oil boom allowed Suharto and his circle of clients to circumvent the economic ministers and subvert the structural power of private capital controllers, the World Bank, the IMF, and other creditor agencies. The widening of policy options during this period of weakened structural power helped bring into much sharper relief capital's decisive capacity to constrain decision makers *before and since* the boom. During that interlude Indonesians witnessed how their country could and would be run when the pressures to be

responsive to a small class of mostly private, highly mobile capital controllers were greatly diminished. And in the same moment they also
caught a rare glimpse of the largely silent and mostly invisible power
relations that form the core of systems based on the private control of
investment resources.

Illustrations

At the end of each of the preceding chapters I summarized other key
points that emerged in the course of the Indonesian study. The main task
that remains is to explore how the approach developed in this book
might be applied to other cases and contexts. In its most general form, a
theory of structural power rooted in mobility centers on the capacity of
an actor or group of actors to withhold or relocate crucial resources and
the political-economic consequences for those who rely on them. In the
specific case of capitalist systems of production, the key consideration is
the ability of investors to deploy capital in ways that jurisdictions and
societies, whether democratic or authoritarian, cannot easily control or
defend against. The range of contexts to which this approach can be
applied not only is extremely broad but has been expanding at a dizzying
pace since the end of World War II. In the rest of this chapter I will not
undertake new analyses or present full case studies. Rather, I offer a
series of sketches designed to illustrate fruitful directions for further
research and theoretical sharpening. Each sketch touches on insights that
can be gained from a focus on structural power linked to mobility. Only
in the final section, centering on comparisons with Nigeria, does attention return to the issues and mediating variables at the heart of the
Indonesian case.

Rethinking the Power of Labor

The weakening of unions and labor movements in advanced industrial
countries is widely recognized.[2] Although labor's power has declined
markedly across Europe and North America, the rate and depth of the

[2] See Cameron 1984, Golden and Pontusson 1992, Lange, Ross, and Vannicelli 1982,
and Jenson and Mahon 1993.

slide have been shaped by institutional, ideological, and historical factors specific to each location.[3] Analysts have emphasized such things as union density, corporatist arrangements, the strength of appeals to justice for a given society, and most recently the role of innovative negotiating strategies by union leaders. A focus on capital mobility would take the analysis in quite different directions. First, it would link the broader decline of labor's strength both at the site of production and over government policy to the ability of capital controllers to threaten (and carry out) the relocation of investment resources to jurisdictions offering more favorable terms. Second, it would invert the meaning of a strong labor movement. High union density, excellent leadership, and solid internal cohesion were the hallmarks of a strong union movement when capital was less mobile. But under current conditions these strengths increasingly translate into disaster as capitalists quietly prepare for relocation even as they negotiate the latest round of contracts with unions. The painful lesson for workers is that strong unions, in the traditional sense, lead to unemployment.

Focusing on mobility would reshape our understanding of the balance of power between labor and capital in still another way. If increasing capital mobility is crucial to explaining labor's overall declining strength, then that decline will vary with the mobility options of investors and employers. In contrast to approaches that mainly help account for variations in union strength across national contexts, this perspective should be particularly useful in explaining variations in strength across sectors or types of firm. Hence, unions facing employers that can cross national jurisdictions with relative ease will feel the full force and devastation of capital's structural power. Those confronting investors that can relocate mainly across subnational lines will also be greatly weakened, though the prospect still exists of organizing out to the limits of the national boundary and pressuring employers with the strike option. Strongest of all are workers who confront highly immobile employers that have very little structural power at their disposal. They would include university employees, those working in city and state bureaucracies, transportation workers, and so on. It is noteworthy that when the relocation threat is unavailable, the standard indicators of union strength reappear as the best predictors of success in contract negotiations.

[3] Streeck 1995.

Recasting the Debates

According to Robert Reich, "The government's role is not just to spread the wealth. It is to build our human capital and infrastructure, and to bargain with global capital on our behalf.[4] Looking at things differently, Herman Daly and Robert Goodall write, "Northern capitalists want Northern laborers to compete directly with Southern laborers. International capital mobility, coupled with free trade of products, stimulates a standards-lowering competition to attract capital: wages can be lowered, as can health insurance, worker safety standards, environmental standards, etc."[5]

An approach emphasizing capital mobility helps make sense of these statements. It also helps us understand why being "competitive" has seemingly crowded out all other goals for a wide range of societies, and why the bases for defining this notion have shifted. Controllers of mobile capital have used their structural leverage not only to win favorable policies from governments at all jurisdictional levels, but also to frame the ideological debates in ways that emphasize a new version of competitiveness in place of economic fairness, justice, "progress," or even more leisure time for workers. It is beyond the scope of this book to detail how such an ideological shift is accomplished. It is possible, however, to hint at the threads a focus on mobility would weave together.

First, it is important to recognize that being competitive or efficient has meaning only with reference to some basis of comparison. When the reference points shift, the meaning shifts.[6] Changes in the spatial and jurisdictional range of production, particularly in manufacturing, are at the heart of the new meaning of the word "competitive" and its force in contemporary society. Here range refers not to the number of jurisdictions involved, but to the variations in their social, economic, and political characteristics. Laborers have long had to compete against each other across national jurisdictional lines. But until the late 1960s and early 1970s that competition was overwhelmingly between jurisdictions that were relatively similar. When the costs of labor and the broader sociopolitical climate did not vary dramatically, it was possible to use

[4] *Euromoney,* suppl. 5 September 1993, 1. The quotation is from Reich 1991. Robert Reich became secretary of labor under President Clinton.

[5] Quoted in Cockburn 1992:489. Until leaving the World Bank in January 1994, Daly was a senior economist in the Environment Department.

[6] Morgan 1993.

productivity as the main gauge of competitiveness and efficiency. That is, laborers could be judged mostly against *themselves* over time. Increases in output and quality per worker would set the standard. And reflecting this, the pact reached between labor and capital across much of the advanced industrial world during the first decades after World War II was that real wages increases ought to be linked to productivity gains.

Several things happened to challenge this arrangement. Direct investors in manufacturing that had initially migrated to postcolonial systems to produce consumer goods for local consumption behind high tariff barriers began flowing to these same areas to produce for export as well. They were joined by a swell of indigenous manufacturers also producing an ever-wider range of goods for export to advanced industrial markets (where higher living standards translate into substantial effective demand). Who could produce, what could be produced, and where the production could be set up all expanded sharply. Not only were the jurisdictions involved in manufacturing more unlike each other than ever before, but the relative insulation of national jurisdictions that had permitted the productivity pact in advanced industrial states was eroded.[7]

As long as the trade regime is open, the "factor price equalization theorem" tells us that this would eventually have occurred even if capital was highly immobile across national jurisdictions. This raises the question that is critical to this story about mobile capital—particularly why labor in North America and Europe has so far proved ineffective in defending against the new ideology of competitiveness. When laborers are compared not with themselves over time but rather with others, the comparisons can be either direct or indirect. The indirect path is through the medium of markets and trade in products. Assuming minimal transport costs, two widgets of comparable quality will define the competitiveness of the laboring populations (and indeed the broader business climate) that produced them through the mechanism of price. A more competitive workforce produces more goods more cheaply, with the lower costs of production being divided between consumers as sav-

---

[7] Rep. Sander Levin, Democrat from Michigan, made the point during a debate over NAFTA: "This is the first time we've tried to put together two economies that have very dissimilar wage structures, five to one or 10 to one." See "CNN Crossfire," transcript 677, 7 October 1992, 1.

ings and capital controllers as higher profits.[8] In contrast, the direct path occurs through mobility, as when plants move to a population of laborers or the laborers move to the employers. In either case laborers that will likely never meet face-to-face find themselves shoulder-to-shoulder in competition for work.

Indirect pressures on labor in advanced industrial states are not new, only more intense now that manufacturers in poor countries have entered the fray. The important thing about indirect modalities of competition is that historically they are highly vulnerable to political attacks and policy barriers. From the days of mercantilism forward, the record of nations is replete with examples of the movement of *goods* being controlled, limited, or banned entirely, because the movement of goods, especially across nation-state lines, is not a defining element of the capitalist system of production. A complete collapse of trade between nations may sink capitalism into a pathetic malaise, but these developments alone would not necessarily threaten the relations at the core of the system of production. Hence the relative openness of the trade regime has long been a highly contested political issue that has frequently divided different segments of capital-controlling classes and has been open to challenges from labor. If capital were highly immobile transnationally, then the source of competitive pressures would be wholly indirect, through trade. And if the historical record is any indication, laboring populations would have a wide range of political levers at their disposal to place high "exploitation" tariffs on goods produced under authoritarian and abjectly poor conditions.

[8] One of the ideological justifications of an open trade regime across national borders is that even if some workers lose their jobs to foreign or relocated producers, consumers benefit from cheaper imported goods made elsewhere. But it is entirely possible that capital controllers could pocket as super profits the new surplus gained from using cheaper labor. In June 1994 the International Ladies Garment Workers Union purchased space on the New York *Times* op-ed page to argue that consumers were not winning. Two workers, Marie Whitt in the United States and Dorka Diaz in Honduras, sewed the same garments for the Leslie Fay Company. Marie Whitt made $7.80 an hour. In a factory without clean drinking water, Dorka Diaz worked a fifty-four-hour week, including forced overtime, alongside girls twelve and thirteen years old, enduring temperatures reaching one hundred degrees. She made thirty-seven cents an hour. The advertisement charged: "Leslie Fay executives claim they can only 'compete' by producing in factories like Dorka's. But identical skirts—one made by Dorka, the other by Marie—were recently purchased at a big retail chain here [in New York]. Both cost $40. Searching the world for ever-cheaper sources of labor is not the kind of competition America needs." See New York *Times*, 29 June 1994, 9.

The direct mode of competition, however, makes such a policy response far more difficult. The important new development in direct competition is that whereas labor remains predominantly mobile within nations, capital now enjoys a far wider capacity to move across national lines and thus across widely varying laboring populations. This is crucial for three reasons. First, if the obstacles to transnational union organization were already great when the jurisdictions competing were more similar, they grew even larger when capital mobility and technology brought systems in essentially different political and economic eras into direct, productive confrontation in the present. Second, it becomes much harder to block the import of goods or levy an exploitation tax when a significant proportion of the goods are produced abroad by capital controllers from "home." The prospects grow even dimmer when we recall that approximately a third of all trade between national jurisdictions occurs within transnational corporations. No matter where they produce goods, capital controllers make full use of their political leverage at home, even to defend privileges and actions injurious to the people and institutions in their home jurisdictions. And third, competition mediated by the movement of *employers* across national jurisdictional lines is linked to one of the defining pillars of capitalism: the right of private property. Not only is the historical record on governing capital unencouraging, but there is every indication that technological changes have made doing so harder than ever. It is hardly surprising, then, that the issue of greater societal control of capital's location options is not debated seriously. A focus on all these factors would help account for how competition and efficiency have been redefined as well as for how a deep disruption in the balance of power between labor and capital in advanced industrial societies has allowed these notions to press other goals and ideological currents to the margins.

Zonal Capitalism

A special economic zone is a subnational area—sometimes walled, but always clearly bounded—in which an intensified effort has been made to create a climate favorable to business.[9] Government policies within and

[9] For preliminary findings based on research conducted since 1991 on special economic zones in Southeast Asia, see Winters 1994a.

for the zone tend to diverge markedly from those applying generally to the national jurisdiction. It is striking that between 1960 and 1990 such zones grew from an insignificant handful spread over just a couple of countries to thousands stretching across the postcolonial world (though concentrated most heavily in Asia and Latin America). Industrial estates, bonded areas, export processing platforms, and other special economic zones are now so widespread that the very character of capitalist industrialization in these emerging areas has been transformed. Instead of a generalized form of industrialization arising in a more diffuse pattern across national territories, the cutting edge and leading sectors of industry and manufacturing are increasingly concentrated in these zones. The term "zonal capitalism" is intended to distinguish this phenomenon from the way capitalist industry arose before or immediately after World War II.

Again, rather than developing a full argument about the rise and significance of zonal capitalism, the objective here is to suggest the ways a focus on changes in capital mobility—and particularly the dramatic rise in the capacity to fragment production processes and relocate manufacturing facilities over great distances—helps make sense of this development. Capital mobility did not, it should be noted, play a role in the initial formation of the earliest special economic zones,[10] but it was the crucial factor in the accelerating rate at which such zones were erected from the 1970s forward and in the changes to their character since then. The increasing capacity of those controlling direct investment for manufacturing to relocate across national lines heightened competitive pressures among host countries to capture the investments for the jobs, technology, and possible export potential they represented.

Creating an attractive investment climate across an entire national jurisdiction proved to be as technically difficult and costly as it was politically and socially destabilizing. The cost of laying down the sort of infrastructure mobile investors demanded (electricity, communications, roads, ports, water facilities, and the like) was prohibitive if carried out in a generalized way across a whole country. The very range of locations

[10] As an institutional or modal form, they appeared first in the United States and Britain as an instrument of city planning (zoning) to lend order to patterns of industrial location and to manage the proximity of industrial and residential areas. Building on the idea of the industrial district or park, the first use of an industrial estate as an integrated platform to attract investors to an area they might otherwise avoid or ignore was by Britain in Northern Ireland in 1958.

that footloose industries could choose among meant that their bargaining position was unusually strong and their demands for responsive policies unusually broad. At a time when economic nationalism was still strong in Asia, Africa, and Latin America, mobile investors were flocking primarily to those locations that found ways to offer exceptionally appealing terms on majority (or even full) foreign ownership of firms, taxation, import and export tariff relief, full and free convertibility of currency, and relief from a host of other restrictive policies intended to force firms to transfer technology, hire and train local managers, and otherwise meet the local development objectives. Rather than introduce these policies for the whole national jurisdiction and risk a backlash from an emerging class of indigenous manufacturers, it was expedient to set aside special zones within which these incentives could be created. This offered host regimes a dual layer of insulation. Policies that domestic capital viewed as threatening (such as the removal of tariff protection or the entry of new competitors) could be sequestered into relatively tiny enclaves, and any distorting or imperial effects of foreign capital could be contained and more easily monitored. It was also considerably easier to provide the needed infrastructure if the effort could be concentrated geographically into zones.

The state took the lead in this first phase of zonal capitalism and industrialization by establishing and operating the estates themselves. But the competitive pressures exerted by mobile capital soon overwhelmed the capacity and resources of the state. Mobile investors complained that special zones planned and managed by governments were built too slowly, were badly run, and generally reflected the political struggles and inefficiencies of the state bureaucracy. By the early 1980s a second phase was already evident in zonal capitalism's evolution. Firms showed a strong preference for locating in privately controlled estates. As a result, governments retreated even further in their development function as mobile capital joined with local partners to take over the construction, management, and ownership of special economic zones. In the meantime, many government-owned estates were sold. Although the rise and spread of industrialization has always been concentrated geographhically, it is impossible to understand the increasingly zonal character of industrialization during the past three decades without reference to the intense pressures manifested in the wider global mobility of capital, especially in the form of direct investment.

The Politics of NAFTA

As with the story of zonal capitalism, many elements of the struggle over the North American Free Trade Agreement (NAFTA) can be illuminated by focusing on the political economy of capital mobility. This section underscores its utility in accounting for the political splits and alliances that arose for and against the treaty, as well as why certain novel policy demands were advanced by those seeking to make the treaty less narrowly responsive to the interests of mobile capital. Beginning first with the issue of major splits, different fragments of capital-controlling classes in the United States have locked horns over the trade regime many times in the past. But the battles surrounding NAFTA mark the first time the new threats inherent in the capacity of *some* capital controllers to relocate their plants and factories across national lines were so squarely at the heart of the conflict.

Table 4 provides a sense of the fairly sharp split within the business community between producers that were highly mobile and those that were relatively immobile. In their vocal opposition to NAFTA, small and medium-sized American manufacturers were not simply making yet another call for protection of the domestic market from cheaper imports. Indeed, in all the commentary and debates surrounding the treaty, it is extremely rare to find American businesses complaining about imported goods produced by *Mexican* manufacturers. What really angered and threatened immobile manufacturers in the United States was the way NAFTA helped *American* producers both operate from Mexico and ship their products back to the United States. In John Cregan's words, "This treaty is a winner for multinational corporations that have the resources to relocate in Mexico."[11] Whereas competition with Mexican firms was deemed reasonable (perhaps because they had yet to pose a major threat), competing with U.S. firms that could ship whole systems of production abroad—involving management, technology, and established continental marketing networks—was viewed as highly unacceptable. The crux of the matter, as immobile producers rightly pointed out, was that NAFTA accelerated the unraveling of a system in which the vast majority of producers of manufactured goods competing for the U.S. market operated either within the United States or within an advanced

[11] Cregan 1992:14A. Cregan, president of the U.S. Business and Industrial Council, emerged as one of the most visible and vocal business opponents of NAFTA.

Table 4. American business positions on NAFTA

Supported treaty	Opposed treaty
American Chamber of Commerce Country's largest umbrella organization for business, dominated by large firms.	**U.S. Business and Industrial Council** Chaired by John Cregan; 1,500 members, mostly medium-sized manufacturers.
U.S. - Mexico Trade Group of the Business Roundtable Chaired by Kay Whitmore, president and CEO of Eastman Kodak. Roundtable represents CEOs from nation's largest firms.	**National Federation of Independent Businesses** 600,000 members, 80 percent employing fewer than 40 workers.
Emergency Committee for American Trade Lobbying group representing 60 CEOs from Fortune 100 firms.	**American Trade Coalition** Broad-based group founded by John Cregan and others.
U.S. Council for International Business Based in New York City, the council represents 300 MNCs.	**Alliance for Responsible Trade** A group in Washington, D.C., that included bodies representing small and medium firms.
U.S.A. - NAFTA Chaired by Sandra Masur, director of international trade policy at Eastman Kodak. An umbrella body dominated by large firms that hired the Wexler Group to spearhead its lobbying effort.	

Source: Data from newspaper reports.

industrial country with a relatively similar standard of living. The agreement made it easier for a producer who once faced a more unified or linked production-consumption space to separate the political-economic milieu in which goods were produced from that in which they were consumed. Quite apart from the impact this separation would have on labor, businesses that could not play the same game were plainly nonplussed. Cregan, speaking on behalf of immobile investors, put the case bluntly during a televised exchange with Carla Hills, the U.S. trade representative, and Kay Whitmore, who represented CEOs of highly mobile firms in the Business Roundtable:

> The problem we have is that we think that this agreement is tilted more towards the Fortune 100 companies, the multinationals, the trans-national companies that have large economies of scale, international divisions of

labor that can have assembly plants in Mexico, [and] enjoy workers for 80 cents an hour. And our companies (and we are a conservative organization) have to stay—are primarily located in this country and they're facing these regulatory burdens, some of the most burdensome that we've ever had, very high tax rates, and I think that's a little bit of a double standard for the government to impose these regulations and these high taxes, and then with a little wink and a nod say, well, if you want to go to Mexico, you can hire workers for 80 cents or a dollar an hour, you don't have to have these regulations, you don't have to have these taxes, and you have an advantage over the medium and small sized manufacturing companies.[12]

Not only was Cregan explicit in citing relative mobility as the major divide among capital controllers on NAFTA, but in all his pronouncements in the media he maintained a narrow focus on American firms that gain the double advantage of producing with cheaper laborers while escaping American regulations (on environment, working conditions, and the like), courts, and tax rates.

It is hardly surprising that major segments of the union and environmental movements were allied in their opposition to NAFTA. What was surprising was that these movements were joined by organizations such as the United States Business and Industrial Council. In somewhat strained overtures to workers, Cregan, who also founded the American Trade Coalition, characterized the job training and worker adjustment programs backed by Clinton and Bush during the 1992 presidential campaign as a worker's version of the golden handshake. A staunch conservative who backed Pat Buchanan for president, Cregan played to labor by saying the programs were "an unequivocal admission by both Clinton and Bush that unemployment will increase as a result of NAFTA," adding, "basically, this is government severance pay, and a warning to many workers that their days are numbered."[13]

Further research will shed light on how deep the waters of this alliance ran. What is interesting here is how the new capital mobility pressed environmentalists, labor, and some segments of U.S. manufacturing capital to pursue overlapping agendas. Because NAFTA's supporters won an early victory in putting the negotiations on a fast track, which favored those players with substantial structural power and disadvan-

---

[12] *McNeil/Lehrer News Hour,* transcript 4431, 12 August 1992, 1.
[13] *International Trade Reporter,* 14 October 1992.

taged those who needed to mobilize other forms of political leverage to be effective, all opponents wanted to slow down the negotiations. "What we have a problem with," Cregan explained, "is the speed with which this was negotiated. I don't understand why we had to have the negotiators locked up in a hotel room for day after day after day, when the only deadline that I can see is really a self-imposed one."[14] Moreover, because the main tension was prompted by threats posed by capital mobility across national boundaries, opponents shared the goal of reducing the differentials across jurisdictional lines that made relocation tempting (or advantageous) in the first place.

But here the similarities, and the bases for alliance, break down. Relatively immobile manufacturers represented by people like Cregan wanted to achieve greater parity by dramatically reducing the "regulatory burden" in the United States. The labor and environmental movements, meanwhile, sought the same end but through opposite means: by building elements into the treaty that not only maintained the regulatory framework of the United States but extended its reach to Mexico.[15] As a presidential candidate Clinton vowed not to support NAFTA unless it included side agreements creating environmental and labor tribunals that could investigate such things as child labor, minimum wages, and toxic-waste cleanup. Since such tribunals would effectively extend American regulations and institutions across all of North America, it is hardly surprising that Mexico and Canada objected on the grounds of national sovereignty. Three months into his presidency, Clinton gutted the tribunals by saying that in place of subpoena and sanction power, they would function through "moral suasion."[16] An alternative proposed by some NAFTA opponents was to extend the reach of U.S. laws and courts *at least* to U.S. companies and managers who relocated to Mexico. It is an interesting proposal in part because it seeks to keep notions of national control over citizens alive even as the nationality of capital and firms becomes more blurred. Although this alternative par-

[14] *McNeil/Lehrer News Hour,* transcript 4431, 12 August 1992, 3
[15] See Robinson 1993.
[16] Mashberg 1993:77. It is apparent that mobile capital was also uncomfortable with the tribunals. Robert L. McNeill, executive vice chairman of the Emergency Committee for American Trade, which represented sixty CEOs from Fortune 100 firms, told the reporter: "We're working on the assumption that there will be a NAFTA, but without tribunals that are given the force of law."

tially addresses the sovereignty concerns and also has precedent in laws like the Foreign Corrupt Practices Act,[17] it was largely ignored.

Almost entirely absent from the debate were any proposals arguing that mobile capital ought to be controlled (much less suggesting how this could be done). Thea Lee, an economist for the Economic Policy Institute, made a start when she argued that the costs of environmental cleanup at the border, worker retraining, and other adjustment assistance be charged to firms relocating to Mexico. Rather than lay the burden on taxpayers, mobile capital should pay relocation and transaction fees.[18] Herman Daly went the furthest. He argued that free trade is a misnomer because it creates the illusion that a fully open trade regime allows anyone to trade anywhere. Recalling United Nations data showing that the world's 15 largest corporations have sales larger than the GDPs of 120 countries and that fully two-thirds of all trade is undertaken by the world's 500 largest global firms (and virtually all of it by the top 1,000), Daly pointed out that deregulating the international trade regime allowed the biggest traders to get even bigger while small and medium firms in every country had to face stiffer competition. "Cosmopolitan global capitalism weakens national boundaries and the power of national and sub-national communities," he noted, "while strengthening the relative power of transnational corporations."[19] Given that the rise of an international government capable of regulating cosmopolitan capital was both doubtful and undesirable, Daly argued, it was evident that capital should be made less mobile and more national. Although these views were carried by the Inter Press wire service, there is no evidence that the articles were picked up by any of the national dailies.

In addition to helping make sense of splits, alliances, and the logic behind different strategies for reducing the impact of NAFTA on the United States, a sensitivity to mobility would also help predict who would be least likely to be actively engaged in the political battles surrounding the treaty. Workers with immobile employers in nontradable sectors like education, construction, health care, government at all jurisdictional levels, and a broad range of services not only would tend to be

---

[17] Stemming from the Lockheed scandal in Japan, this law holds Americans criminally liable in U.S. courts for engaging in corporate bribery in any country.

[18] *International Trade Daily*, 22 September 1992, 1. The EPI is a think tank funded by the labor movement.

[19] Chatterjee 1994:1.

more insulated from the structural power of capital controllers (for reasons suggested earlier), but would also be less likely rise to a challenge like NAFTA. Unions such as the American Federation of State, County, and Municipal Employees (AFSCME), the American Federation of Teachers (AFT), and the National Education Association (NEA) were extremely slow to react to NAFTA. Just two days before Congress was to vote the treaty up or down, the AFSCME finally held a major rally against it in Washington, D.C.[20] When Gerald McEntee, international president of the union, explained the logic behind their opposition, the best he could muster was an argument about the indirect repercussions of the treaty on AFSCME members: "To the extent that NAFTA negatively impacts on employment and wages, it will directly affect government tax revenues. Federal, state, and local governments will lose tax revenues from businesses that relocate and from individuals who become jobless or agree to lower wages and reduced benefits in order to preserve their jobs at any price. Thus NAFTA will shrink tax revenues, likely forcing governments to lay off employees and cut programs, precisely at the moment when the demand for entitlement benefits and government services will rise."[21] According to one observer, the reason many unions were slow to organize resistance to the treaty as negotiated "is that many unions thought it of little concern to them. The public service unions, the teachers, didn't fear their jobs trickling south, and so AFSCME and the AFT were among Clinton's earliest supporters. Construction unions were similarly indifferent."[22]

Nigeria

To further develop the range of the capital mobility approach, let us turn to the case of Nigeria since independence. For a variety of reasons

[20] Although other unions were fully mobilized and applying pressure on Clinton and Bush during the 1992 presidential election, the AFSCME did not make its first pronouncements on NAFTA until May 1993. In August 1993, the Public Services International, of which the AFSCME is the largest member, adopted a resolution in opposition to NAFTA at its twenty-fifth World Congress in Helsinki, Finland. Agreements like NAFTA, the resolution stated, have the potential to "cause massive job loss, economic dislocation, and erosion of social and human rights." See Rivera 1993:1. For a report on the equally late reaction by the NEA, see *Daily Report Card,* 17 November 1993, 1.

[21] Rivera 1993.

[22] Cockburn 1992:489.

Nigeria is an excellent context for comparisons with Indonesia. Like Indonesia, it is a postcolonial state with a huge population comprising multiple ethnic groups speaking scores of mutually unintelligible languages. Oil has played a crucial role in the political economy of both states. Moreover, authoritarian military governments have dominated both countries during most of their postindependence histories. But despite these similarities, it is the differences that are most prominent and interesting analytically. This section considers how these differences sharpen and deepen the theoretical tools and insights already developed in the Indonesian case. The most important lessons to be learned from a parallel study of Nigeria center on the interplay between the intensity of the structural pressures generated by controllers of mobile capital and the capacity of policymakers to respond effectively to those pressures.

Although Suharto clearly tried at various times to pursue dual and quite contradictory agendas, he nearly always ended up being responsive to strong structural constraints rather than resisting or ignoring them. If one were to consider only a case like Suharto's Indonesia, it would be easy to develop a rather mechanistic and deterministic mode of thinking—such that when structural pressures imposed by capital are great and the consequences of failing to respond positively are likely to be politically and economically devastating, then even policymakers who may not *want* to create a more favorable policy climate for mobile capital will be compelled to do so. The Nigerian case supplies a corrective to such easy conclusions. Although the structural pressures on Nigeria were in some ways even more intense than those on Indonesia, favorable responses to those controlling the capital the country desperately required were not forthcoming.

For a variety of political and institutional reasons, the Nigerian system proved far less *capable* of producing policy responses. This does not mean structural pressures were absent; the evidence is overwhelming that the pressures were perceived and understood. And it is equally evident that the Nigerian system has paid a heavy political and economic price for failing to respond. This book opened with the caution that pressures and constraints do not lead in any necessary or automatic way to policy outcomes that relieve the pressures or recognize the constraints. A host of factors mediate not only the intensity of the pressures but also the willingness and capacity of policymakers to respond effectively. Two of these factors are particularly relevant to Nigeria:

1. A high degree of institutional and organizational incoherence—marked by a high turnover of officials, little policy-making continuity, frequent coups, or a weak center for decision making—can lead to unresponsive state policies despite the clear presence of structural pressures from those controlling investment resources.
2. A jurisdiction in which the opposition to the regime in power is unorganized, co-opted, fractured, destroyed, or otherwise rendered ineffectual will be less vulnerable to pressures exerted by capital controllers than one in which the societal forces of opposition are united and well equipped to react to economic stress. This includes fragmentation along regional, racial, religious, ethnic, or ideological lines.

A sensitivity to these considerations is crucial for understanding why similar structural pressures resulted in quite divergent patterns of response. And it is in the nuances of these mediating factors, moreover, that one finds much of the richness of an approach focused on capital mobility.

The first crucial difference between Indonesia and Nigeria centers on the concentration of effective political power at each system's center. Although both countries represent an amalgam of ethnicities and groups, key historical experiences have shaped how ethnicity operates politically and institutionally. It is striking that despite Indonesia's scattered geography, power over the entire system has been heavily concentrated in the institutions based in Jakarta. It is equally striking that despite the preponderant governing role played by the military in Nigeria since independence, power remains more diffused and fragmented. The political expression of ethnicity is a major factor in this divergence.

Alhough both countries performed in similarly patrimonial-distributive ways during the oil boom years (with the exception that Suharto's concern about danger from the countryside resulted in significant investment in agriculture and irrigation), their reactions to the oil bust starting in 1982 were decidedly dissimilar. Indonesia managed to reduce its dependence on the mining and export of fossil fuels for government revenue and foreign exchange. Nonenergy goods leaped from 20 percent of total exports at the height of the oil boom to 60 percent by 1993, with 42 percent of this from manufactures. Over the same period, oil and gas exports from Nigeria *increased* from 96 to 98 percent. Manufacturing remained at only 8.6 percent of GDP in Nigeria, whereas it rose to twice that level in Indonesia.[23] The wealthy and privileged aside, Nigerians have paid a high price both economically and politically for the system's incapacity to respond with policies to attract and retain capital at a time when the state's own oil-based resources were dropping in value. Peter Lewis reports that since the early 1980s, "Per capita income in Nigeria has dropped 75% and the economy has experienced virtually no real growth. Nigeria's nonoil sectors are perhaps the least productive among comparable developing countries [including Indonesia], and Nigeria has one of the most skewed and unstable oil-exporting economies in the world."[24] By the end of the 1980s, Nigeria's value added in manufacturing was half that of Pakistan, a quarter that of Venezuela, and a fifth that of Indonesia. Nigeria's first political response to the pressures of the oil bust was to stage yet another military coup in 1983. A structural adjustment program was finally attempted in 1986 but was "near collapse" just six years later.

Even those who argue that communal and regional divisions are growing less salient in Nigeria's political economy admit that no single factor is more important for explaining how the country responds to various challenges and opportunities.[25] Before sketching how these ethnic divisions shaped Nigeria's response to constraints, we need to rehearse some basic details of the Indonesian case. The fascinating fact about ethnic politics in Indonesia is how muted are the tensions across groups, regions, and even religions. The reasons are many and complicated, but a few key points can be offered for comparison and contrast with Nigeria. About the same time the British were finally taking control of the area today called Nigeria, a group of young Indonesian intellectuals drawn from different parts of the archipelago were meeting to launch a nationalist movement that would eventually bring to a close nearly three centuries of widening Dutch hegemony. Even though the Javanese were by far the largest ethnolinguistic category, the activists had already decided early in this century to adopt the neutral trade language of Malay-Indonesian as the national language. A second point is that the struggle for independence itself involved considerable violence as the

[23] *Economist* 328, 7825 (1994): 7

[24] Lewis 1994:437.

[25] See, for instance, Diamond 1988. By the early 1990s, ethnic tensions appeared to run as deep as ever. According to one observer, "Nigeria has not looked so close to the edge in years." See *Economist* 328 7825 (1994): 12.

Dutch refused to give up peacefully in 1945, despite their own country's devastation from the German occupation of Holland. Indonesia's army arose and was commanded regionally, yet it fought from the start for a national cause against a common enemy. This eased the transition, fully achieved by the early 1970s, to a truly national armed forces based in Jakarta with loyalties less to regional divisions dating from the war of independence than to fellow officers graduating from the military academies in the same class. Even when revolutionary movements based outside Java sprang up in the late 1950s, they were never secessionist in character. Instead they were intended to shift the locus of power within Indonesia away from the archipelago's most populous but least endowed island.[26]

A third point is that while communal divisions do exist in Indonesia, they have been greatly overshadowed by ideological cleavages based on class. In 1965 Indonesia had the largest Communist Party outside a communist country, and it was during the annihilation of this threat from below that upward of a million people were massacred. And finally, easily the deepest communal division cuts not regionally or ethnically but racially—between the overwhelming majority of poor Indonesians of Malay descent and the tiny slice of the citizenry of Chinese descent that controls the bulk of the country's local capital. Since persons of Chinese descent are barred from leadership in the military and the bureaucracy, this cleavage does not find expression in the state's two key institutions of control and legislation. The upshot of all of these factors is that despite being ethnically more diverse than Nigeria, Indonesia is considerably less torn by ethnic divisions. Solidarity within the military, the primary coercive apparatus, has been high since the late 1960s, but especially since 1974 when Suharto crushed the last significant challenge from competing generals. Suharto, who was credited at home and abroad with crushing the PKI in 1965, was able to pull tremendous power into his own hands as he systematically dismantled all competing societal institutions. By the time the oil boom ended, his political position was secure enough to permit him to shift national policies in a rapid and even radical fashion.

---

[26] The clear exceptions are rebellious regions either never fully incorporated into the Dutch colonial territory (Aceh) or acquired by invasion after independence (the former Portuguese colony of East Timor).

The contrasts with Nigeria are striking. Beginning with the colonial legacy, British colonial policy heightened the sense of division among the major communities making up Nigeria. The colony was formed as recently as 1900. The northern portion was administered through a system of indirect rule that kept most power vested in Muslim emirs. The south was administered separately, even after an official amalgamation was undertaken in 1914. As Sam Oyovbaire explains, it was not until 1947 that leaders in the north and the south finally met for formal discussions about affairs of state. So divided was British administration of the colony that people joked at the time, "If Nigerians were to leave Nigeria [of the period to the 1940s], the British would go to war with each other."[27] In 1939 the British decided to split the south into western and eastern sections, further exaggerating the weight and size of the north. Each of three parts of the colony was dominated by a major ethnolinguistic group, with the Yoruba in the west, the Igbo in the east, and the Hausa-Fulani in the north—outnumbering the west and east combined. To make divisions and identifications even sharper, the British isolated the emirs of the north from Christian missionaries, who aggressively spread Western education, cultural influences, and even economic opportunities across the south.

Ethnicity and regional-religious divisions have played a role in both of the mediating factors under discussion. They have reduced the strength of the governing center and conditioned the range of feasible responses to challenges and opportunities. But they have also diluted and divided societal responses to dislocation and economic decline by giving prominence to vertical-ethnic interpretations and responses over horizontal-class reactions based on ideological grounds that straddle regions and ethnicities. Taking these in turn, the focus is first on the civilian leadership.

"At its inception," Lewis argues, "the Nigerian state lacked a core of authority, and the nation's elites were divided by powerful cultural and spatial allegiances." Characterizing postindependence Nigerian politics as predominantly "neopatrimonial," Lewis notes that the patron-client relations at the core of the system have been conditioned in such a way that ethnicity and regional identities form the principal bases for clientalist affiliations. "Communal networks suffuse the institutions of the

---

[27] Quoted in Oyovbaire 1993:12.

state, and allocative decisions by government are influenced by invidious sectional competition."[28] Relations among Nigeria's three main ethnic groups are so tense that the last census was taken in 1963. Another was attempted in 1973 but caused such an uproar that its results had to be discarded to prevent an outbreak of communal violence. "No one has yet claimed full factual knowledge of the number of communities or ethnic groups in Nigeria," Oyovbaire points out. Some scholars have claimed there are over four hundred. Two government commissions investigated the issue of ethnic minorities in 1957 and 1975, but the results were inconclusive.[29] The depth of ethnic divisions has blocked the emergence of Suharto-style personal rule. Instead, a much more fluid and shifting pattern of "ethnic accommodation" has arisen to deal with group jealousies and ambitions. Lewis writes: "Nigeria's neopatrimonial system has developed in the context of shifting elite coalitions, collegial leadership and administrative devolution. State resources have been controlled by a heterogenous political class cemented by factional alliances and ethnic accommodation, rather than by a single personage or a cohesive party leadership."[30] Government officials may exercise considerable power in shaping clientelist structures, but no single group has managed to dominate the system. Rather, a distributive game of balancing communal access to state goodies best characterizes the operation of the Nigerian state. "Consequently," Lewis writes, "major regional groups expect equivalent chances to capture state largesse and to control some portion of the state organization. A form of moral economy obtains: contentious sectional elites do not expect equity, but they do hold a claim on fair opportunity in the struggle for resources. Historically, the violation of this implicit compact has eroded the legitimacy of regimes and incited civil conflict."[31]

When sharply declining oil revenues restored the structural leverage of capital controllers in demanding responsive policies, the Nigerian state was badly equipped to match Suharto's shift to his team of economic ministers who could deliver laws and reforms, most of which impinged directly on key state patrons and their clients. Nigeria's patron-client center was so parcellized along regional and ethnic lines that a parallel

[28] Lewis 1994:442
[29] See Oyovbaire 1993:6.
[30] Lewis 1994:442.
[31] Lewis 1994:440.

response would have involved complex negotiations for shared deprivation in place of shared spoils. "State autonomy is limited," Lewis emphasizes, "both in the realm of policy formulation and at the infrastructural
level. The unstable administrative and political framework undermines
the pursuit of a coherent strategy of development, and pervasive clientelist pressures impede effective resource allocation."[32] As the Indonesian
case study in this book has suggested, the central tension in the country's
political economy since the mid-1960s has been over the terms of economic access and opportunity. Those defending allocation through a
clientelist network radiating outward from President Suharto have struggled against those demanding allocation by more impersonal market
forces. The first system favors political supporters and regime clients
down to the village level, while the second favors those controlling capital, production facilities, and networks of distribution. So pervasive are
ethnic-regional cleavages in Nigeria that they crowd out these classic
tensions associated with political-economic transitions to market
capitalism.

Often the military is viewed as an institution of last resort that will rise
above societal cleavages and pursue the "national" interest in a profes-
sional and regimented manner. Although the evidence suggests that communal divisions are more muted in the Nigerian armed forces, they
remain a salient factor. The Nigerian military was organized during the
British period as a constabulary designed mainly for internal control and
policing of the colony.[33] For most of the preindependence era, military
planning and budgeting were done separately in the north and south,
though the two arms of the military were merged into the West African
Frontier Force. From the earliest days of recruitment, there was a high
concentration of Igbo among the officers, with northerners making up
the bulk of the rank and file. After independence a conscious attempt
was made to use quotas in commissions and recruitment to achieve a
balance of 50 percent from the north and 25 percent each from the west
and east. By the first military coup in 1966 little progress had been made
toward these more balanced proportions.[34] Moreover, unlike the situation in Indonesia, because independence was achieved without going to
war with the British there was no turbulent nationalist struggle through

---

[32] Lewis 1994:440.
[33] On the history of the Nigerian armed forces see Ukpabi 1987 and Luckham 1971.
[34] A useful summary of these developments can be found in Ekoko 1990.

which soldiers and officers from different parts of the colony could forge lasting bonds through battles against a common enemy. Instead, the Nigerian armed forces had their birth of fire in the three-year *civil war* that erupted in 1967 when the Igbo attempted to establish an independent state in the oil-rich east. Thus, whereas Nigeria managed to match Indonesia in the slaughter of perhaps a million people in the latter half of the 1960s, the primary challenge was not communist-ideological, but rather ethnic-regional.[35]

As the Nigerian armed forces have entered more deeply into the country's political conflicts, the predominantly ethnic foundations of those conflicts were increasingly refracted back into the military itself. "The officers corps has been increasingly politicized, breaking into several factions and cliques and destroying its traditional *esprit de corps*," A. E. Ekoko argues, with the result that "political and ethnic considerations loom larger."[36] Between 1960 and 1993 Nigeria endured five successful military coups, at least four attempted coups, six different military leaders, and only nine years without soldiers in power. The first coup in 1966 had strong Igbo elements and involved the murder of the premiers in the north and west but spared Igbo leaders in the east. Hundreds of Igbo living in the north were murdered in retaliation. A second coup that same year brought to power a Christian from the Muslim-dominated north as a compromise candidate.[37]

The situation had not improved much by the late 1980s. At the 1987 graduation ceremony for officers at the Command and Staff College, President Babangida, himself a general, admitted that "the military cohesion exhibited cracks due to ethnic, religious, political, and class leanings." Discipline was undermined by what he termed "godfatherism," and the military's sense of nationalism and patriotism were "deeply

---

[35] Material factors played a crucial role in precipitating the Biafran war. From 1940 to 1960, the regional governments of the north and west favored high levels of direct state control over revenue because their own production of groundnuts and cocoa was the main source of export revenue. As petroleum revenue began to come on line in the 1960s and the north and west realized they had virtually none of the country's reserves, they reversed their positions in favor of surrendering most state revenue to the central government and having shares distributed to the regions based on population size. Just after declaring its secession, eastern Nigeria instructed the foreign oil companies to pay £20 million to it rather than to the federal government. As a majority shareholder in Shell-BP, the British government vetoed the payment. See Rupley 1981:257–277.

[36] Ekoko 1990:12.

[37] Diamond 1988:45.

truncated and diluted by sectional and parochial loyalties."[38] As he was swearing in members of his Armed Forces Ruling Council in 1989, Babangida admonished his generals: "You are not representing your states, tribes, religions or any geographic expression. Your constituency is the Nigerian nation, period."[39] A few months later the president offered reassurances about unity within the armed forces, saying there were "no cracks in any wall, the wall is as strong as ever." Shortly thereafter rebel soldiers attacked Babangida's Lagos base at Dodan barracks and announced the overthrow of the government "on behalf of the patriotic and well-meaning peoples of the Middle Belt and southern parts of the country." The coup leaders, who were predominantly Yoruban, voiced regional and Christian complaints. Their first governing act was to announce the expulsion of five Muslim states in the north from the Nigerian federation. A general loyal to Babangida managed to foil the attempted coup just seven hours after it was begun.[40]

Larry Diamond's assessment of the impact of ethnic and regional divisions on the armed forces parallels that of Lewis on the Nigerian state in general. Unlike the case in Indonesia, where President Suharto—himself a general who staffed his authoritarian regime with military figures from top to bottom—succeeded in accumulating enormous power without a single coup attempt in three decades, the more deeply fractured Nigerian context forbids the emergence of such a strongman. "Nigeria's volatile ethnic and religious diversity has made it difficult to institutionalize authoritarian rule," Diamond writes. The rotation of military leaders alleviates the tendency of groups to see the regime as solidly against them. An entrenched Suharto-style regime cannot be transplanted to Nigeria because "the ethnic identity of the few top leaders assumes exaggerated importance, and the distribution of power and resources takes on an aura of permanence, which makes it much more fundamentally threatening to groups that feel excluded or inadequately included."[41]

[38] Ekoko 1990:12.

[39] *Reuters*, 13 February 1989, 1.

[40] *Economist*, 26 April 1990. As recently as August 1993 the armed forces found themselves responding to attacks from the press, which is estimated to be 90 percent Yoruban owned, that army commissions and salary decisions were ethnically biased. See "Army Denies Reports of Commissioning Based on Ethnicity," *BBC*, 4 August 1993.

[41] Diamond 1988:68. For reasons quite specific to each country's history, the ideological foundations for entrenched military rule differ significantly. The Indonesian armed forces claim to have a legitimate *dwi-fungsi* or dual function in national life, given that they

By constraining and dividing power at the center, these factors impinged directly on the relative capacity of the Nigerian state to respond as Indonesia did to very similar structural pressures when the oil boom ended in the 1980s. As I mentioned above, ethnic and regional divisions also conditioned the nature of the societal response to the dislocations and decline that came in the wake of the state's inability to create a more inviting climate for capital controllers. One of the prime reasons state leaders introduce market-friendly policies—even when they are clearly detrimental to regime supporters, who benefited enormously when officials carved up the economy and doled out access—is a strong concern that failing to satisfy the demands of capital controllers will reduce investment levels, which will reduce job creation, slow production, and cut off access to credit. Once this economic decline is set in motion, political decline usually follows close behind. It is plain that the punishment capital can inflict has been delivered in Nigeria. But in an ironic twist, the same ethnic and regional cleavages that undermined the capacity of the military-dominated state to respond in a sustained way with policies capital controllers judged favorable also diluted and fragmented the pressures the Nigerian population could exert against state leaders. Indeed, it is not entirely clear that the economic devastation described by Lewis and others can even be interpreted by Nigerians in a way that could result in a frontal challenge to the country's governing elites.

In a sense, ethnic divisions have reduced the dangers to the federal government of Nigeria because economic dislocation and declining standards of living tend to be seen in communal and regional terms rather than along class or even urban-rural lines. Jealousies and resentments run more horizontally than vertically, so that the primary Igbo concern is whether the Yoruba are doing as badly, and both look with suspicion at the Hausa-Fulani to make sure the rough times are not caused by the northern states' grabbing more than their share.[42] The shifting and ro-

---

arose from the people and struggled in tandem with civilian officials to gain independence from the Dutch. The Nigerian military has far less historical material to justify its hold on power. "It is revealing of the nature of the society and its political culture," Diamond notes, "that every Nigerian military regime has committed itself, at least verbally, to an eventual return to civilian rule, and no regime that has seemed to betray this democratic commitment has been able to survive."

[42] Nigeria's experience with privatization is emblematic of the problem. When the federal government under Babangida announced its intention in 1987 to privatize 275 federally owned firms, the reaction was framed in communal terms. From the outset

tating nature of distributive politics at the country's center compounds the already formidable obstacles to class-based identifications and challenges posed by strong ethnic divisions that map almost perfectly onto Nigeria's thirty states. Instead of being confronted with a broad, potentially revolutionary threat to the state, Nigeria is left to deal with more isolated regional rebellions and attempts at secession that demand what Nigerians appear to have raised to a fine art—a regional balancing act. The contrast with Indonesia is striking. Because ethnic and regional divisions are shallower, and because the precedent of the PKI showed that class-based challenges to the country's elites could be mounted effectively, the dangers of failing to adopt reforms that generated new investment and production in the early 1980s were far higher. Thus Suharto not only felt capital's pressures more acutely, he also had at his disposal a stronger governing center with which to act.

The Increasing Power of Capital

In the closing decades of the twentieth century we have witnessed the beginning of a "locational revolution." As a phase in the development of capitalism, it promises to be as disruptive economically and as transformative politically as the Industrial Revolution that began more than a century ago. Then as now, populations of direct producers, political elites, and those controlling the investment resources everyone depends on were confronted with new forms of production as well as shifting sources and allocations of wealth and power. While industrialization unfolded in the North, most of the rest of the world either was excluded or took part as colonized suppliers of raw materials or consumers of imported goods. This arrangement not only fueled the wealth of the North but also permitted labor to struggle against capital over the surplus from production (not to mention reshaping the broader political-legal milieu) without having to contend with direct competition from an almost endless supply of workers in the colonies who were far poorer and had no hope of gaining wider political leverage. Colonies and col-

---

northerners were suspicious of the scheme because southerners had far more capital with which to bid for shares. The Muslims in the north argued that if southerners succeeded in grabbing all the state firms, the north would be even more economically disadvantaged. See Lewis 1990:210–233.

onizers were deeply intertwined and yet in important respects were quite insulated from each other. The great strides northern laborers made both economically and politically were promoted by this insulation.

Capital mobility played a crucial part in maintaining the hermetic seal on the struggles unfolding in the North from the beginning of the Industrial Revolution until the first decades after World War II. It is not that capital was immobile during this period. On the contrary, for centuries capital had circulated in large quantities over great distances. It was the *form* capital mobility assumed and its impact on the spatial distribution of production that were the key. Even as finance and portfolio capital moved widely and rapidly, direct investment in factories and plants remained strongly concentrated in Europe, North America, and somewhat later, Japan until the closing decades of this century. Only then did the location options for production expand dramatically, and only then did the insulation between workers in now profoundly dissimilar contexts begin to wear thin.

For labor in advanced industrial countries, the party is over (if we may so term the bitter and often brutal struggle they have waged against propertied classes). It is not yet clear how devastating the new capital mobility and the new geography of production are going to be. But if the trends of declining power and wealth for workers in North America and Europe continue for several decades at their current pace, there is reason for considerable alarm. Giovanni Arrighi disagrees, however, and suggests that a longer-range and more global perspective is needed. The relocation of capital and jobs, he argues, represents not "a reduction in the overall social power of the world proletariat" but rather "a transfer of social power from one segment of the world proletariat to another segment." He adds that "the tendency of the first half of the twentieth century towards a spatial polarization of the social power and mass misery of labour in different and separate regions of the world-economy has begun to be reversed."[43] Although certainly correct in pointing out that the relocation of firms or productive processes is simultaneously a loss for one pool of laborers and a gain for another, Arrighi skirts the issue that for the time being (and probably for a considerable time to come) the ability of investors to pit laborers that are more politically and economically advantaged against those living under conditions of poverty and dictatorship represents a clear and dramatic *net gain* in the

[43] Arrighi 1990:51–2.

power of capital controllers in advanced industrial states and, until laborers make headway both politically and economically in postcolonial states, a net gain globally as well. Given that political elites in authoritarian states routinely argue that concessions cannot be made to labor because every effort must be made to maintain and expand their ability to attract mobile investors, a more pessimistic view than Arrighi presents may be warranted.

That organized labor and the Left in general are everywhere feeling defeated and even immobilized by the sharp increase in capital's structural power during the past two decades is clear and was probably the prime factor motivating David Gordon to write his critique of the "new international division of labor" (NIDL) orthodoxy. While admitting that the problem is real, Gordon maintains that the global mobility of investors must be kept in perspective. "Yes, they have huge resources. And yes, they can still take their capital out on strike if they dislike our behaviour at the bargaining table. But they are much less invulnerable, with far less security about the future, than many on the left appear to believe." The NIDL orthodoxy has, in Gordon's view, "helped foster . . . a spreading political fatalism in the advanced countries. If we struggle to extend the frontiers of subsistence and security at home, one gathers, we shall stare balefully at capital's behind, strutting across the continents and seas, leaving us to amuse ourselves with our unrealized dreams of progress and the reality of our diminishing comparative advantage." "I disagree with these political inferences," Gordon writes. "The opportunity for enhanced popular power remains ripe."[44]

To say "remains ripe" probably overstates the opportunities of the past, but it certainly exaggerates the possibilities for the present and the decades immediately ahead. This is not to suggest that capital controllers are positioned so sweetly that they have no grounds for worry. As in every era marked by huge disparities of power, wealth, influence, and status, the political economy contains deep contradictions that will eat away at the edifice of the system until at least some of the conflicts are resolved. One contradiction lies in the disjunction that has arisen between the best locations to produce goods and the best locations to sell them. If decline in advanced industrial contexts outpaces improvements in living standards across the postcolonial world (and not merely the mathematical expressions of higher GDPs per capita, but meaningful

[44] Gordon 1988:25, 64.

distribution), then the disjunction could lead to a crisis of production and consumption as job deterioration in the industrial centers saps effective demand that is not replaced by equally effective demand elsewhere.

Unlike earlier phases in capital mobility, this most recent phase has introduced a particularly strong (though still latent) force that undermines the legitimacy of private property as a basic institution of capitalism. Partly reflecting the extent of capital immobility in the past, a myth prevails in most communities that capital has nationality. Tied to this myth is an expectation that even as investors pursue their self-interest, the net welfare of the rest of the community ought to be advanced along the way. An entire capitalist ideology was built around the notion that self-enriching propertied classes serve a social function as the managers of the society's capital, operating efficiently and yielding abundance and innovation. The new capital mobility threatens to shatter this myth as people increasingly witness jobs and factories relocated to other national jurisdictions, with all the benefits accruing to capital controllers (and perhaps distant workers) and none to their fellow citizens. The chance increases that class tensions will sharpen, improving the odds that capital controls or other limits on mobility could move onto the national political agenda as communities struggle to survive.

Related to this is still another contradiction for capital controllers. Even as states become just so many investment sites jockeying to attract investors, they remain the defenders and guarantors of private property, with no supranational entities threatening to replace them in this crucial function. But with forces undermining the legitimacy of private property as communities are increasingly pressed to take defensive actions, it becomes less certain that the home nation-state can be counted on to rescue distant capital controllers who experience difficulties. And finally, even if private property is so fundamental to capitalist systems that it must be treated as a structural factor, it remains a social construct that can be challenged, reshaped, and even undone should any or all of the contradictions mentioned here precipitate a deep political or social crisis. These considerations notwithstanding, the locational revolution is still a relatively new political-economic force. Considerable work lies ahead in examining how power balances will continue to shift, as well as determining what strategies those most injured by these changes will adopt.

REFERENCES

American Embassy. 1975. "Nationalizing—Indonesian Style." Jakarta. Airgram to U.S. Department of State, 8 April.

——. 1979. "Indonesia's Investment Climate." Jakarta, 12 April.

Anderson, Benedict R. O'G. 1983. "Old State, New Society: Indonesia's New Order in Comparative Historical Perspective." *Journal of Asian Studies* 42 (3): 477–496.

——. 1990. "The Idea of Power in Javanese Culture." In *Language and Power.* Ithaca: Cornell University Press.

Anderson, Perry. 1974a. *Lineages of the Absolutist State.* London: New Left Books.

——. 1974b. *Passages from Antiquity to Feudalism.* London: New Left Books.

Aron, Raymond. 1950. "Social Structure of the Ruling Class." *British Journal of Sociology* 1 (March–June): 1–17, 126–144.

Arrighi, Giovanni. 1990. "Marxist Century, American Century: The Making and Remaking of the World Labour Movement." *New Left Review* 179 (January–February): 29–63.

Astbury, Sid. 1984. "Positive Measures Are Needed to Stimulate a Sagging Economy." *Asian Business,* February, 59.

Awanohara, Susumu. 1984. "The Perennial Problem." *Far Eastern Economic Review,* 6 September, 26–27.

Bank Indonesia. 1967. "Indonesian Investment Conference, Geneva, 2–4 November 1967." Internal document.

——. 1988. *Selected Key Policy Issues in the Indonesian Economy.* Proceedings and papers of the Bank Indonesia–IMF Institute Seminar on Financial Programming and Policy. Jakarta, 17–28 November.

Baran, Paul. 1957. *The Political Economy of Growth.* New York: Monthly Review Press.

Bates, Robert H., and Da-Hsiang Donald Lien. 1985. "A Note on Taxation, Development, and Representative Government." *Politics and Society* 14 (1): 53–70.

Baxter, J. M. 1984. "Equipment Dealing and Leasing: Some Comments on the Indonesian Market." *East Asian Executive Reports* 6 (6): 14.

Begg, Hugh, and Stuart McDowall. 1987. "The Effect of Regional Investment Incentives on Company Decisions." *Regional Studies* 21 (5): 459–470.

Biersteker, Thomas J. 1987. *Multinationals, the State, and Control of the Nigerian Economy*. Princeton: Princeton University Press.

Block, Fred. 1977a. *The Origins of International Economic Disorder: A Study of United States International Monetary Policy from World War II to the Present*. Berkeley: University of California Press.

———. 1977b. "The Ruling Class Does Not Rule: Notes on the Marxist Theory of the State." *Socialist Review* 7 (3), no. 33: 6–28.

———. 1980. "Beyond Relative Autonomy: State Managers as Historical Subjects." In *The Socialist Register*, 227–242. London: Merlin Press.

Bluestone, B., and B. Harrison. 1980. *Capital and Communities: The Causes and Consequences of Private Disinvestment*. Washington, D.C.: Government Printing Office.

Boatman, John. 1988. "Indonesia: Purchasing Power Handed to Ministers." *East Asian Executive Reports* 10 (4): 6.

Bowles, Samuel, and Herbert Gintis. 1983. "The Power of Capital: On the Inadequacy of the Conception of the Capitalist Economy as 'Private.'" *Philosophical Forum* 14 (3–4): 225–245.

Brasier, Marilyn. 1981. "An Investor's Guide to the Indonesian Corporate Income Tax." *East Asian Executive Reports* 3 (5): 3.

Briggs, Jean A. 1981. "Not to Worry." *Forbes*, 6 July, 121.

Bryan, Bryan. 1987. "The State and the Internationalisation of Capital: An Approach to Analysis." *Journal of Contemporary Asia* 17 (3): 253–275.

Buchanan, James M., Robert D. Tollison, and Gordon Tullock, eds. 1980. *Toward a Theory of the Rent-Seeking Society*. College Station: Texas A&M University Press.

Bunker, Stephen G. 1987. *Peasants against the State: The Politics of Market Control in Bugisu, Uganda, 1900–1983*. Urbana: University of Illinois Press, 1987.

Business International. 1968. "Indonesia: A Briefing Paper." Business International Indonesian Roundtable, Djakarta, 8–13 September. New York: Business International.

———. 1975a. "Indonesia: Business Opportunities in a Resource-Rich Economy." Business International Asian Research Report, October. Hong Kong.

———. 1975b. "Business Strategies for Developing Asia, 1975–1985." Business International Asian Research Report, November. Hong Kong.

———. 1979a. "Prospects for Profits." 16 February. Hong Kong.

———. 1979b. "Briefing Paper: Business International Roundtable with the Government of Indonesia." 24–26 April. Jakarta.

———. 1981. "Marketing in Indonesia: Roadmap to the Consumer, Industrial, and Government Sectors." Business International Multiclient Research Study, May. Jakarta.

———. 1982. "Prospects for Profits." 19 March. Hong Kong.

Cameron, David R. 1984. "Social Democracy, Corporatism, Labor Quiescence,

and the Representation of Economic Interests in Advanced Capitalist Society." In *Order and Conflict in Contemporary Capitalism*, ed. John H.
Goldthorpe. Oxford: Clarendon Press.

Cardoso, Fernando Henrique, and Enzo Faletto. 1979. *Dependency and
Development in Latin America*. Berkeley: University of California Press.

Castle, James. 1980. "Avoiding 'Possible Nightmare': Indonesia Wakes up to
Reality." *Asian Business* 16 (11):55.

Chatterjee, P. K. 1965. "Taxation of Foreign Investment in India." In *Basis of
Taxation in the Context of Developing Indian Economy*, ed. R. S. Chelliah.
Bombay: Popular Prakashan.

Chatterjee, Pratap. 1994. "Trade: Will the WTO Bring 'Free' Trade or Only 'Big'
Trade?" *Inter Press Service*, 12 April, 1.

Cockburn, Alexander. 1992. "Clinton, Labor and Free Trade: The Executioner's
Song." *Nation* 255 (14): 489.

Conybeare, John. 1988. *U.S. Foreign Economic Policy and the International
Capital Markets: The Case of Capital Export Controls, 1963–74*. New
York: Garland.

Cooke, Kiernan. 1984. "Investors in Indonesia Hold Fire," *Financial Times*, 31
July, 7.

——. 1985. "Trouble-Shooter Who Aims to Rationalise System." *Financial
Times*, 24 April, 6.

Cowper, Richard. 1984. "Indonesia 'to Adjust Newly Introduced Tax Code.'"
Financial Times, 31 October, 7.

Cregan, John P. 1992. "This Agreement Is a Loser." *USA Today*, 14 August, 14A.

Crenson, Matthew. 1971. *The Un-politics of Air Pollution*. Baltimore: Johns
Hopkins University Press.

Crouch, Harold. 1988. *The Army and Politics in Indonesia*. Rev. ed. Ithaca:
Cornell University Press.

Dahl, Robert A. 1961. *Who Governs? Democracy and Power in an American
City*. New Haven: Yale University Press.

——. 1985. *A Preface to Economic Democracy*. Berkeley: University of California Press.

Dahl, Robert A., and Charles E. Lindblom. 1953. *Politics, Economics and Welfare*. Chicago: University of Chicago Press.

Dahrendorf, Ralf. 1959. *Class and Class Conflict in Industrial Society*. London:
Routledge and Kegan Paul.

Davey, Kenneth. 1989. "Central-Local Financing Relations." In *Financing Local
Government in Indonesia*, ed. Nick Devas et al., 169–190. Southeast Asia
Series 84. Athens, Ohio: Monographs in International Studies.

Davies, Derek. 1966. "The Sultan's Problems." *Far Eastern Economic Review*,
no. 181, 16 June, 519–522.

Davies, Kathryn. 1983. "Singapore Reassesses Links with Indonesia." *Financial
Times*, 19 May, 7.

Devas, Nick, et al. 1989. *Financing Local Government in Indonesia*. Southeast
Asia Series 84. Athens, Ohio: Monographs in International Studies.

Diamond, Larry. 1988. "Nigeria: Pluralism, Statism, and the Struggle for
Democracy." In *Democracy in Developing Countries: Africa*, ed. Larry

Diamond, Juan J. Linz, and Seymour Martin Lipset, 2:33–91. Boulder: Lynne Rienner Publishers.

Domhoff, G. William. 1978. *The Powers That Be: Processes of Ruling Class Domination in America.* New York: Random House, Vintage Books.

——. 1983. *Who Rules America Now? A View for the Eighties.* Englewood Cliffs, N.J.: Prentice-Hall.

Doner, Richard F. 1986. "The Dynamism and Complexity of State Autonomy." Paper presented at the annual meeting of the International Studies Association, Atlanta, 6–8 November.

Dunning, J. H. 1973. "The Determinants of International Production." *Oxford Economic Papers,* n.s., 25: 389–436.

Early, Edwin F. 1991. "Toward the Commercial Union of Argentina, Brazil and Uruguay: Past Dynamics, Future Prospects." Paper presented at the thirty-second annual convention of the International Studies Association, Vancouver, 21 March.

Eisinger, Peter K. 1988. *The Rise of the Entrepreneurial State: State and Local Economic Development Policy in the United States.* Madison: University of Wisconsin Press.

Ekoko, A. E. 1990. "The Historical and Socio-political Environment of Nigerian Defence Policy." In *Nigerian Defence Policy: Issues and Problems,* ed. A. E. Ekoko and M. A. Vogt. Lagos: Malthouse Press.

Elkin, Stephen. 1985. "Pluralism in Its Place." In *The Democratic State,* ed. Roger Benjamin and Stephen Elkin. Lawrence: University of Kansas Press.

Ensor, Richard. 1979a. "Rachmat Saleh and His Trophies." *Euromoney,* suppl., January, 20.

——. 1979b. "The Rocky Road to Growth." *Euromoney,* suppl., January, 2.

Evans, Peter B. 1979. *Dependent Development: The Alliance of Multinational, State, and Local Capital in Brazil.* Princeton: Princeton University Press.

——. 1985. "Transnational Linkages and the Economic Role of the State: An Analysis of Developing and Industrialized Nations in the Post–World War II Period." In *Bringing the State Back In,* ed. Peter B. Evans, Dietrich Rueschemeyer, and Theda Skocpol, 192–226. Cambridge: Cambridge University Press.

Fainstein, Norman I., and Susan S. Fainstein, eds. 1982. *Urban Policy under Capitalism.* Beverly Hills, Calif.: Sage.

Felix, David, and Juana Sanchez. 1989. "Pooling Foreign Assets and Liabilities of Latin American Debtors to Solve Their Debt Crisis: Estimates of Capital Flight and Alternative Pooling Mechanisms." *Research in International Business and Finance* 7:43–61.

Frank, André Gunder. 1967. *Capitalism and Underdevelopment in Latin America.* New York: Monthly Review Press.

Frieden, Jeffry. 1981. "Third World Indebted Industrialization: International Finance and State Capitalism in Mexico, Brazil, Algeria, and South Korea." *International Organization* 35:407–431.

——. 1988. "Classes, Sectors, and Foreign Debt in Latin America." *Comparative Politics* 21 (1): 1–20.

———. 1991. "Invested Interests: The Politics of National Economic Policies in a World of Global Finance." *International Organization* 45: 24–41.

Friedland, Roger, and William T. Bielby. 1981. "The Power of Business in the City." In *Urban Policy Analysis,* ed. Terry Nichols Clark, vol. 21. Beverly Hills, Calif.: Sage.

Fröbel, Folker, Jurgen Heinrichs, and Otto Kreye. 1978. "The New International Division of Labour." *Social Science Information* 17 (1): 123–142.

Galbraith, John Kenneth. 1956. *American Capitalism: The Concept of Countervailing Power.* Boston: Houghton Mifflin.

———. 1970. "Countervailing Power and the State." In *Business and Government: The Problem of Power,* ed. Howard D. Marshall, 39–53. Lexington, Mass.: D. C. Heath.

Gelb, Alan, and Associates. 1988. *Oil Windfalls: Blessing or Curse?* World Bank Research Publication. Oxford: Oxford University Press.

Geldner, Marian. 1986. "Integrating the Theories of International Trade and Foreign Direct Investment." In *Research in International Business and Finance,* ed. H. Peter Gray, vol. 5. Greenwich, Conn.: JAI Press.

Gill, Stephen R., and David Law. 1988. *The Global Political Economy.* Baltimore: Johns Hopkins University Press.

———. 1989. "Global Hegemony and the Structural Power of Capital." *International Studies Quarterly* 33: 475–499.

Gingerich, Duane J. 1982. "Tendering in Indonesia: The Legal Framework." *East Asian Executive Reports* 4 (11): 7.

Glasberg, Davita Silfen. 1989. *The Power of Collective Purse Strings: The Effects of Bank Hegemony on Corporations and the State.* Berkeley: University of California Press.

Goldberg, Ellis. 1990. "Border, Boundaries, Taxes and States in the Medieval Islamic World." Paper presented at University of Washington Conference on Revenue and State.

Golden, Miriam, and Jonas Pontusson, eds. 1992. *Bargaining for Change: Union Politics in North America and Europe.* Ithaca: Cornell University Press.

Goldscheid, Rudolf. 1958. "A Sociological Approach to Problems of Public Finance." In *Classics in the Theory of Public Finance,* ed. R. Musgrave and A. Peacock. New York: Macmillan.

Goodman, John B., and Louis W. Pauly. 1993. "The Obsolescence of Capital Controls? Economic Management in an Age of Global Markets." *World Politics* 46 (1): 50–82.

Gordon, David M. 1988. "The Global Economy: New Edifice or Crumbling Foundations." *New Left Review* 168 (March–April): 24–64.

Guisinger, Stephen E., et al. 1985. *Investment Incentives and Performance Requirements: Patterns of International Trade, Production, and Investment.* New York: Praeger.

Habermas, Jürgen. 1975. *Legitimation Crisis,* Trans. Thomas McCarthy. Boston: Beacon Press.

Haggard, Stephan. 1990. *Pathways from the Periphery: The Politics of Growth in the Newly Industrializing Countries.* Ithaca: Cornell University Press.

Hammer, Richard M., James T. Elliot, and Philip J. Shah. 1985. "An Update on Indonesia's New Tax Laws." *A-P Tax and Investment Bulletin,* September, 366.

Haner, F. T. 1980. *Global Business: Strategy for the 1980s.* New York: Praeger.

Harink, Vincent G. 1984. "Do Recent Tax Changes Reduce Foreign Investment?" *East Asian Executive Reports,* 6 (8): 8.

Hawley, Amos H. 1950. *Human Ecology: A Theory of Community Structure.* New York: Ronald Press.

Helleiner, Eric. 1994. *States and the Reemergence of Global Finance.* Ithaca: Cornell University Press.

Hill, Hal. 1988. *Foreign Investment and Industrialization in Indonesia.* East Asian Social Science Monographs. Singapore: Oxford University Press.

Hill and Knowlton, Inc. 1985. "Global Direct Investment: Past, Present and Future Trends." Study prepared by the International Division, Hill and Knowlton, August.

Hirschman, Albert O. 1970. *Exit, Voice, and Loyalty: Response to Decline in Firms, Organizations, and States.* Cambridge: Harvard University Press.

Howell, Chris. 1992. *Regulating Labor: The State and Industrial Relations Reform in Postwar France.* Princeton: Princeton University Press.

Huntington, Samuel P. 1968. *Political Order in Changing Societies.* New Haven: Yale University Press.

Indonesian Embassy. 1967. "Foreign Investment in Indonesia." Special issue. Washington, D.C.

Jenson, Jane, and Rianne Mahon, eds. 1993. *The Challenge of Restructuring: North American Labor Movements Respond.* Philadelphia: Temple University Press.

Jessop, Bob. 1982. *The Capitalist State: Theories and Methods.* New York: New York University Press.

——. 1983. "The Democratic State and the National Interest." In *Socialist Arguments,* ed. David Coates and Gordon Johnston. Oxford: Martin Robertson.

Keohane, Robert O. 1984. *After Hegemony: Cooperation and Discord in the World Political Order.* Princeton: Princeton University Press.

Khoury, Sarkis J. 1990. *The Deregulation of the World Financial Markets: Myths, Realities, and Impact.* New York: Quorum Books.

Krasner, Stephen D. 1976. "State Power and the Structure of International Trade." *World Politics* 28 (3): 47–61.

——. 1978. *Defending the National Interest.* Princeton: Princeton University Press.

——, ed. 1983. *International Regimes.* Ithaca: Cornell University Press.

——. 1985. *Structural Conflict: The Third World against Global Liberalism.* Berkeley: University of California Press.

Lange, Peter M., George Ross, and Maurizio Vannicelli, eds. 1982. *Unions, Change and Crisis: French and Italian Union Strategy and the Political Economy, 1945–1980.* New York: Allen and Unwin.

Latham, Earl. 1952. "The Group Basis of Politics: Notes for a Theory." *American Political Science Review* 46 (June): 376–397.

Leechor, Chad, Harinder S. Kohli, and Sujin Hur. 1983. *Structural Changes in World Industry: A Quantitative Analysis of Recent Developments.* Washington, D.C.: World Bank.

Levi. Margaret. 1981. "The Predatory Theory of Rule." *Politics and Society* 10 (4): 431–465.

———. 1988. *Of Rulers and Revenue.* Berkeley: University of California Press.

Lewis, Chris. 1980. "After the Misused Boom." *Asian Business* 16 (3): 54.

Lewis, Peter M. 1990. "State, Economy, and Privatization in Nigeria." In *The Political Economy of Public Sector Reform and Privatization,* ed. Ezra N. Suleiman and John Waterbury, 210–233. Boulder, Colo.: Westview Press.

———. 1994. "Economic Statism, Private Capital, and the Dilemmas of Accumulation in Nigeria." *World Development* 22 (3): 437–451.

Lindblom, Charles E. 1977. *Politics and Markets.* New York: Basic Books.

———. 1982. "The Market as Prison." *Journal of Politics* 44 (2): 324–336.

Lipietz, Alain. 1982. "Towards Global Fordism." *New Left Review* 132: 33–47.

Lipset, Seymour M. 1960. *Political Man: The Social Bases of Politics.* Garden City, N.Y.: Doubleday.

Loeb et al. 1977. "The Climate for Foreign Investment in Indonesia [Confidential]." A report produced by Kuhn Loeb and Co., Lazard Frères et Cie, and S. G. Warburg and Co., February.

Lonsdale, John. 1981. "States and Social Processes in Africa: A Historiographical Survey." *African Studies Review* 24 (2–3): 139–225.

Luckham, Robin. 1971. *The Nigerian Military: A Sociological Analysis of Authority and Revolt, 1960–1967.* African Studies Series 4. London: Cambridge University Press.

MacIntyre, Andrew. 1991. *Business and Politics in Indonesia.* Sydney: Allen and Unwin.

Mandel, Ernest. 1978. *Late Capitalism.* London: Verso Press.

Marshall, Howard D., ed. 1970. *Business and Government: The Problem of Power.* Lexington, Mass.: D. C. Heath.

Martens, Robert. n.d. "Nudging the Tiller: Indonesia Reverses Course." Interview with U.S. ambassador Marshall Green. [Martens was a political officer in Jakarta from 1963 to 1966. Conducted under the auspices of the Foreign Service History Center at George Washington University as part of the center's oral history project.]

Mashberg, Tom. 1993. "How to Save a Trade Deal: Trade a Few Deals." *Boston Globe,* 2 May, 77.

Mas'oed, Mohtar. 1983. "The Indonesian Economy and Political Structure during the Early New Order, 1966–1971." Ph.D. diss., Ohio State University.

Mathieson, Donald J., and Liliana Rojas-Suarez. 1993. "Liberalization of the Capital Account: Experiences and Issues." IMF Occasional Papers Series 103.

Maxfield, Sylvia. 1990. *Governing Capital: International Finance and Mexican Politics.* Ithaca: Cornell University Press.

McCawley, Peter. 1977. "Indonesia's New Balance of Payments Problem: A Surplus to Get Rid Of." Paper presented at Work-in-Progress Seminar, Department of Economics, Research School of Pacific Studies, Australian National University.

McGreevy, T. E., and A. W. J. Thomson. 1983. "Regional Policy and Company Investment Behaviour." *Regional Studies* 17 (5): 347–358.

McKenzie, Richard B. 1979. *Restrictions on Business Mobility: A Study in Political Rhetoric and Economic Reality.* Washington, D.C.: American Enterprise Institute.

McVey, Ruth. 1992. *Southeast Asian Capitalists.* Studies on Southeast Asia. Ithaca: Cornell Southeast Asia Program.

Migdal, Joel S. 1988. *Strong Societies and Weak States: State-Society Relations and State Capabilities in the Third World.* Princeton: Princeton University Press.

Miliband, Ralph. 1969. *The State in Capitalist Society.* London: New Left Books.

Millstein, Ira M., and Salem M. Katsh. 1981. *The Limits of Corporate Power: Existing Constraints on the Exercise of Corporate Discretion.* New York: Macmillan.

Milner, Helen. 1988. *Resisting Protectionism: Global Industries and the Politics of International Trade.* Princeton: Princeton University Press.

Ministry of Finance. 1989. "Summary of Deregulation Policy since 1983." Photocopied. Jakarta.

Mitnick, Barry M. 1980. *The Political Economy of Regulation: Creating, Designing, and Removing Regulatory Reforms.* New York: Columbia University Press.

Morgan, Mary S. 1993. "Competing Notions of 'Competition' in Late Nineteenth-Century American Economics." *History of Political Economy* 25 (4): 563–604.

Neary, J. P., and S. van Wijnbergen, eds. 1986. *Natural Resources and the Macroeconomy.* Oxford: Basil Blackwell.

Nelson, Mark A. 1988. "Jakarta Modifies Policies on Government Procurement." *East Asian Executive Reports* 10 (6): 20.

Neustadt, Richard. 1976. *Presidential Power: The Politics of Leadership, with Reflections on Johnson and Nixon.* New York: Praeger.

Nordlinger, Eric. 1981. *On the Autonomy of the Democratic State.* Cambridge: Harvard University Press.

O'Brien, Richard. 1992. *Global Financial Integration.* London: Pinter.

O'Connor, James. 1973. *The Fiscal Crisis of the State.* New York: St. Martin's Press.

———. 1987. *The Meaning of Crisis: A Theoretical Introduction.* New York: Basil Blackwell.

Offe, Claus. 1972a. "Advanced Capitalism and the Welfare State." *Politics and Society* 2: 479–488.

———. 1972b. "Political Authority and Class Structure: An Analysis of Late Capitalist Societies." *International Journal of Sociology* 2: 73–108.

———. 1974. "Structural Problems of the Capitalist State; Class Rule and the Political System; On the Selectiveness of Political Institutions." *German Political Studies* 1: 31–57.

Offe, Claus, and Volker Ronge. 1975. "Theses on the Theory of the State." *New German Critique*, 137–147.

Offe, Claus, and Helmut Wiesenthal. 1985. "Two Logics of Collective Action." In *Disorganized Capitalism*, ed. Claus Offe. Cambridge: MIT Press.

Oyovbaire, Sam Egite. 1993. "Structural Change and Political Processes in Nigeria." *African Affairs* 82 (326): 3–28.

Palmer, Ingrid. 1978. *The Indonesian Economy since 1965: A Case Study of Political Economy.* London: Frank Cass.

Pangaribuan, Robinson. 1988. "Perkembangan Kekuasaan Sekretariat Negara Dalam Jajaran Politik Nasional, Periode 1945–1987." Master's thesis, Faculty of Political and Social Sciences, University of Indonesia.

Panglaykim, J. 1966. "Optimism in Djakarta." *Far Eastern Economic Review*, no. 182 (23 June): 606–608.

Park, Robert E. 1936. "Human Ecology." *American Journal of Sociology* 42 (1): 1–15.

Peet, Richard, ed. 1987. *International Capitalism and Industrial Restructuring: A Critical Analysis.* Boston: Allen and Unwin.

Pemberton, John. 1994. *On the Subject of "Java."* Ithaca: Cornell University Press.

Perrons. D. C. 1981. "The Role of Ireland in the New International Division of Labour: A Proposed Framework for Regional Analysis." *Regional Studies* 15 (2): 81–100.

Peterson, Paul E. 1981. *City Limits.* Chicago: University of Chicago Press.

Pfeffer, Jeffrey. 1981. *Power in Organizations.* Boston: Pitman.

Pfeffer, Jeffrey, and Gerald S. Salancik. 1978. *The External Control of Organizations: A Resource Dependence Perspective.* New York: Harper and Row.

Polanyi, Karl. 1944. *The Great Transformation: The Political and Economic Origins of Our Time.* Boston: Beacon Hill Press.

Posthumus, G. A. 1972. "The Intergovernmental Group on Indonesia." *Bulletin of Indonesian Economic Studies* 8 (2): 50–58.

Poulantzas, Nicos. 1969. "The Problem of the Capitalist State." *New Left Review* 58: 67–78.

———. 1975. *Political Power and Social Classes.* Translated by Timothy O'Hagen. London: New Left Books.

Presthus, Robert. 1964. *Men at the Top.* New York: Oxford University Press.

Prowse, Michael. 1993. "Heretical Thoughts on Currencies: America." *Financial Times*, 6 September, 3.

Przeworski, Adam. 1980. "Social Democracy as a Historical Phenomenon." *New Left Review*, July–August, 27–58.

Przeworski, Adam, and Michael Wallerstein. 1988. "Structural Dependence of the State on Capital." *American Political Science Review* 82 (1): 11–29.

Pura, Raphael. 1985. "Indonesia Tries to Reform Tax System." *Asian Wall Street Journal*, 1 February.

Reich, Robert B. 1988. "Corporation and Nation." *Atlantic Monthly,* May, 76–81.

———. 1991. *The Work of Nations: Preparing Ourselves for Twenty-first Century Capitalism.* New York: Alfred A. Knopf.

Rivera, Janet. 1993. "AFSCME Press Release." *PR Newswire,* 5 August, 1.

Roberts, P. W. 1985. "Mobile Manufacturing Firms: Locational Choice and Some Policy Implications." *Regional Studies* 19 (5): 475–481.

Robinson, Ian. 1993. *North American Trade as if Democracy Mattered: What's Wrong with NAFTA and What Are the Alternatives?* Ottawa: Canadian Centre for Policy Alternatives.

Robison, Richard. 1977. "Capitalism and the Bureaucratic State in Indonesia, 1965–1975." Ph.D. diss. University of Sydney.

———. 1986. *Indonesia: The Rise of Capital.* Sydney: Allen and Unwin.

———. 1989. "Structures of Power and the Industrialisation Process in Southeast Asia." *Journal of Contemporary Asia* 19 (4): 371–397.

Rose, Arnold. 1967. "Confidence and the Corporation." *American Journal of Economics and Sociology* 26 (3): 231–236.

Ross, Robert J. S. 1987. "Facing Leviathan: Public Policy and Global Capitalism." In *International Capitalism and Industrial Restructuring,* ed. R. Peet, 248–269. Boston: Allen and Unwin.

Rubin, Steven M. 1988. *Tax-Free Exporting Zones: A User's Manual.* Special Report 1135. London: Economist Publications.

Ruggie, John G. 1983. *The Antinomies of Interdependence: National Welfare and the International Division of Labor.* New York: Columbia University Press.

Rupley, Lawrence A. 1981. "Revenue Sharing in the Nigerian Federation." *Journal of Modern African Studies* 19 (2): 257–277.

Sacerdoti, Guy. 1980. "Red Tape under Repelita." *Far Eastern Economic Review,* 31 October, 52–54.

Sassen, Saskia. 1988. *The Mobility of Labor and Capital: A Study in International Investment and Labor Flow.* Cambridge: Cambridge University Press.

Schumpeter, Joseph. 1954. "The Crisis of the Tax State." In *International Economic Papers,* ed. A. Peacock, et al. New York: Macmillan.

Scott, A. J. 1987. "The Semiconductor Industry in South-east Asia: Organization, Location and the International Division of Labour." *Regional Studies* 21 (2): 143–160.

Scott, Bruce R., and George C. Lodge, eds. 1985. *U.S. Competitiveness in the World Economy.* Boston: Harvard Business School Press.

Sekretariat Negara, R. I. 1988. "Laporan Pelaksanaan Tugas—Tim Pengendali Pengadaan Barang/Peralatan Pemerintah." Implementation Report— Government Procurement Team. Jakarta.

Shinn, Yoon Hwan. 1989. "Demystifying the Capitalist State: Political Patronage, Bureaucratic Interests, and Capitalists-in-Formation in Soeharto's Indonesia." Ph.D. diss., Yale University.

Skocpol, Theda. 1980. "Political Responses to Capitalist Crisis: Neo-Marxist Theories of the State and the Case of the New Deal." *Politics and Society* 10 (2): 155–201.

Snoy, Bernard. 1975. *Taxes on Direct Investment in the EEC: A Legal and Economic Analysis*. New York: Praeger.

Sparrow, Bartholomew H. 1990. "Raising Taxes and Going into Debt: A Resource Dependence Model of U.S. Public Finance in the 1940s." Paper presented at the annual meeting of the American Political Science Association, San Francisco.

Stallings, Barbara. 1985. "International Lending and the Relative Autonomy of the State: A Case Study of Twentieth-Century Peru." *Politics and Society* 14 (3): 257–288.

———. 1986. *Banker to the Third World: U.S. Portfolio Investment in Latin America, 1900–1985*. Berkeley: University of California Press.

Storper, Michael, and Richard Walker. 1989. *The Capitalist Imperative: Territory, Technology, and Industrial Growth*. New York: Basil Blackwell.

Streeck, Wolfgang. 1995. "German Capitalism: Does It Exist? Can It Survive?" In *Modern Capitalism or Modern Capitalisms?* ed. Colin Crouch and Wolfgang Streeck. London: Pinter.

Sullivan, John H. 1969. "The United States and the 'New Order' in Indonesia." Ph.D. diss., American University.

Syrett, S. J. 1987. "The International Trading of Policies: The Portuguese Experience of Local Employment Initiatives." *Regional Studies* 21 (5): 475–479.

Time, Inc. 1967. *To Aid in Rebuilding a Nation*. Proceedings of the Indonesian Investment Conference. New York: Time.

Truman, David B. 1951. *The Governmental Process*. New York: Random House.

Ukpabi, S. C. 1987. *Mercantile Soldiers in Nigeria: History and Origins of the Nigerian Army*. Zaira, Nigeria: Gaskiya Press.

United Nations. 1993. *World Investment Report*.

U.S. Department of Commerce. 1986. "Indonesia: Economy Faces Negative GDP Growth This Year; Twelve Product Areas Offer Best Export Prospects; Business Looks Abroad." U.S. Dept. of Commerce, vol. 9, 21 July.

U.S. House of Representatives. 1969. *Foreign Affairs Act of 1969*. Hearings before the House Committee on Foreign Affairs, 10 June.

U.S. Senate. 1968. *Foreign Assistance Act of 1968*. Hearing before the Senate Committee on Foreign Relations, 14 May.

———. 1978. *The Witteveen Facility and the OPEC Financial Surpluses*. Hearings before the Subcommittee on Foreign Economic Policy of the Committee on Foreign Relations, U.S. Senate, 95th Cong.; 1st sess. Washington, D.C.: GPO.

USAID. 1982. "Indonesian Private Sector Contributions to Development—a Background Paper for AID." Discussion document to accompany the mission's FY 1984 macroeconomic paper, June. AID Indonesia.

Useem, Michael. 1979. "The Social Organization of the American Business Elite and Participation of Corporate Directors in the Governance of American Institutions." *American Sociological Review* 44 (4): 553–572.

———. 1984. *The Inner Circle: Large Corporations and the Rise of Business Political Activity in the U.S. and U.K.* New York: Oxford University Press.

Wade, Robert. 1990. *Governing the Market: Economic Theory and the Role of*

Government in East Asian Industrialization. Princeton: Princeton University Press.

Walker, R., and M. Storper. 1981. "Capital and Industrial Location." *Progress in Human Geography* 5 (4): 473–509.

Ward, M. F. 1982. "Political Economy, Industrial Location and the European Motor Car Industry in the Postwar Period." *Regional Studies* 16 (6): 443–453.

Webb, Michael C. 1991. "International Economic Structures, Government Interests, and the International Coordination of Macroeconomic Adjustment Policies." *International Organization* 45: 456–477.

Wellons, Phillip A. 1977. *Borrowing by Developing Countries on the Eurocurrency Market.* Development Centre Studies. Paris: Development Centre of the OECD.

Whitt, J. Allen. 1979. "Toward a Class–Dialectic Model of Power." *American Sociological Review* 44 (1): 81–99.

——. 1980. "Can Capitalists Organize Themselves?" In *Power Structure Research,* ed. G. William Domhoff, 97–114. Beverly Hills, Calif: Sage.

Winters, Jeffrey A. 1988. *"Indonesia: The Rise of Capital*—a Review Essay." *Indonesia* 45: 109–128.

——. 1991. "Structural Power and Investor Mobility: Capital Control and State Policy in Indonesia, 1965–1990." Ph.D diss., Yale University.

——. 1994a. "Zonal Capitalism." Manuscript.

——. 1994b. "Power and the Control of Capital." *World Politics* 46 (3): 419–452.

Wood, Robert C. 1968. The Local Government Response to the Urban Economy." In *City Politics and Public Policy,* ed. James Q. Wilson, 69–96. New York: John Wiley.

Wood, Robert E. 1980. "Foreign Aid and the Capitalist State in Underdeveloped Countries." *Politics and Society* 10 (1): 1–34.

World Bank. 1966. "Import Requirements of Indonesia for 1967 in the Sectors of Transport, Agriculture, and Industry." Recommendations by a mission of the International Bank for Reconstruction and Development, November. Washington, D.C.

——. 1980. "Indonesia: Selected Issued [*sic*] of Industrial Development and Trade Strategy." "Confidential" report 3182-IND, 15 December. Jakarta: East Asia and Pacific Regional Office, World Bank.

Wright, Erik Olin. 1978. *Class, Crisis and the State.* London: Verso Press.

Yoffie, David B. 1993. *Beyond Free Trade: Governments, Firms, and Global Competition.* Boston: Harvard Business School Press.

Young, Ruth C. 1986. "Industrial Location and Regional Change: The United States and New York State." *Regional Studies* 20 (4): 341–369.

Index

Page numbers in italics refer to tables.